Hh Ii Jj Kk Ll Mm

Uu Vv Ww Xx Yy Zz

Handwriting in America

HANDWRITING
IN AMERICA

A Cultural History

TAMARA PLAKINS THORNTON

Yale University Press   *New Haven and London*

Designed by Sonia L. Scanlon.
Set in Caslon type by Tseng Information
Systems, Inc.
Printed in the United States of America by
Edwards Brothers, Inc., Ann Arbor,
Michigan.

Library of Congress
Cataloging-in-Publication Data
Thornton, Tamara Plakins, 1957–
Handwriting in America : a cultural
history / Tamara Plakins Thornton.
p.   cm.
Includes bibliographical references
and index.
ISBN 0-300-06477-2 (alk. paper)
1. Writing—United States—Psychological
aspects—History.   I. Title.
Z40.T46   1996
652'.1'09—dc20   96-6282
CIP

A catalogue record for this book is available
from the British Library.
The paper in this book meets the guidelines
for permanence and durability of the
Committee on Production Guidelines for
Book Longevity of the Council on Library
Resources.

10 9 8 7 6 5 4 3 2 1

In memory of my grandparents
Alexander Fischgrund and Helene Klein Fischgrund,
whose lives are inscribed in my own.

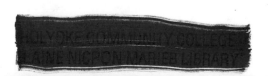

CONTENTS

My first experiences with handwriting were not happy ones. From kindergarten through second grade, I was enrolled in an experimental program in which children were taught to read with the aid of computers; in 1961 we called them talking typewriters. My teachers were quite expert in teaching their young charges how to touch-type—every morning, we lined up to have our fingernails painted in colors that matched the ones on the computer keyboard—but they were far less successful when it came to handwriting instruction. From the start, I was a clumsy printer, and things only got worse when I was expected to learn cursive. I found script awkward, even painful, and was much happier at the keyboard, where "real" writing took place, and I could compose poems for our class newspaper. I never did acquire a proper hand. In fourth grade, I was often kept in from recess to practice my cursive letters, but I still got C's in penmanship. I didn't care about those grades, though, since I was convinced that poor handwriting had nothing to do with intelligence or, indeed, with any ability of any worth. I believe I took a certain pride in those C's.

Except for the part about computers, my story is a common one for my generation, but what I have discovered in the course of writing this book is how thoroughly my experiences with handwriting were shaped by the era in which I grew up. Until the 1920s, for example, a first-grader would have been almost as likely to learn printing as to use a computer. When children learned how to write, they *began* with cursive. There would also have been no question that the "second R" meant penmanship, not, as with my early attempts at poetry, original composition. And in the eighteenth century, I probably would not have learned to read and write at the same time but separately and consecutively, as two distinct skills. In fact, as a girl, I might never have learned to write at all; and if I had, the script I acquired might well have been a particular script that was reserved for females.

It is also true that the attitudes I held toward handwriting were unmistakably mid-twentieth century. Foremost among these was my secret conviction that good penmanship does not matter, that if anything it denotes a person who is fearful or incapable of being in any way unusual. Of course, what lies behind that conviction is the belief that handwriting in some way reflects personality, most especially those qualities that differentiate one person from everyone else. Faithful imitation of penmanship models—what teachers would call good handwriting—thereby signals conformity and ordinariness, while breaking all the penmanship rules, even to the point of illegibility, is a mark of individuality. Yet none of this reasoning would have made sense to a seventeenth-century American, not the assumption that every person's handwriting is unique, not the link between handwriting and personality, not the premium placed on individuality, not even the conception of individuality as such. These ideas emerged in the intervening centuries, each in its own time and place, its own historical context.

I certainly did not set out to study handwriting. That happened by accident, when I chanced across an eighteenth-century advice book for merchants that included a discussion of handwriting among its prescriptions. It advised men of commerce to adopt a particular style of handwriting that epitomized in its aesthetic characteristics the ideal traits of the mercantile class as a whole: boldness, efficiency, practicality. I was used to thinking of handwriting style as something unconsciously and individually generated; the notion that one would deliberately affect a style—and, what is more, a style that represented the collective character of a group to which one belonged—struck me as bizarre. And then I was off. I had fallen down the rabbit hole into a world where things became curiouser and curiouser, and I have been chasing the white rabbit ever since.

The historian Robert Darnton has remarked that "the best points of entry in an attempt to penetrate an alien culture can be those where it seems to be most opaque."[1] The conundrums presented by the history of handwriting in America are just such serendipitous openings into the past, just such rabbit holes. Like the little door to a much larger world that awaited Alice at the bottom of the rabbit hole, the history of handwriting only seems to be a small subject. Once I grasped its internal logic, I realized that it holds broad significance for the study of American culture. Handwriting is important first of all because it mattered to people in the past, in ways deeply embedded in their cultures. And it carried larger meanings and served broader functions; in particular, it embodied, regulated, and generated notions of the self.

In exploring the relation between handwriting and culture, we can take our cue from scholars who are working in a relatively new and tremendously fertile field that encompasses the history of literacy, reading, the book, and print.[2] One of the key insights emerging from this field is that reading as a practice has a history of its own, for readers have not read the same way in all times and places. They have read out loud or in silence, in company or in solitude, in devotion or for leisure. They have read a single text intensively and repeatedly or many texts quickly and but once. And, of course, the ability to read has varied with class, race, gender, occupation, and religion. How people have read has depended partly on the physical nature of what they read, so historians take a new interest in reading matter as physical object, examining, for example, a book's format and the relation between text, markings, and illustrations. Ultimately, both the physical texts and how people have read them have been shaped by the cultural assumptions that govern the practice of reading. And so historians seek to reconstruct the purposes reading was thought to serve and the meanings with which it was invested.[3]

Handwriting also has a history of its own. Writers have not written in an identical manner in all times and places. Handwriting has been variously practiced as copying or composing; as a skill distinct from or linked to reading; as a single competence—writing script—or a multiple one, writing many hands. As was the case with the ability to read, whether one could write had much to do with whether one was a man or a woman, a merchant or a laborer, a townsman or a farmer. Nor have the physical artifacts of handwriting remained constant, most obviously, writing instruments but also the scripts themselves. And most fundamental, the cultural assumptions governing the practice of writing have both changed over time and competed among themselves at any given time. Thus handwriting has been understood as a mercantile tool, a female accomplishment, or a craft; as an inherently male practice or a gender-neutral one; as a manual skill or an intellectual, even moral, endeavor; and as a form of social discipline or individual self-expression.

One task of this book, then, is to put writers and handwriting in a historical context in much the same way scholars have historicized readers and reading. In another respect, however, this book must step outside that scholarship, for historians of literacy, print, and reading have largely ignored handwriting as a historical phenomenon with its own distinctive cultural functions and meanings. Ironically, it was the scholars who were investigating the dimensions of literacy who first drew attention to handwriting when they established that the skills of reading and writing were historically distinct, but they have employed this knowledge mainly to evaluate and adjust reading literacy statistics derived from signature data.[4] In conjunction with scholarship that characterizes the printing press as inherently revolutionary, these literacy studies have been used to establish the boundaries of what are perceived as two distinct worlds, a folk world steeped in orality and an elite world steeped in print. There is little conceptual room for handwriting in this schema. Walter Ong, for example, characterizes "chirographic" culture as either a less-intense form of "typographic" culture or as essentially oral, unable to make the break with the spoken word that print would soon accomplish.[5] Other historians take exception to this model, some stressing the permeability of the line separating literate from nonliterate, printedness from orality, others concentrating on the notion that any medium of communication, whether word of mouth or printing press, carries with it predetermined cultural consequences. This outlook does make room for handwriting. Roger Chartier, for example, insists on the continuities between handwritten manuscripts and printed texts, but because his conceptual focus remains the history of reading, he does not distinguish the practice of handwriting from the practice of reading it.[6]

What needs to be recognized is that long after Gutenberg cast his movable type, the use of pen and ink persisted, and even when print became ubiquitous, people continued to write by hand. Even more important, handwriting existed as something apart from both orality and print and something other than a medium incidental to the practice of reading. It occupied its own cultural domain, where it was capable of serving distinct cultural purposes and carrying distinct cultural messages. Furthermore, it maintained this ability even as—indeed, I shall argue, precisely because—print saturated American society and consciousness. In this study I seek to recover that domain of script and to explore handwriting's unique meanings and functions in a wide range of phenomena: the scripts themselves, in all their aesthetic variety and social shadings; penmanship pedagogy, from the training offered by colonial writing masters to the Palmer method; the theory and practice of handwriting analysis, or graphology, as it came to be called by the end of the nineteenth century; the hobby of autograph collecting; the social perception of forgery; the legal interpretation of handwriting evidence; and the twentieth-century revivals of historic calligraphy.

What emerges from these explorations is the consistent identification of handwriting with the self that produces it. We are perhaps most familiar with the contemporary version of that identification, handwriting analysis. Even those who do not subscribe to graphological theories are aware of the practice of reading character from script, and probably many assume in some casual way, as I did in the fourth grade, that there is a correspondence between personality and handwriting style. But this is only one way to conceive of the relation between handwriting and the writer, and a relatively recent one at that. In the nineteenth century, for example, writing masters regarded penmanship training as a way to form legions of that Victorian favorite, the man of character. At the same time, autograph collectors and handwriting experts examined signatures as signs of individuality, which was defined as genius by the former, physiological uniqueness by the latter. Indeed, that there is any relation between handwriting and writer is a relatively modern notion, established securely only in the eighteenth century, ironically, the era in which print first achieved a kind of critical cultural mass. This is no coincidence. It was print that endowed handwriting with its own, new set of symbolic possibilities; script emerged as a medium of the self in contradistinction to print, defined as characteristically impersonal and disassociated from the writer. Handwriting thus became a level of meaning in itself, quite apart from the sense of the text, and the sense that it transmitted took as its subject the self.

Once the association between script and self took hold, there were any number of scenarios that could be played out in light of it. Historically, the possibilities have hinged on three issues. First, how have people conceptualized the self: as externally assigned or internally generated, generic or individuated, physiological or characterological in essence? Second, what ends have these conceptions of self served? Have they been used to reinforce the existing order of things, to challenge it, or to achieve some working rapprochement with it? And finally, in what ways have people understood handwriting to function as a medium of the self? As a deliberate act or a spontaneous gesture, a product of the conscious will or the unconscious mind, an artifact of physiology or of the soul? How people have chosen to answer these questions in times past has depended on the natures of their societies, the kinds of changes they faced, and the strategies they used to speed, resist, or accommodate to these changes. A history of handwriting, then, must be set in the context of such broad social and economic phenomena as the shift from a rank-ordered society to one that was nominally egalitarian and pluralistic and the rise of market, industrial, and corporate capitalism. It must also be set in the context of such closely linked cultural phenomena as the homogenizing and standardizing effects of new economic realities, the changing definitions of manhood and womanhood, and the growing authority of scientific expertise.

In seeking the answers to these questions I argue that the issues they engage—the nature of the self, the purpose of its definition, and the relation between script and self—should not be separated from one another. When people defined the self, regulated and controlled it, expressed and released it, they did so not as an abstract intellectual exercise but in the very ways they lived. We should not study handwriting as a phenomenon that reflects changing conceptions of the self but as one of the places where the self happened. Penmanship pedagogues and their pupils, graphologists and their clients, handwriting experts and the law courts in which they testified, autograph collectors and calligraphers all knew that.

Of course, it was not their usual practice to hold forth on the nature of the self, although much to the delight of the historian, a few did just that. But most often, whatever formulations of these issues they arrived at were articulated in terms specific to their conceptions of handwriting. Two aspects of handwriting in particular functioned in this capacity. First, the skill of handwriting involves both mental and physical processes; it sits astride the cusp of mind and body. Second, as handwriting is the work of an individual writer but executed in imitation of a standard model, it straddles the cusp of individuality and conformity. These sets of oppositions, between mind and body and between individuality and conformity, define the continua along which representations and practices of handwriting have lain, and these axes in turn define the conceptual space in which the self has been delineated.

Here are the boundaries of the domain in which script culture has operated. Here is the world behind the little door. Now then, "READ ME."

Handwriting in America

CHAPTER ONE

The Lost World of Colonial Handwriting

"Let us suppose the mind to be, as we say, white paper void of all characters," wrote John Locke in his *Essay Concerning Human Understanding* of 1690. Thus he introduced his now-famous notion of the human being as a tabula rasa, who acquires reason and knowledge through experience. Not two years before he published this essay, Locke had had more literal dealings with blank paper and blank tablets—he paid £1 10s. for the former and £15 15s. for engraving the latter—when he was teaching the children of Benjamin Furley how to write. As he explained in *Some Thoughts Concerning Education* of a hypothetical pupil: "The way to teach him to Write, without much trouble, is to get a Plate graved, with the Characters of such an Hand as you like best. . . . Such a Plate being graved, let several Sheets of good Writing-Paper be printed off with Red Ink, which he has nothing to do, but to go over with a good Pen fill'd with Black Ink, which will quickly bring his Hand to the formation of those Characters, being at first shewed where to begin, and how to form every Letter." For the Furley children, Locke had engraved the letters of the alphabet, along with an alphabetical series of twenty-four proper names, many of them taken from the Furley family.[1] If for the young Furleys the process of acquiring knowledge was to be one of passive inscription, the process of acquiring writing skills would be the opposite: an active effort, aimed at transcription. Yet ironically the end product was the same, a fully formed self, symbolized in the first instance by a tablet bearing the marks of experience and in the second, by the accurately copied name proper to oneself.

On the surface, it would appear that Locke's concerns in writing the two essays were very different. How could the development of the human self and the acquisition of writing skills have anything to do with each other? Yet in the seventeenth, and especially the eighteenth, century these issues were intertwined, shaping the ways handwriting was perceived and practiced. Locke was not the only one to link the written character with the human character. Benjamin Franklin noted in his autobiography that he often drew his mind back to the life course he had set for himself, and although he fell short of his goals, yet "as those who aim at perfect Writing by imitating the engraved Copies, tho' they never reach the wish'd for Excellence of those Copies, their Hand is mended by the Endeavour, and is tolerable while it continues fair & legible."[2]

Just what colonial men and women read in handwriting—not the text but the handwriting itself—has long since vanished from the page, leaving us a blank white paper to ponder. To recover those lost messages, we must first consider how widespread was the ability to write and how that ability was acquired, by what sorts of people and for what ostensible purposes. We must, in other words, place handwriting within a historically specific and culturally defined system of literacy. Ever-greater numbers and kinds of people learned to write in these centuries, but in a rank-ordered society, it was inconceivable that the written texts of the humble and the exalted would be executed toward identical ends or accorded the same degree of cultural authority. In this context, penmanship pedagogy and practice served to regulate both the cultural functions of and the cultural significance attached to the handwritten word. The regime of copying, typified by Locke's copytexts, was just one of the means used to accomplish these ends. So too were the withholding of penmanship skills and the "marking" of handwriting with telltale signs of class and gender.

To reconstruct the colonial world of handwriting, we must also attend to its setting within the world of the printing press. Here the eighteenth century is especially critical. Just as literacy skills expanded in this century, so did the presence of printed material. More important, print underwent a qualitative change, now defining a medium that was characteristically abstract, impersonal, and, it was sometimes feared, duplicitous. The quantitative growth of printing edged out the use of script in many instances, but the qualitative change in print lent new meaning to handwriting, providing script with a symbolic function even as it diminished its practical utility. If print entailed self-negation, then by contrast script would entail the explicit presentation of self. The printed page might be "void of all characters," but the handwritten one would present the self to its readers. Thus would the Furleys appear before the world.

THE USES OF WRITING

In colonial America, the ability to read was treasured largely as the ability to gain direct access to Scripture. To ensure that children achieved Bible literacy, reading instruction took place at age six or seven, before the child assumed any substantial burden of work, in an informal, domestic (and therefore female) environment. Typically, children were taught by their mothers or another female relative at home or at a dame school run by another woman. Acquired in this manner, the ability to read was relatively widespread, although we must be attentive to change over time and differences among groups and regions. Levels of reading literacy were significantly higher in the eighteenth century than in the seventeenth. New England tended to have higher literacy rates than the colonies to its south, and literacy rates were higher in urban areas than in the countryside. And in any particular time and place, the ability to read was generally far more common among men than women. Where circumstances were most unfavorable for the acquisition of reading skills, about 60 percent of the adult male population could read, but only half or even a quarter of that proportion of women. At the other extreme

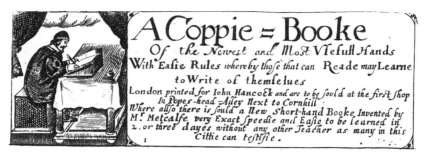

Of the Newest and Most Vsefull Hands
With Easie Rules whereby those that can Reade may Learne
to Write of themselues
London printed for Iohn Hancock and are to be sould at the first shop
In Popes-head =Alley next to Cornhill.
Where allso there is sould a New Short-hand Booke Invented by
Mr. Metcalfe very Exact speedie and Easie to be learned in
2. or three dayes without any other Teacher as many in this
Cittie can testifie.

1. A seventeenth-century copybook for people who can read but not write.

is late eighteenth-century New England, where nearly all men and women could read.[3]

Writing, however, was another story. Because reading and writing were understood to serve entirely different ends, instruction in one was divorced from instruction in the other. Reading was taught first, as a universal spiritual necessity; writing was taught second, and then only to some. That women were entrusted with reading instruction is just one indication that reading was perceived as an elementary skill, calling for no other abilities either to teach or to acquire it. So too were the teaching methods employed. To learn to read, children memorized and recited first letters, then syllable combinations, then complete words with careful attention to proper pronunciation. Typically, they advanced to reading the Psalter (the Book of Psalms), and thence to the Bible. This approach followed upon the uses to which reading literacy was to be put, the intensive reading, often out loud, of a limited number of religious texts. It followed as well upon the perception of the written word as something to be received from without rather than generated from within. The end product of this system of instruction was the ability to read the printed word, not to write—not even to read handwriting.[4]

Abundant evidence attests to the existence of this limbolike state of literacy. Penmanship self-instruction manuals, for example, purported to provide teaching "whereby those that can Reade may Learne to Write of themselves" (fig. 1) and, in the case of one copybook published explicitly "for the benefit of the new planted Vineyards of the Lord Jesus in Virginea, Sommer Ilands, and New England," to instruct "How One That can reade, may with a little helpe learne to write of himselfe." Writing masters refused instruction to complete illiterates, as when Samuel Giles, a teacher of writing and arithmetic in New York City, stipulated that "no Children will be taken but such as have already been taught to Read, and are fit for Writing," or when Boston writing master John Proctor insisted that he had "refused none of the

Inhabitants Children, but such as could not Read in the Psalter." Indeed, as late as 1817 the British and Foreign School Society reported that some of its pupils could read well but could not write at all. Perhaps even stranger is that group—likely the same one—that could read printed but not handwritten material. An English copybook of the seventeenth century presented handwritten alphabets so that children "may be capable of reading Written as well as Printed Hands." And one Sis Hopkins was quoted as saying she could "read readin' but couldn't read writin'."[5] Even into the nineteenth century, there existed a body of American men and women who could read printed matter but who could neither produce nor even make sense of the handwritten word. And the faintest echo of the traditional continuum is heard in the 1914 classic *Tarzan of the Apes,* when the hero teaches himself to read from a schoolbook but is stymied by a set of letters executed in script.[6]

Some readers, however, did continue on to learn how to write. Just who did reflects a conception of writing as a narrowly defined social, or more often vocational, skill, of limited use to the general populace. Clergy, it was conceded, needed to compose sermons, physicians to write out prescriptions, and lawyers to pen legal documents. Well-bred men and, by the eighteenth century, women as well, kept private journals and wrote personal letters, rituals critical to the formation of self-conscious social elites and largely confined to those classes. Most important, the workings of commerce entailed a tremendous amount of written material: daybooks, ledgers, waste books, invoices, bills of lading, receipts, and all manner of business correspondence. Thus Bible-reading backwoods farmers, otherwise literate artisans living beyond the pale of market activity, and most women usually did not need to know how to write and often could not. Those readers who had also learned to write included members of the learned professions—clergymen, physicians, and lawyers, as well as their hired "hands," legal scriveners, notaries public, and engrossers; the well-born of both sexes and their private secretaries; and, above all, merchants and their clerks and bookkeepers.[7]

"Whoever would be a *Man* of *Business,* must be a Man of *Correspondence,*" wrote Thomas Watts in 1716, "and Correspondence can never be so commodiously, or at all to the Purpose maintain'd, as by the Use of the Pen: So that WRITING is the *First* Step, and *Essential* in furnishing out the *Man of Business.*" Watts, who ran a private business academy in London (fig. 2), rated arithmetic the second and accounting the third skill incumbent upon the would-be merchant to acquire.[8] We would be wise to take our cue from Watts in placing penmanship instruction of the colonial era not among the "three R's" of nineteenth-century common-school education, but as one of this mercantile triumvirate of commercial skills that held sway through the eighteenth century. The association of penmanship with commerce is clear

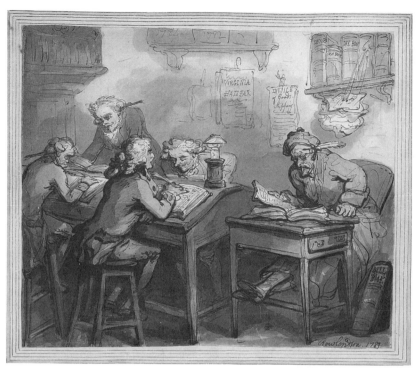

2. The merchant as penman, from Thomas Rowlandson, "A Merchant's Office," 1789.

not only in all aspects of penmanship education but also in the nature of the academic settings where handwriting was taught, the profile of penmanship pupils, the content of teaching materials, and the ancillary activities of writing masters.

Colonial Americans who wished to learn to write had to quit the female, domestic environment of reading instruction to seek out the expertise of a writing master. There were no writing mistresses.[9] Many writing masters offered private courses of instruction; others taught in public schools or private academies; some published copybooks and manuals that could be used for self-instruction. The first option presented itself most often, although not exclusively, in the commercial entrepots of the seaboard. Colonial newspapers abound with advertisements for private instruction in penmanship, almost always in association with training in arithmetic and accounting. In Boston, for example, John Vinal offered to teach "Writing, vulgar and decimal Arithmetic, several Branches of the Mathematics, and Book-keeping after the best Methods." Owen Harris, whose quarters were located "opposite to the Mitre Tavern in Fish-street near to Scarletts-Wharf," added other subjects appropriate to a clientele oriented to maritime trade: "Writing, Arithmetick in all its parts; And also Geometry, Trigonometry, Plain and Sphaerical, Surveying, Dialling, Gauging, Navigation, Astronomy; The Projection of the Sphaeres and the Use of Mathematical Instruments." In the port city of Philadelphia, Andrew Lamb likewise appended nautical subjects to the standard instruction in "Writing, arithmetick, vulgar and decimal," and "merchants accompts, the Italian method, by double entry." Among the planter gentry of South Carolina, however, it was not navigation but dancing that George Brownell and John Pratt offered in conjunction with penmanship, arithmetic, and double-entry bookkeeping.[10]

Private courses of instruction attracted boys seeking to enter the counting-house, as well as adult students looking to transfer into or advance in mercantile pursuits; hence, the offer of night classes. Richard Green explained that "for the Benefit of Persons confin'd in Business in the Day-Time, . . . that they may be taught Writing, Arithmetick, Algebra, Navigation, Gauging, Book-keeping, &c. &c.," he would teach "during the Winter Season, from Candlelight till Half an Hour past Eight o'Clock in the Evening." To "those employ'd in Business all the Day," Peter Pelham was another who offered candlelight instruction in "Writing and Arithmetick," along with "the best Virginia Tobacco cut, spun into the very best Pigtail, and all other Sorts; also Snuff, at the cheapest Rates."[11]

In spite of this mercantile orientation, writing masters advertising their services could not afford to ignore another potentially lucrative clientele—females. Some penmen took girls on with the promise of a mercantile training less complete but not dissimilar to that of their brothers, offering instruction in not only handwriting but also arithmetic and accounting. Most, however, represented a fair hand as a female "accomplishment" on par with dancing, music, or, most appropriate, needlework. "Then let the Fingers, whose unrivall'd Skill, Exalts the Needle, grace the Noble Quill," ran a common copybook ditty. Penmanship training for girls, then, was more commonly paired with embroidery than with bookkeeping. When in 1774 William and Sarah Long opened their school for young ladies in New York, they proposed to instruct their charges in "reading, writing, arithmetic, needlework &c. Also the TAMBOUR completely taught in GOLD, SILVER, SILK, and COTTON." To attract and accommodate their female pupils, writing masters offered instruction segregated from male students; stressed "epistolary correspondence" as the goal of penmanship education; and, above all, represented fine penmanship as a mark of fine breeding.[12]

When we turn to the public schools and private academies of colonial America, most of which simply excluded girls from their student bodies, we return to the definition of penmanship as a primarily mercantile subject. The pattern is clearest in Boston, where by 1684 public secondary education had split into a grammar school track offering instruction in classical languages to Harvard-bound scholars and a writing school track for boys who planned to enter the world of commerce. In addition to tackling mercantile arithmetic and accounts, writing school students spent years acquiring and perfecting their penmanship skills. Boys at the two Latin schools learned to write too, of course, but not from their regular schoolmaster. Instead, a writing master was brought in to instruct them in penmanship.[13]

The rigid bifurcation of schools into grammar and writing tracks was not universal, but schools commonly lumped together the subjects befitting a merchant and separated them from those befitting a gentleman. We can see this division, for example, in the decision of the Salem, Massachusetts, school committee to exclude writing and arithmetic from the grammar school curriculum. And we can see it too in "An Act for the Founding and Erecting of a Free School for the Use of the Inhabitants of South Carolina," which, envisioning instruction in the standard mercantile trio, called for the appointment of "a fit person to teach the youth of this province to write, and also the principles of vulgar arithmetic and merchants accounts." The division holds as well in the prospectus of the Philadelphia Academy, "wherein Youth will be taught the Latin, Greek, English, French, and German Languages, together with History, Geography, Chronology, Logic, and Rhetoric; also Writing, Arithmetic, Merchants Accounts, Geometry, Algebra, Surveying, Gauging, Navigation, Astronomy, Drawing in Perspective, and other mathematical Sciences." And that division is maintained in a Virginia cleric's notice that he had engaged a private tutor "properly qualified to teach the learned languages, as well as writing and accounts" and in a Virginia parish's search for a "Schoolmaster well qualified to teach Writing and Arithmetic; if *Latin* also, the more agreeable, and the Salary enlarged."[14]

The materials used in handwriting instruction reinforced the links between penmanship and commerce. The standard penmanship "textbook" was the copybook, a collection of engraved specimens of model handwriting to be imitated by the pupil. Once past the initial stages of copying letters and single words, students worked on full sentences, usually maxims, and many of these pithy sayings commented on the proper conduct of commerce and the character of the merchant. Copybooks also often included such mercantile forms as bills of exchange, bills of lading, letters of credit, receipts, invoices, and bookkeeping entries, while ciphering books, on the other hand, consisting of painstakingly transcribed arithmetical rules and mercantile-oriented problems, served as calligraphical showpieces (figs. 3, 4).[15] Accounting and arithmetic textbooks might also act as copybooks. Such works as John Ayres's *Arithmetick and Writing,* John Colson's *Arithmetical Copy Book,* and Joseph Champion's *Tutor's Assistant in Teaching Arithmetic* consisted of calligraphi-

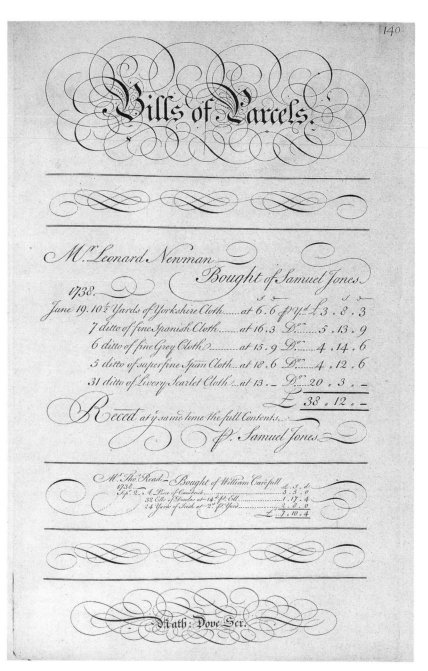

3. The mercantile orientation of penmanship: copy matter from a popular eighteenth-century penmanship treatise.

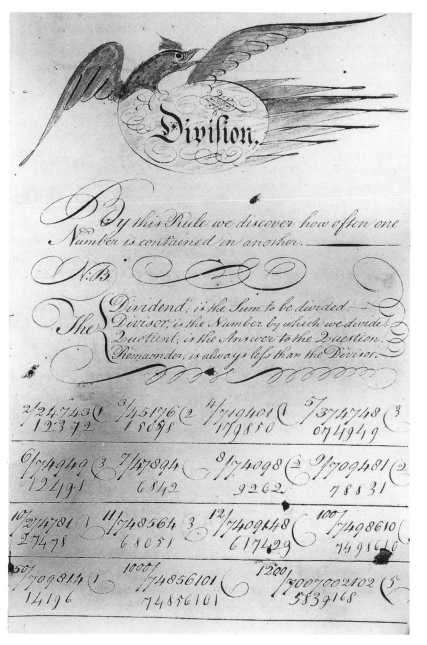

Division,

By this Rule we discover how often one Number is contained in another.

N.B.

The
Dividend, is the Sum to be divided.
Divisor, is the Number by which we divide.
Quotient, is the Answer to the Question.
Remaonder, is always less than the Divisor.

2/24743 (1	3/45176 (2	4/719401 (	5/374748 (3
12372	15058	179850	074949

6/74949 (3	7/47894 (	8/74098 (2	9/709481 (2
12491	6842	9262	78831

10/274781 (1	11/748564 (3	12/7409148 (	100/7498610 (
27478	68051	617429	7498610

50/709814 (1	1000/74856101 (	1200/7007002102 (5
14196	74856101	5839168

4. Arithmetic calligraphically rendered in an eighteenth-century ciphering book.

cally rendered text in which enough space was left to complete the arithmetic problems in carefully executed penmanship. Even those arithmetic and accounting texts that did not offer training in penmanship were often written by writing masters—small wonder, as many writing masters operated private academies that featured a full business curriculum. Hence instruction in penmanship tended to overlap with instruction in arithmetic and accounting.[16]

In titling their works, writing masters knew their clientele: *The Accomplish't Clerk or Accurate Penman, The Merchants Penman, The United Pen-Men for Forming the Man of Business, Mercantile Penmanship*.[17] Members of their audience hoped to learn penmanship on their own, by purchasing self-tutoring manuals, some in penmanship alone, others in the full complement of business subjects. *The American Instructor: Or, Young Man's Best Companion,* the first work published in America to contain copybook material, was typical of these comprehensive self-instructors. Purporting "to qualify any Person for Business, without the Help of a Master," it included instruction in penmanship, of course, but it also contained chapters on such topics as "How to write Letters on Business," a "short and easy Method of Shop and Book-Keeping," and the proper "Forms of Indentures, Bonds, Bills of Sale, Receipts, Wills, Leases, Releases, &c."[18] There could be no mistaking the mercantile nature of writing literacy.

THE CRAFT OF PENMANSHIP

The links between penmanship and the countinghouse were tight, making the ability to write less universal than the ability to read but something other than a mark of gentle breeding. Merchants might have wealth but they were not aristocrats. Further depressing the potential prestige of penmanship was the common perception of the writing master as a person who worked with his hands, a craftsman. Although English writing masters might commission portraits in robe and wig (fig. 5), and although a couple of them could even boast a coat of arms, by and large they came from modest, if not lowly, origins. John Ayres began life as a footman, William Chinnery was the son of a common cordwainer, and Abiah Holbrook of Boston, probably the most accomplished writing master in colonial America, was the son of a keg maker. Some of these men combined instruction in penmanship with the practice of other crafts. John Baskerville was both a calligrapher and a japanner of tinwares, while John Langton appeared at least as proud of his accomplishments in "the Noble Art of Glass-Painting, Staining, and Tinging" as of those in penmanship. They set up shop as other craftsmen did, under a sign—the hand and pen was a favorite in London—that symbolized their expertise.

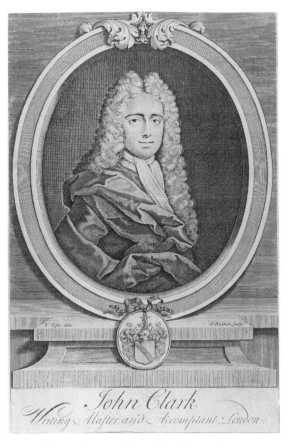

John Clark
Writing Master and Accomptant, London

5. Aristocratic pretensions of an eighteenth-century
writing master.

Most telling, with few exceptions penmen acquired their skills through an
apprenticeship.[19]

In England, so great was the perception of penmanship as a lowly mechanical skill that an illegible hand stood as the mark of gentle breeding.
Shakespeare's Hamlet admitted that he "once did hold it, as our statists do, /
A baseness to write fair, and labored much / How to forget that learning" and
reflected positively on the skill of penmanship only as it had ultimately done
him "yeoman's service." Two centuries later, Thomas De Quincey noted that
French aristocrats of the 1790s purposefully "and even ambitiously" cultivated a poor hand, "as if in open proclamation of scorn for the arts by which
humbler people oftentimes got their bread." In 1802 the Reverend William
Barrow commented that "Quintilian has told us, that the nobility in his time

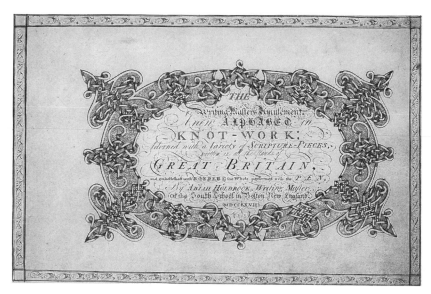

6. A master craftsman's showpiece.

despised, or affected to despise, the mechanical dexterity of writing a fine hand: and not many years ago the same affectation had an extensive influence on people of fashion in England. A letter was often considered as the more genteel; the less conveniently it could be read." In America, where elite status often rested on mercantile wealth, such attitudes carried less weight, but even there, writing masters had to overcome a mild prejudice against fine penmanship. "It is much to be regretted," complained writing master John Jenkins in 1813, "that it has become of late years in a degree fashionable to write a scrawling and almost unintelligible way."[20]

The perception of penmanship as a craft becomes even more understandable when we consider the mechanics of writing in the seventeenth and eighteenth centuries. Until steel pens became available (in the middle third of the nineteenth century), learning to write included instruction in the physical manipulation of writing tools and materials. The novice penman learned to cut a proper nib from a goose, raven, or crow quill with a penknife, no easy task. Poorly cut quills dried up quickly, carried the ink unevenly across the paper, or otherwise made execution of a proper script impossible, and even well-cut quills required constant sharpening. If the pen was not ready-made, often neither was the ink, forcing penmen to learn to mix ink from the proper ingredients in the right proportions. With pen and ink ready, the young penman then turned his attention to the paper. He might be required to rule guidelines in pencil, and he certainly had to learn how to treat the paper with powdered pumice or sandarac, variously known as gum sandrick or pounce, so as to prevent the ink from soaking in. Penmanship treatises of the colonial era thus gave consideration not only to handwriting itself but also to the physical process of preparing pen and ink and ensuring a tidy product. A rhyme commonly found in these treatises summarized the directions:

> A Pen-Knife Razor Metal, Quills good Store;
> Gum Sandrick Powder, to Pounce Paper o'er;
> Ink, shining black; Paper more white than Snow,
> Round and Flat Rulers on yourself bestow,
> With willing Mind, these, and industrious Hand,
> Will make this Art your Servant at Command.[21]

Furthermore, the execution of handwriting required no small degree of manual dexterity and skill—the "industrious hand"—again, because of the nature of writing tools. In addition to producing proper letter shape and slope, students in the quill and ink era had to control the passage of ink onto the paper in order to execute hairline upward strokes (ascenders) and contrasting thick, ink-laden descenders. Some writing masters taught their pupils how to strike and flourish—that is, how to decorate their hands with elements ranging from simple curlicues and spirals to fanciful birds, dragons, and angels. And, of course, everything had to be done without spotting and smudging.

Colonial writing masters understood that students required a good deal of practice even to approximate their own level of proficiency. Hence the main pedagogical method involved the copying of handwriting models. These might be set by the writing master at the top of a sheet of paper or slate, demonstrated on the blackboard, taken from an engraved copybook, or (by the end of the eighteenth century) provided in the form of printed copy slips, in all cases, to be imitated over and over again down the length of the page or slate. Recognizing the challenge this presented to beginning pupils, especially young children who lacked adult levels of physical coordination, writing masters often allowed beginners to use pencil or chalk and slate, to trace models with a dry pen, or to execute copies in an oversized script. Mastery of these skills was signaled much the way expert competence in other forms of craftsmanship was represented, through the execution and display of virtuoso specimens (fig. 6).[22]

It was the bane of the writing master's existence to be perceived as little better than a master craftsman. To counter such perceptions as best they could, writing masters took pains to detail the ancient origins and historical significance of handwriting. If we were to believe John Bancks, God himself bestowed the gift of penmanship on humanity, although "whether the Memphian Priests, or Hebrew Sage" were the initial recipients was still a matter of conjecture. According to the usual account, handwriting made all civilized intercourse possible. "Hail happy Art!" rejoiced Bancks of "The Scholar's Treas'ry, and the Merchant's Guide":

> Learning, thro' thee, descends to distant Times,
> And Commerce travels o'er remotest Climes:
> Thou chain'st Events which Ages widely part,
> Convey'st the Lover's Wish, reliev'st the lab'ring heart.[23]

While stressing the social utility of practical penmanship, writing masters wanted penmanship to be revered as something more than useful. It was clearly impossible to ignore the commercial applications of their skill—and, after all, these applications were the writing master's bread and butter—but could not penmanship be useful and beautiful at the same time? Might it not be a skill "where Use and Ornament Unite in One," as John Bancks insisted in 1743, "To serve, or grace, the Counter or the Throne"? Most writing masters agreed with Bancks and thus invoked such fashionable aesthetic principles as variety, symmetry, and proportion to describe the products of their art. This is not to say that anyone else bought their line. It was written of the eighteenth-century penman Thomas Tomkins that he "dreamed through life that penmanship was one of the fine arts, and that a writing master should be seated with his peers in the [Royal] Academy." Unable to obtain membership in this society of artists, he lowered his sights to an invitation to their annual dinner. "Many a year passed," the tragic story continues, "every intrigue was practiced, every remonstrance was urged, every stratagem of courtesy was tried," but alas, with no luck. Thus expired the hapless penman "for want of a dinner!"[24]

THE REGULATION OF LITERACY

"Three things bear mighty Sway with Men," read a common eighteenth-century copybook maxim, "The Sword, the Scepter, and the PEN."[25] There is, in fact, no necessary connection between power and literacy. For centuries, Europe had been ruled by largely illiterate warriors and statesmen. Nor does the spread of literacy among the population necessarily have democratizing or leveling effects, giving all who can read equal authority and social position. As Keith Thomas has argued in the case of early modern England, the rise in literacy added only a cultural dimension to well-established hierarchies of status, wealth, and power.[26] Nevertheless, by the time Anglo-Americans practiced their penmanship to this couplet, they knew full well that in their society at least, there certainly was a connection between the ability to write and the opportunity to rule. A brief thought to those who could not write—

mostly humble or female or nonwhite members of society—confirmed that social truth. Under these circumstances, literacy skills would have to be imparted and practiced in such a way as to regulate the cultural and social meanings attached to them. Men of standing would of course be fully literate, but in addition, the practice and products of their literacy would have to be understood as expressions of their rank and power. Conversely, those with little status and authority would either have to remain illiterate or their literacy skills would need to be in some way discounted.

Withholding literacy was the most direct way of regulating the social and cultural weight attached to it. In some cases, those in power were conscious of the subversive potential of being able to write, and they deliberately prohibited those under their power from learning. Slaveholders, for example, did not relish the idea of slaves forging freedom papers or passes. But there may have been a less overtly conspiratorial rationale for keeping a substantial portion of the population unable to write. The historian Richard D. Brown argues that if seventeenth-century colonial elites were able to maintain a near monopoly on primary sources of information, passing news down the social scale at their discretion, it was because they believed that only those at the top of society needed and could make responsible use of such intelligence. Literacy skills may have been withheld from certain groups on the analogous theory that humbler members of society had no use for full literacy, nor could they be trusted to use their ability to write in socially beneficial or innocuous ways. Thus, literacy skills, like information, would be imparted on a "need-to-know" basis, and some people, it was believed—African-Americans, Native Americans, humble whites, women—did not need to know how to write.[27]

Prescribing the uses of writing literacy was another way of ensuring that those who did know how to write did nothing disruptive with their skill. Historians of the printed word have amply demonstrated the limited uses to which reading was put in colonial America, the major one being the intense and repeated study of the Bible and related religious works. Far less has been said of how the uses of writing were strictly prescribed and proscribed, but we should by no means equate the ability to write with the means of authorship. Penmanship pedagogy discouraged such an equation; certainly copybooks taught students how to write, but more strictly speaking, they taught students how to copy writing. The model bills of lading and ledger entries they contained largely defined the boundaries of the world of writing that the ordinary student would one day enter. Even where we might expect greater levels of self-expression, such as in correspondence, forms were prescribed almost as carefully as they were in more mundane mercantile writing. Some copybooks included model letters, both business and personal, and the many self-help books of the eighteenth century, from the general *American*

Instructor to the more specialized manuals of letter writing, provided even more epistolary forms.[28]

The practice of copying penmanship models shaded into a generalized habit of copying by hand. Colonial Americans copied sermons and lectures, passages from medical books and legal writings, poetry and essays. Print copies of these texts were nonexistent, scarce, or expensive, so that copying made practical sense. But the practice of transcription also reinforced the notion of reading as the passive inscription of authoritative texts into one's inner being and of writing as the subsequent copying of those texts. If reading was the internalization of received truths, then writing was simply its reexternalization.[29] Few members of society ever went beyond an understanding of writing as copying or transcribing to the practice of original composition. Those who did were people with social power and cultural authority—literary wits, elite letter writers, statesmen, clerics, and scholars—and it was fitting for their pens to produce works that were qualitatively different from those of lower status.

It was not only the content of writings that varied with one's standing in society, however. The very style in which one formed letters was also determined by one's place in society and therefore acted as a third mechanism of controlling the social and cultural meanings attached to writing literacy. Open a penmanship treatise of the seventeenth or eighteenth centuries, and you will find not one, single cursive script but an entire range of hands, each reserved for—and therefore a marker of—a specific occupation, gender, or class (fig. 7). To understand the conceptual underpinnings and the practical workings of this system of multiple hands, we must look at the development of handwriting in England, where the system existed in its purest form.[30]

During the Middle Ages, the institutions under whose auspices almost all writing took place—the church, the royal court, and the judiciary—determined what scripts were to be used by prescribing particular hands as proper to official use. The Exchequer, for example, mandated that the pipe-roll hand be used to record transactions with the king's debtors. Although ecclesiastical hands differed from administrative ones and these again from legal hands, all were variants on a native Gothic script.

From the Elizabethan era, other uses of literacy, hence other groups of writers, made their appearance and expanded their influence. These groups of writers, first, social elites (both male and female), and then a rapidly growing corps of merchants, discarded an older Gothic hand, known generically as secretary in the sixteenth and seventeenth centuries, in favor of a completely new set of hands that had arrived from Italy. These new scripts were originally developed by Florentine humanist scholars (who claimed only to have reintroduced them from ninth-century exemplars), then given official sanction and hence a wide and lasting influence by Vatican officials. The development of handwriting in England, and ultimately in its colonies, from the late sixteenth to the nineteenth centuries entails, in its grossest aspect, the displacement of the native, Gothic forms of script by those derived from the humanistic scripts of Renaissance Italy.

This process of displacement, however, was gradual and complex, and even at the end of the colonial period, it was not complete. Until the latter part of the 1600s, the Italian hands flourished mainly among the high-born and the scholarly. Queen Elizabeth, for example, mastered the italic chancery cursive as a young woman, as did King Charles I as a young man. The adoption of the new hands among the well-born was neither wholesale nor immediate, however, and the Gothic and Italian forms coexisted in a variety of ways. The secretary hand was commonly used for English-language texts, for example, the italic for Latin texts. A gentleman's private amanuensis characteristically employed the secretary hand, with the gentleman reserving italic for his signature, postscripts, and any letters he might pen personally. And many a gentleman's letter simply oscillated from one to the other. In seventeenth-century America, we see a mixed use as well. In Massachusetts, Cotton Mather used a Gothic cursive, but John Winthrop wrote in the Italian hand—sometimes. The governor also made use of secretary and, even more confusingly, was known to alternate back and forth within a single sentence. The overall trend was clear, however. By the end of the 1600s, native Gothic scripts were archaic, the Italian-derived scripts the rule.[31]

Meanwhile, the Italian hands had evolved into scripts suitable for men and those suitable for women. If in the late 1500s members of the British nobility, male and female alike, had acquired a modish italic chancery, by the 1600s the roman hand had become increasingly associated with the fair sex, and by the early 1700s it was considered appropriate only for the ladies. John Langton clearly shared the same sense of propriety when in 1727 he dedicated his *Small Italian Hand* to "the R[t]. Honb[le]. The Lady Elizabeth Cecil." And George Bickham, reflecting on the early seventeenth-century writing master Lucas Materot from the vantage point of the eighteenth century, characterized the Frenchman as a penman whose mastery of the Italian hand made him "the Darling of the Ladies."[32] Gentlemen did not revert to a Gothic hand, but their brand of italic differed stylistically from that of their female counterparts.

The greatest boost in the fortunes of the Italian hands came not from the well-born, however, but from men of commerce and finance. At the end of the sixteenth century, merchants, tradesmen, and bankers adopted stripped-down versions of the italic as modified by French and Dutch writing masters. The mercantile round text, round hand, and running hand derived from Italy,

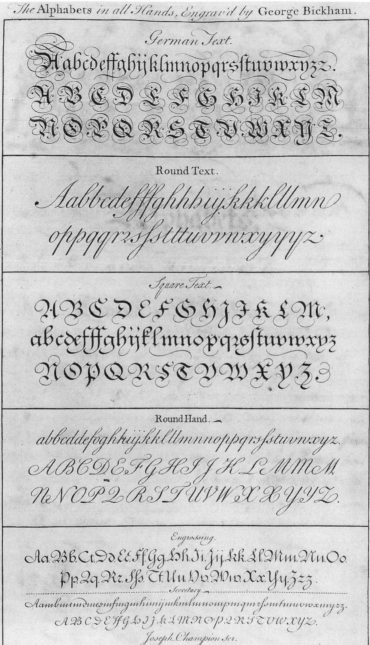

7. The multiple hands of the eighteenth century.

Old English Print.

Aabcdefghijklmnopqrſsſstuvwxyz.xc.

ABCDEFGHJKLMNOP

QRSTUWXYZZJC.

Italick Print.

Aabcdefghijklmnopqrſstuvwxyz.æœ

ABCDEFGHIJKLMNOPQR

RSTUVWXYYZÆ.

Roman Print.

Aabcdefghijklmnopqrſstuvwxyz.

ABCDEFGHIJKLMNOPQ

RSTUVWXYZ.

Italian Hand.

aabbccddeefffoghbijkkllmmnoppgrſsſstuvwxyzz.

ABCDEFGHIJKLLMMN

NOPQRSTUVWWXYZZ.

Court Hand.

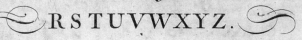

The Chancery

Aa Bb Cc Dd Ee Ffff Gg Hh Jiij Kk Llll Mm Nn

Oo Pp Qq Rr Sſs St Yuv Ww Xx Yy Zz.tt Champion Scrip.

to be sure, but they were aesthetically distinct from the gentlemen's italic, much as the gentlemen's italic was from the ladies'. Thus, by the eighteenth century the new but now dominant classes of writers—gentlemen, ladies, and men of affairs—each practiced related but discrete variants of the Italian hand. The older Gothic forms, including the court, chancery, and engrossing hands, survived only as legal hands.[33]

Learning to write was thus a complicated business in the seventeenth and eighteenth centuries. Ordinary folk—a fully literate farmer, for example, or a simple country tradesman—would learn only a single hand. Other writers, however, might well have to learn several. Some scripts could be dismissed as inappropriate; an eighteenth-century gentleman would steer clear of a ladies' italic just as certainly as a merchant would ignore the legal hands. But otherwise, penmanship education might well entail the laborious mastery of successive scripts.

Just how much of this byzantine system of hands survived the journey across the Atlantic must be considered. Clearly, colonial Americans living in seaboard towns had opportunity to master a variety of scripts. Scholars at Boston's three public writing schools, for example, learned anywhere from five to eight hands. Private writing masters advertised instruction in "all the hands of Great Britain," all "the most modish as well as necessary Hands," and "divers Sorts of Writing, viz. English and German Texts; the Court, Roman, Secretary & Italian Hands." The many copybooks imported from England featured multiple hands, and penmanship models published in America, beginning with the *American Instructor* of 1748, afforded similar instruction. As late as 1808 Henry Dean of Salem, Massachusetts, published a copybook featuring current or mercantile running hand, round and round text, Italian, German text, engrossing and running secretary, square text, court, set and running chancery, roman print, italic print, and black English letter.[34] While most boys and girls would not have been trained in multiple hands, then, it seems highly likely that they would have known of their existence, much as even poorly educated Americans would at least have heard of Latin and Greek.

Although colonial Americans were aware of a great variety of hands, American writing masters simplified the complex repertoire of their English counterparts, in practice if not in theory. The reasons were many. For one, as the older Gothic forms lost favor in England, the number of scripts in common use decreased, even in the mother country. Then too, the colonies lacked England's highly developed administrative and judicial systems, so that the legal hands were simply irrelevant. More to the point, given the attenuated social structure of the colonies—in particular the lack of a titled aristocracy, a gentry distinct from a mercantile elite, and a rigid structure in the professions—penmanship instruction reflected a simplified social agenda. American writing masters were competent in a range of hands, but they were called upon to teach only some of them. In actual practice, the potential multiplicity of hands divided into overlapping pairs of opposites: mercantile versus epistolary, practical versus ornamental, male versus female. These divisions were by no means absolute. It is clear that some girls received training in business hands, while writing masters, ever eager to raise the status of their skill from craft to art, itched to instruct mercantile students in ornamental penmanship. Nevertheless, the system of classifying hands by class, occupation, and gender remained intact in its conceptual essentials.

Just what should we make of this now unfamiliar system of differentiation? What were its purposes and meanings? As we have seen, the seventeenth and especially the eighteenth century witnessed increasing levels of literacy; elbowing their way into the groups with a long-standing ability to write—merchants, professionals, and private secretaries to the well-born—were the well-born themselves, both male and female, along with increasing numbers of more ordinary folk whose links with the world of commerce or with the apparatus of the state recommended the skill of penmanship to them. Tagging handwriting with the social identity of its producer prevented any potential confusion of social status that would have occurred had all handwriting been executed in the same script. Thus the gentleman signaled his social superiority to his private secretary when he signed a letter in an au courant italic, leaving the body of the letter unmistakably the product of a hired hand who had been relegated to the old-fashioned, workmanlike secretary hand. Should our gentleman write the letter entirely by himself, it would not be confused for one by his wife, which would have been executed in a ladies' roman, or for one by a merchant, executed in a round hand. And although common artisans and farmers might learn the same round hand, they were unlikely to embellish it with the ornate capitals and flourishes taught in the mercantile courses of the seaboard cities. At a glance, then, a fully literate stranger could evaluate the social significance of a letter—from a male? a female? a gentleman? a clerk?—simply by noting what hand it had been written in. The appropriate degree of authority granted to the handwritten word, to literacy in the largest sense, was inscribed into the very words themselves, guaranteeing that literacy would carry neither socially promiscuous meanings nor culturally disruptive uses. Thus the system of multiple hands joined the withholding of literacy training and the regimen of copying as mechanisms to control the meanings attached to the skill and product of writing literacy.

What does it mean to talk of handwriting in an age of print? Does script become obsolete with the invention of the printing press? At the very least, is it rendered socially inoperative and culturally meaningless? Certainly the historiographical focus on the ability to read and the products of the press would tend to suggest that reading literacy and print—or their folk-culture opposites, illiteracy and orality—are the real players in the drama of Western history since Gutenberg. Writing literacy and script are generally either absent from the cast of characters or have bit parts. What we must keep in mind, however, and what will be related here, is first, the extent to which the presence of print remained marginal until the eighteenth century and second, how the emergence of print worked to define a set of meanings and functions for handwriting.

The first printing press in Britain's American colonies was established in Massachusetts Bay Colony in 1639, a mere nine years after the founding of the colony. But we should not interpret the early date to mean that colonial Americans clamored for more presses. There was no sense of urgency, no critical need to be met as quickly and broadly as possible. Throughout the whole of the seventeenth century, only five presses found their way to the seaboard colonies—more, one should add, than could be found in England. What printers there were operated under the watchful eye of governmental and clerical authorities, and they produced a relatively small number of works with limited, traditional cultural purposes, including proclamations, law codes, sermons, and other religious writings. Nor did the printed materials imported into seventeenth-century America represent a print revolution, bringing with them new ways of experiencing the world. Importers of English imprints recognized that the greatest demand was for much the same kind of material already being printed in the colonies, namely, religious books. Books of humor and magic and stories of wonders and adventures also made their way from England, but these served to maintain the vitality of popular beliefs that originated prior to and existed independent of print. Indeed, as the historian David Hall has argued, the currency of these genres shaped what did appear in print, so that Puritan sermons read as godly versions of the sensationalist narratives churned out by London presses. Print was something more than a twinkle in Gutenberg's eye, but it did not yet wield the full powers of its maturity.[35]

A further sign that the press did not rule is the existence of an alternative means of publication, scribal publication.[36] In seventeenth-century Britain, country gentlemen subscribed to handwritten newsletters filled with London news and gossip; men gathered at coffeehouses to read the latest handwritten lampoon of state or court; the well-born of both sexes distributed their literary productions in handwritten form; and musicians sold their compositions, again in handwritten form, to musically inclined families of means. Copies might be penned by their authors or by authors' secretaries and clerks. Alternatively, originals might be circulated, sometimes with the understanding that copies could be—or indeed should be—made. Scribal publication might also be undertaken as a commercial enterprise, complete with well-staffed scriptoria churning out dozens and even hundreds of copies of a single text.

We should not imagine that scribal publication functioned as a poor second choice to press publication. Economics may have played some role in the choice between script and print—in small editions, print was more expensive—but not all scribal editions were small, and purchasers were apparently willing to pay a premium for the handwritten form. Indeed, scribal authors and readers actively preferred the handwritten form. What made print less appealing and script more so were the associations each medium carried. Print was public, openly available to all with the money to buy it; furthermore, in an age of government censorship it was regulated by the state. In other words, there was no controlling the readership but there was plenty of control over the authors. In contrast, handwritten texts circulated among an exclusive, handpicked audience, most usually a circle of social equals with similar tastes and interests. And because the texts were privately distributed, they were uncensored. Scandalous gossip, anti-government propaganda, pornography—all were free to circulate in handwritten form. If print was the realm of social promiscuity and ideological control, script was the realm of exclusivity, privacy, and freedom.

In some cases, the nature of the author recommended the qualities of one medium over another. For women, print publication was culturally tantamount to prostitution, an unseemly exposing of oneself to every buyer. By confining her literary productions to an exclusive, deliberately selected audience, the female avoided compromise. Male courtiers, anxious to dissociate themselves from the pecuniary motives of professional poets and the tawdry productions of broadside balladeers, also avoided what one literary historian has called the stigma of print and one Tudor poet termed "the publique tipographicall theatre."[37] In other cases, the nature of the text determined the medium. Script best suited materials of a politically or morally controversial nature. It also made sense for private or confidential materials, such as the London newsletters country gentlemen relied on to keep abreast of metropolitan affairs. Even when the circulation of these newsletters climbed dramatically and their publishers began to print them, the suggestion of private confidence was maintained by setting them in a script typeface.

By the early 1700s print publication had largely, though not entirely, eclipsed scribal publication, just one sign of the printing press's increasing dominance. There were many others. As we have seen, the new century saw a marked increase in literacy that reflected and created a growing market for printed goods. This market was served by an ever-larger number of printers and printing presses, producing ever-greater numbers of such traditional materials as religious books, broadsides, and almanacs, as well as such new forms as newspapers and magazines. What was not printed in the colonies might be imported from England. Gentlemen ordered gilt-tooled, leather-bound volumes for their libraries, while shopkeepers and specialty booksellers stocked a wide variety of English imprints, including religious works, schoolbooks, novels, practical advice manuals, and the cheap and popular romances, adventure stories, and folk amusements known as chapbooks.[38]

Just as critical, the medium of print changed in character, developing into what the literary scholar Michael Warner has termed a technology of publicity. After 1720, relates Warner, printed newspapers and political pamphlets made their appearance, but these did not so much reflect the development of a public sphere as reconstitute it. Under the older understanding of the public sphere, conflict was inevitably personal and socially disruptive. In face-to-face confrontations or heated exchanges of letters, men clashed on the basis of their personal interests and in the context of their personal relationships. The use of print might exacerbate conflict or lead to consensus, but only arbitrarily and incidentally, not inherently. By contrast, under the reconfigured definition of the public, publication in print was conceptualized as the way public discussion usually and ideally takes place and the mechanism whereby the public itself is constituted. These conceptual transformations established new conditions under which print operated. Opinions expressed in print would be validated only inasmuch as their authors renounced the specifics of their personhood in favor of an abstract citizenship in the public sphere. There would be no personal exchanges; they would be conducted on the premise and legitimized on the condition that unknown—and by definition unknowable—others read and participate in them. What validated and characterized the medium of print was above all its impersonality.[39]

Over the course of the eighteenth century, even typefaces underwent a gradual but significant shift to the impersonal, a shift that involved a move away from calligraphical, somatic models of design to rational, mathematical models. In the first centuries of printing, there were strong aesthetic links between script and print. Many of the most prominent typeface designers were also writing masters: Ludovico degli Arrighi, of the Italian Renaissance; the Parisian Pierre Moreau, active in the mid-1600s; and John Baskerville, an eighteenth-century Englishman. Even more critical, calligraphical forms served as models for their typographical equivalents. In Gutenberg's Germany, for example, Gothic typefaces were modeled on contemporary Gothic scripts. By the end of the 1400s, roman and italic typefaces, based respectively on the formal and informal humanistic scripts of fifteenth-century Italy, made their appearance. As late as the eighteenth century, the hairline upstroke and thick downstroke of the running hand was mimicked in the contrast of thick and thin elements in the new, so-called modern typefaces.[40]

Typographers and printers acknowledged the role handwriting models played in their craft. For a typeface to approximate the "true shape" of letters, wrote Joseph Moxon in his *Mechanick Exercises on the Whole Art of Printing* (1683–84), it must approximate geometric figures as modified by "the Course and Progress of the Pen." A century later, Benjamin Franklin made the same point in commenting on two typefaces newly designed by the Italian typographer Giambattista Bodoni. "I do not presume to criticise your Italic Capitals; they are generally perfect," wrote Franklin in 1787. "I would only beg leave to say, that to me the form of the *T* in the world *LETTRE* of the Title Page seems preferable to that of the *T* in the word *Typographie* in the next Page as the downward stroke of *T, P, R, F, B, D, H, K, L, I,* and some others, which in writing we begin at the top, naturally swells as the pen descends; and it is only in the *A* and the *M* and the *N* that those strokes are fine, because the pen begins at the bottom."[41]

As long as typographers and printers sought to reproduce in hot metal what writing masters executed with pen and ink, they did so with the understanding that ultimately the design of both script and type was based on the same aesthetic principle: consonance with the idealized dimensions of the human body. Renaissance treatises analyzed letter forms, script and type, as their proportions conformed to those of the body, either literally rendered or abstracted into squares and circles (figs. 8, 9). Even the terminology used by calligraphers and typographers reflected this anthropomorphism. Thus, letter forms had faces, heads, necks, and bodies.[42]

Increasingly over the course of the eighteenth century, however, and accelerating into the early nineteenth, script and print diverged, both as executed and, more important, as conceptualized. Certainly the "fat face" typefaces first introduced around 1810 for newspaper headlines, timetables, and advertising had no calligraphical precedent. But by then typographers had reconceived the design principles of their craft, ditching the traditional somatic model for a rationalized, mathematical one. The establishment in 1692 of a French royal commission to reform typography heralded that shift. The commission was charged with redesigning the roman typeface on an analytical grid consisting of 2,304 squares. The rationalization of print was furthered in the eighteenth century by the development of standardized type sizes, separated by steps of equal magnitude, and expressed in numerical units ("seven-

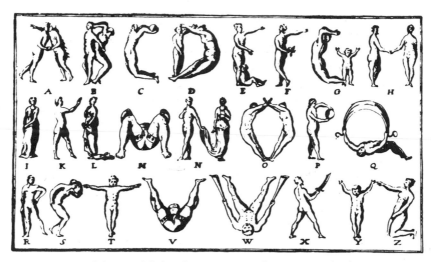

8. A human alphabet, from a seventeenth-century copybook.

point") rather than the traditional descriptive terms ("mignone").[43] No such transformation occurred in handwriting aesthetics. The two had taken separate paths.

Walter Ong characterizes the differential aesthetics of print and script as inherent to the media. "Printed texts look machine-made," he writes, "as they are." By contrast, "chirographic control of space tends to be ornamental, ornate, as in calligraphy." Ong asserts that "typographic control typically impresses more by its tidiness and inevitability: the lines perfectly regular, all justified on the right side, everything coming out even visually. . . . This is an insistent world of cold, non-human facts."[44]

Michael Warner argues that it is the absence of this link with the human body that determines what "counts" as print to begin with. Many have assumed that quantity and accuracy are the defining characteristics of print, but Warner maintains that the mass production of identical copies was neither a necessary consequence nor the sole province of print technology. Many early printers, he points out, produced material in smaller quantities than their scribal contemporaries. Similarly, he contends that printed copies of the same texts often differed from one another in small but nonetheless significant details, so that handwritten copies, executed according to rigid standards of consistency, might actually resemble each other more than their printed counterparts. What defined printing, then, and distinguished it from handwriting, was not the scale or quality of production, but its "negative relation to the hand." Even today, Warner argues, the production of duplicates by means of carbon paper is not considered printing, because of its origin

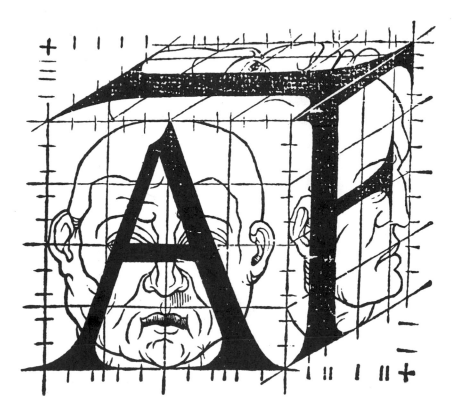

9. The somatic proportions of letters, from a sixteenth-century treatise on typography.

in a manual process; the photocopying of duplicates, on the other hand, *is* conceptualized as a form of printing. Thus print is defined in opposition to handwriting.[45]

Given that calligraphic models and principles of design informed typography as it was first practiced and conceived, the dissociation of print from script was apparently not instantaneous. Nevertheless, sometime in the eighteenth century the cultural trajectories of print and script were set by their respective relations to the hand, and from that time they did diverge. Print lost any association with the hand just as pointedly as script retained it. This association of script with the physical executor of the script endowed handwriting with a unique set of cultural meanings and functions. For if print was defined by its dissociation from the hand, the body, and the corporeal individual that created it, then handwritten matter necessarily referred back to the hand, the body, and the individual in new ways. Handwritten texts could be read for both substance and form. Words transmitted their authors' ideas;

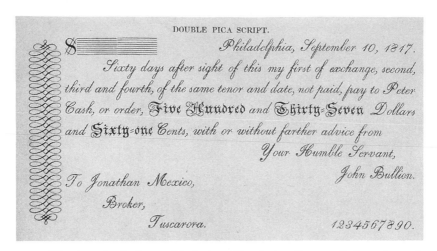

10. The place of script in a world of print: a "handwritten" mercantile form, from a printer's specimen book, 1816.

scripts, the authors themselves. Hence we should not interpret the "triumph of print" as the banishing of script to the cultural margins but as a critical moment of definition for the script medium. As men and women exploited the impersonality of print to its fullest, they came to understand handwriting in contradistinction to print and to make handwriting function in contradistinction to the press, as the medium of the self.

One telling consequence of that characterization of handwriting was the seemingly anomalous persistence of the use of script where mechanical replication would seem to have made sense. Why, in the late eighteenth and early nineteenth centuries, did members of elite literary circles prefer to disseminate their belles lettres in manuscript form? Why not send calling cards to the printer for mechanical reproduction instead of laboriously executing dozens in pen and ink or paying a professional calligrapher to do the same? And surely it would have made sense to print such frequently used mercantile forms as the trade card or the sales receipt, leaving spaces, if necessary, for the particulars of individual transactions. After all, legal forms had been printed in America from at least the early eighteenth century. Even when traditionally handwritten forms did yield to the economic logic of mechanical reproduction, they were not always set in the usual print typefaces. Calling cards, trade cards, and mercantile forms were often engraved to look like script, much as they were in penmanship copybooks of the day. And when these same texts were set in type, it was likely to be in specially designed script typefaces (fig. 10).[46]

The literary historian David Shields suggests that, in the case of belles lettres manuscrits, authors deliberately rejected the public nature of print in favor of the "exclusive communications and privy pleasures" provided and symbolized by the handwritten form, for much the same reason that many authors and readers selected scribal publication in the seventeenth century. But it is unwise to generalize these conclusions and align script with the private sphere and print with the public. For one, it was understood that some ostensibly private, handwritten material might well become public. Thus, it was not unusual for private mercantile correspondence to circulate among the merchant class as a whole and to end up in public print. Then too, there were other handwritten forms—the bill of exchange, for example—that were surely artifacts of the public sphere.[47] The error occurs in focusing on print solely as it symbolizes the public sphere and then defining the meaning of handwriting by default. What is overlooked is the positive association of script with the self. Where such association was socially or culturally desirable, handwriting became the "logical" medium of writing, regardless of its technological limitations, whether the communication was of a private or public nature. In the eighteenth century, calling cards, trade cards, mercantile letters, even the mundane bill of exchange involved just such a presentation of the self—before society, before one's clientele, before one's business associates—and handwriting acted as the proper vehicle for that enterprise.

The association of handwriting with the self took on special significance as the impersonality of the print medium came to be regarded as hazardous (fig. 11). By the eighteenth century, as print took hold, many in the Anglo-American world expressed concern over the potential pitfalls of human communication. The problem was an old one. Even in the sixteenth and seventeenth centuries, argues the historian Jean-Christophe Agnew, the emergence of a market economy and society in Britain and America had fostered the theatricalization of self-presentation and the sense that self-interested motives lay concealed behind masks of disinterestedness. But if the potential duplicity of human appearances had long been of concern, its embodiment in the perils of print was new.[48] Print, engrossing an ever-greater share of public communication, was indeed a dangerous medium on this count. Choices among typefaces had always been made with reference to the nature of the *text*—Latin or vernacular, religious, legal, or fictional; with respect to the *author*, type presented a blank countenance behind which the authorial presence was impossible to detect. Now, the impersonal, mechanical aesthetics of the new typeface designs presented the visual counterpart of that unsettling blankness. In both cases, the opacity of print opened up the possibility of its duplicity, for who knew what lay behind the expressionless face of type?[49]

Benjamin Franklin expressed just this sense of uneasiness in a letter to

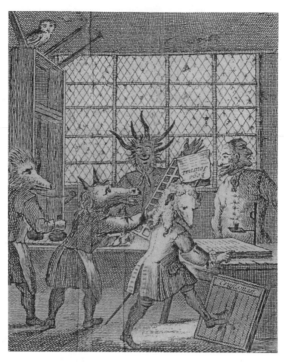

11. The duplicity of print, epitomized by the Janus-faced
printer (right).

Noah Webster in 1789. The problem with modern printing practices, he argued, is that they thwart our ability to make sense of the text, both visually and substantively. They conceal more than they reveal. Franklin complained about the use of gray rather than black ink, claiming that "new Books are printed in so dim a character as to be read with difficulty by old Eyes, unless in a very strong light and with good Glasses." He rued that, in a misguided attempt to present a more "even, regular appearance," printers no longer capitalized proper nouns. It was "the same fondness for an even and uniform appearance of characters in a line" that had led printers to discontinue the use of italics for emphasis and to discard the long s in favor of the short, round one. "Certainly the omitting [of] this prominent letter makes the line appear more even," Franklin wrote of the obsolete s, "but renders it less immediately legible; as the paring all Men's Noses might smooth and level their Faces, but would render their Physiognomies less distinguishable." In this disfigured typeface—the physiognomy of print—the face of the author remained concealed, and with it, the author's true motivations and sentiments.[50] Thus the new aesthetic standard for typeface, which stressed abstract, mathematical regularity above all, interfered with print as a medium of sincere human expression.

Some envisioned typographical solutions to the opacity of print. One school of literary critics argued that poetry should be typeset so as to reveal patterns of oral delivery. They reprinted couplets, the sense and sound of which straddled both lines, into two visually unequal and unrhyming lines that approximated the actual reading of the poem. Less seriously, in a tongue-in-cheek essay of 1787, Francis Hopkinson proposed "an improvement in the art of printing, so as to make it expressive not only of an author's narrative, opinions, or arguments, but also of the peculiarities of his temper, and the vivacity of his feelings." This would be accomplished by representing the growing "degree of vociferation" of newspaper disputes with progressively larger and therefore angrier types, beginning with long primer and ending with five-line pica, "which, indeed, is as far as the art of printing, or a modern quarrel can well go" (fig. 12). William Thornton suggested the introduction of a special symbol to mark a text as ironic, while Franklin recommended the Spanish use of the question mark, at both the beginning and the end of the sentence, to similarly clue the reader into the authorial temper.[51]

These typographical reforms never came about. Men and women of the eighteenth century found other ways of dealing with the blankness of print. One was to reject print for the spoken word. In what has been termed an elocutionary revolution, mid-eighteenth-century rhetoricians proposed a model for public speaking that deemphasized the text itself and stressed instead the public expression of private sentiments engendered by the text. What made oratory a more sincere medium of expression was its reliance on the speaker's body—the nuances of his voice, his facial expressions, his gestures—which was assumed to be more expressive of the self and opposed to the "dead letter" of print.[52]

Like speech, handwriting was perceived as a transparent medium of the self. Unlike typeface, with its mathematical design, the handwritten alphabet reflected its human origins in its somatic proportions. Human bodies executed letters that in turn resembled the human body. There was also a sense in which handwriting as an act, not just an aesthetic form, partook of the human body. Eighteenth-century penmanship manuals conditioned their readers to focus as much on the movement that produced handwriting as on the visual effect of the completed script. When viewing a script, one could imagine how it had been executed—with a leisured motion of the hand in the case of the gentleman, a delicate touch or a bold arm in the case of other writers. In representing handwriting as a form of gesture, contemporaries granted it many of the same functions of their elocutionary practice, regarding it as an undisguised expression of the self through bodily movement.

whilſt a paſſionate man, engaged in a warm controverſy, would thunder vengeance in

French Canon

It follows of courſe, that writers of great iraſcibility ſhould be charged higher for a work of the ſame length, than meek authors; on account of the extraordinary ſpace their perfor-mances muſt neceſſarily occupy; for theſe gigantic, wrath-ful types, like ranters on the ſtage, muſt have ſufficient elbow-room.

For example: Suppoſe a newſpaper quarrel to happen be-tween * M and L. M begins the attack pretty ſmartly in

Long Primer.

L replies in

Pica Roman.

M advances to

Great Primer.

L retorts in

Double Pica.

And ſo the conteſt ſwells to

Raſcal, Villain

* Left ſome ill-diſpoſed perſon ſhould miſapply theſe ini-tials, I think proper to declare, that M ſignifies Merchant, and L Lawyer.

Coward,

12. The duplicity of print, typographically remedied.

The eighteenth-century notion that writers could not disguise themselves in the medium of script was embodied in a practical way in the law courts. In the seventeenth century, men and women had certainly perceived differ-ences among hands but did not regard them as either so fundamentally or so uniquely linked with their writers as to make handwriting style a permanent or reliable indicator of identity. Hence legal practice and theory held that the only sure proof a man had penned a particular document was a witness. "The similitude of hands is nothing," argued Algernon Sidney in his treason trial of 1683, for "we know that bonds will be counterfeited, so that no man shall know his own hand." Five years later, in another trial, it was similarly argued that "it is an easy matter for any man's hand to be counterfeited; . . . frequent daily experience shows how easily it may be done." By the same token, if style could not establish identity, then identity did not determine style. If handwriting could be forged at will, it could also be changed at will. Thus having received "a fatherly admonition" regarding "the forme of my writing," a student at Oxford replied in 1622 that "if I had knowen before I could easily have altered [it], and hence forth will daylie show that I can easily change it."[53]

In the eighteenth century, these notions did not completely disappear, but they were increasingly challenged. Whereas it had been taken as a given that the same hand could be executed by more than one writer (forgery) and, conversely, that one writer could vary his style so as to execute many different hands, there now arose the perception that each person's hand was unique—indelibly marked by the self and therefore undisguisable. Much as Benjamin Franklin represented the opacity of print by comparing rationalized typeface to a disfigured physiognomy, so the uniqueness and transparency of script was likened to that of the human face. In his 1726 treatise on evidence, Geoffrey Gilbert expressed the novel opinion that "men are distinguished by their handwriting as well as by their faces, for it is very seldom that the shape of their letters agree any more than the shapes of their bodies." Accordingly, argued Gilbert, the identity of a writer and the possibility of forgery could indeed be resolved by an examination of handwriting style. Peering out of the page of script was the face of the writer.[54]

THE PRESENTATION OF THE SELF

Because handwriting revealed the self, what made handwriting important was the impression of self it left with readers, and what made it good was the degree to which it faithfully represented the writer. But what kind of self was presented in penmanship? What aspects of the writer needed to be represented in his or her handwriting? For members of the Anglo-American world, men and women were social beings, whose places in the social order were determined by their gender, status, and occupation and whose social identity was defined accordingly. Proper presentation of one's public self therefore consisted in the faithful representation of one's place in society. That meant donning the visible signs of one's gender and rank: in clothing, speaking, and carrying oneself in ways appropriate to one's station in life. Included among the arts of self-presentation, and sharing in aspects of its major elements—dress, speech, and deportment—was handwriting.[55]

To the well-born, the writing master could be categorized not only with the accountant or the craftsman but also with the fashionable tailor and the dancing master. "To Write a Good Hand is a fine Accomplishment," argued penman John Clark, "and is as useful to the Gentleman and Scholar, as the man of Business." Clark compared a poor hand to "a Stammering Tongue," and a good one to "a Graceful manner of Speaking." He recommended to an aristocratic client that to endow his son "with Gentlemanlike Qualifications, suffer him not to neglect that of Writing well . . . tho' 'tis not likely, he may want it for a maintenance."[56]

Such sentiments reflect more than the self-promotion of a writing master hungry for both business and prestige. In reality, Clark's advice was often heeded. When Lord Chesterfield attempted to mold his son into a perfect gentleman, he advised him on dress, scolded him for poor enunciation, urged him to seek out the services of a dancing master, recommended he learn the art of carving—and took him to task on his penmanship. "Your handwriting is a very bad one," he wrote in 1750, "and would make a scurvy figure in an office-book of letters, or even in a lady's pocket-book." We have no record of his son's reply, but no doubt Chesterfield looked for a letter similar to the one George Shelley included in his copybook of 1714. "In obedience to your Command I send this to inform you what Advances I have made in my Writing," read the hypothetical letter from a dutiful son to his father. A good hand, conceded the son, was not easy to acquire, "but this is no discouragem[t]. to me Since you have frequently told me that to write a good hand would be more servicable to my Designs, than any other Learning."[57]

Ladies as well as gentlemen were urged to attend to their penmanship as part of their public self-presentation. In yet another perhaps hypothetical letter included in a penmanship copybook, a well-born lady is praised for having educated her daughter in music, singing, dancing, good conversation, and the art of penmanship. Addressing "the Ladys of Great Britain," writing master Thomas Ollyffe regretted that "it is the misfortune of yo[r]. Sex not to be intrusted with a Liberal Education, yet," he added, "there are many Embellishments allow'd you w[ch] are as useful as Ornamental, . . . among which writing a fair hand is one of the most necessary Qualifications."[58] As we have seen, many colonial writing masters promised to instruct girls in what was generally regarded as one of the female accomplishments.

For the mercantile community, self-presentation was especially critical, for one's public persona was literally one's livelihood. Credit, as many a copybook made clear in its maxims, was the lifeblood of commerce, and credit was granted and withheld on the basis of a man's public reputation. "Who steals my Purse, steals Trash; 'tis something, nothing," quoted one such popular copybook precept. "'Twas mine, 'tis his, & has been Slave to Thousands. But he that filches from me my Good Name, Robs me of that which not Enriches him, And makes me Poor indeed." That self-presentation was involved is clear from penman John Ayres's comparison of mercantile reputation to "a Glass [that] being once Crackd will never be otherwise y[n] Crazy." Ayres

clearly regarded handwriting as one element of self-presentation; when reputation is lost, he wrote, "yo^u are like a canceld writing, of no value." Similarly,
another copybook asserted that while the merchant's credit is not in doubt,
his handwriting is a "portable Coin."[59]

There was nothing generic, however, about good penmanship. To be sure,
gentlemen, ladies, and merchants sought to distinguish their penmanship
from that of common folk, but they also sought to distinguish their hands
from one another. When Lord Chesterfield complained of his son's penmanship that it was "neither a hand of business, nor of a gentleman; but the
hand of a schoolboy writing his exercise," he was admonishing his son not
merely to write more legibly but to write the hand appropriate to his gender,
his occupation, and his class. Similarly, mercantile advice books urged men
of commerce to shun penmanship refinements appropriate for gentlemen in
favor of a straightforward "Clerk-like Manner of Writing." And where men
might be urged to cultivate a "good" or "fine" hand, women were urged to
cultivate a "fair" one.[60]

We see then that the system of multiple scripts did more than regulate
the meaning of literacy. Incorporating a logic that defined human beings as
players on a social stage, it also served as a mechanism whereby handwriting
faithfully represented the self. As each human being performs a socially differentiated part, so is each given a different "script." Conversely, by reading
that script for its social information one could learn all there was to know
about the writer. Here at last was a sincere medium of selfhood.

Typeface, we recall, bore no such connection to the writer. It was selected
only with reference to the nature of the text. Before the invention of the
printing press, the same principle had applied to the selection of hands—
some hands for Latin texts, others for vernacular, and so on—but although
the principle held for the new medium of print, it was gradually discarded
for the medium of script. The social identity of the writer, rather than the
nature of his or her text, determined the hand. In the sixteenth century, what
recommended a particular hand to a particular social group had more to do
with the origins of the script than the characteristics of the group that used
it. Aristocrats took to the Italian hands, for example, because they carried the
associations of the Italian Renaissance with them, thus marking those who
used them as proper courtiers. But increasingly in the seventeenth and most
pointedly in the eighteenth century, scripts took their character directly from
those who used them. Each hand was regarded as the aesthetic embodiment
of the corporate character of the social, occupational, or gender group that
made exclusive use of it.

Let us look at the legal hands. By the eighteenth century, these were completely archaic, hence incomprehensible to even a well-educated audience.

Indeed, as early as 1674 Edward Cocker's *Young Lawyer's Writing Master* promised instruction in reading, as well as writing, these inscrutable scripts. That lawyers were never popular figures is well known, but legal scriveners, whose specialty was to pen documents in the impenetrable scripts required by law, were likewise reviled. In their case, it seems that the animosity arose from the layperson's utter inability to fathom those scripts and therefore the law itself. Thus the visual inaccessibility of the law hands was emblematic of the mystery and monopoly of the legal profession.[61]

The link between the style of a script and the public, corporate character of the group for which it was reserved is even more clear in the case of scripts used by women. "Ladies' hands" were diminutive and ornamental, like the ladies themselves, lacking both power and utility. Often they required the penwoman to go back over her script and add decorative shading to her letters, suggesting her leisured status. Ladies' hands were also considered easy both to learn and to execute; they symbolized female physical delicacy, intellectual inferiority, and constitutional flightiness. James Radcliffe noted that the Italian hand had "been peculiarly practised by the ladies" because of "the easy pressure which the pen requires to execute" it, while Edward Cocker wrote of the italic hand that as "it is a Hand Generally known and most easie to attain, . . . we recommend it to the imitation of Women-kind." Martin Billingsley was even more explicit. The roman hand, he explained, "is conceived to be the easiest hand that is written with Pen. . . . Therefore it is usually taught to women, for as much as they (having not the patience to take any great paines, besides phantasticall and humoursome) must be taught that which they instantly learne."[62]

If we listen to Billingsley's description of roman characters, it is difficult to avoid the impression that he was describing not the letters but their executrixes. He writes, for example, of their "visible rotundity," of how the "stems of the Letters in this Hand, must wave and bend naturall," and "the Bodies of all Letters herein must be full." By the end of the eighteenth century, when the aesthetics of the female body no longer called for suggestions of robust fecundity and sensuality, Radcliffe could write that the Italian hand "seems, indeed, best adapted to the *fair sex*, in the slenderness of its characters" and "in the delicacy which appears in the formation of them." In their very aesthetic components—the size and shape of the letters, the extent of decoration, the relative ease of execution—the ladies' hands represented the corporate character of "Women-kind."[63]

To some extent, the female scripts suggested the actual writing process as practiced by women, a process that was painstaking and therefore time-consuming. Most of the female "effect" of these scripts, however, had to do with the aesthetics of the product. More than any other component of female self-presentation, penmanship thus resembled dress. Like clothing, it was an object in itself, easily dissociated from the person. It could be displayed and admired, even in the absence of the lady, as pleasingly feminine. Not so with the male hands. Here penmanship was understood as an aspect of physical carriage. Rather than focusing on the visual effect of the completed script, commentators noted the movement that produced the handwriting. What we look for in penmanship, read the *Universal Penman,* is "what we admire in fine Gentlemen; an Easiness of Gesture, and disengag'd Air." The trick was to make the handwriting gesture look effortless; to do so required work. "True ease in writing comes from art, not chance," explained the writing master, "As those move easiest, who have learned to dance." Thus contemporaries admired a gentleman's hand inasmuch as it was "loose, careless," or "free and easy."[64]

This deliberate insouciance was the essence of the gentleman's self-presentation. It reflected the nonchalant manner of the aristocrat, gained by exposure to the most refined courts and salons at home and abroad. Thomas Jefferson had something of this courtier ideal in mind when he commented that George Washington "wrote readily, rather diffusely, in an easy, correct style. This he had acquired by conversation with the world, for his education was merely reading, writing, and common arithmetic, to which he added surveying at a later day." Here then was the "easiness of Gesture" recommended as one of the essentials of a fine gentleman's manner. The other characteristic attributed to fine gentlemen, and by extension recommended as vital to a gentlemanly hand, was, we recall, "the disengag'd Air." In the realm of manners it consisted in a studied inattention to appearances that only men secure in their social station could afford. In the realm of penmanship, it consisted in a certain carelessness, a lack of concern to execute the script just right. Illegibility represented not only a rejection of manual labor but also the logical extreme of freedom and ease.[65]

To some extent, the aesthetics of the mercantile hands resembled that of the aristocratic hands. Merchants, like gentlemen, were urged to adopt a script "flowing with a kind of Artificial Negligence"; it is clear that there was no small degree of social imitation here. But contemporaries also recognized that the mercantile hand must positively exude the mercantile character, for as business correspondence was the lifeblood of trade, so must that correspondence establish confidence in the merchant as a man whose life and soul, whose very character, breathed commerce. In its content, a business letter was to be stripped-down and no-nonsense. Similarly, the "Clerk-like Manner of Writing, fit for the Dextrous Dispatch of Business" was to be above all fast, efficient, and legible. The running and current hands (the very names are suggestive) achieved these effects in their greater slope and degree of connectedness and by their relative lack of decoration. In describing his business hands, Charles Snell rejected decorative flourishing—what he described as "*Owls, Apes, Monsters,* and *Sprig'd Letters*"—as completely inappropriate. "*Merchants* and *Clerks,*" he insisted, "are so far from admitting those *wild Fancies,* and the *Strokes* they have so *plentifully struck* through the *Body* of their WRITING, as a Part of PENMANSHIP; that they *despise* and *scorn* them." Instead, agreed Thomas Watts, what was called for was "Plain, Strong, and neat *Writing* . . . among Men of *Business;* with whom all *affected* Flourishes and quaint Devices of Birds and Bull-Beggars, are as much avoided as Capering and Cutting in Ordinary Walking."[66] Mercantile scripts thus stood in contrast to the dandyish, even effeminate, scripts of the gentleman.

As was the case with aristocratic hands, commentators focused on the physical execution of these scripts, but what defined the penmanship gesture of the merchant, like the merchant himself, was not so much ease and carelessness as a forthright self-assurance and sense of command. Not *free* and *easy* but *bold* and *masterly* were the terms most often used to describe mercantile penmanship. This handwriting befit members of the merchant class, at least as they imagined and idealized themselves as men who, in the words of Daniel Defoe, "may more truly be said to live by their Wits than any people whatsoever." In the beginning, explains Defoe, foreign commerce is "all Project, Contrivance, and Invention," to be hazarded only "by the help of strange and Universal Intelligence"—handwritten mercantile dispatches—so a "True-bred Merchant" is "the most Intelligent Man in the World, and consequently the most capable, when urg'd by Necessity, to Contrive New Ways to live."[67] Thus is the merchant uniquely adventuresome, risk taking, able to manipulate the world for private and public benefit, characteristics manifest in his bold and masterly hand.

As many a historian will tell you, reading the handwriting of the colonial era is no straightforward proposition. While the cursives of the 1700s present few problems, the enigmatic Gothic scripts of the first half of the seventeenth century make the novice start in apprehension and squint in confusion. The first step in decoding early documents is often a lesson in paleography.

There is a deeper sense, however, in which colonial handwriting is illegible to the modern reader. Quite apart from the meaning of the particular text is the significance of the handwriting itself, intuitively apprehended by contemporaries but lost to us now. It disappeared in part because handwriting existed within a historically specific and culturally defined system of literacy that is no longer in existence. Reading and writing were not two aspects of one skill but entirely distinct accomplishments, which were taught separately to different groups of people in different pedagogical settings for different purposes. Penmanship was represented as a mercantile skill on par with book-keeping, a female accomplishment analogous to embroidery, and an element of public self-presentation that partook of aspects of both dress and deportment. Given these multiple contexts, learning to write did not mean acquiring a single, standardized script but making a suitable choice among hands. The system of multiple scripts had the effect of regulating the implications of literacy, guaranteeing that the writing produced by different categories of writers would be accorded culturally appropriate, socially innocuous degrees of authority.

Exactly what colonial men and women read in handwriting is lost to us for another reason as well. Just as we must place handwriting within the contemporary system of literacy, so must we place it in the context of the rise of print, for by the eighteenth century handwriting was accorded its particular meanings and functions in contrast to the medium of print. Where print was defined by dissociation from the hand, script took its definition from its relation to the hand. Where print was impersonal, script emanated from the person in as intimate a manner as possible. Where print was opaque, even duplicitous, script was transparent and sincere. In the new legal standard for handwriting identification, the somatic aesthetics of calligraphical design, and the system of multiple hands, handwriting functioned as a medium of the self.

As we shall see, it is this association of script with self that had the most lasting implications for handwriting in America. Indeed, that association holds today, so much so, in fact, that it comes as something of a surprise to discover it did not always exist. If this chapter has shown anything, though, it is that assuming a continuity between the colonial period and our own time is dangerous. If we thought we knew what the term *script* denoted, we may have had to revise our notions in the face of such oddities as readers who could not write, the classification of penmanship with embroidery, and the ranking and gendering of hands. Similar cautions apply to the term *self*. Seventeenth- and eighteenth-century men and women regarded handwriting as a form of self-presentation but not self-expression. Individual style or sentiment played no role in the careful copying of an authoritative original in a socially appropriate hand, but those aspects of the individual that constituted identity in the eighteenth century—gender, status, and occupation— were inscribed by the pen as surely as the ostensible message of the text.

CHAPTER TWO

Men of Character,
Scribbling Women

Penmanship in
Victorian America

In 1845 writing master James French issued two copybooks, a *Gentlemens' Writing Book*, bound in blue, and a *Ladies' Writing Book*, bound in pink. In the former, French's male students practiced their mercantile running hand with such phrases as "A neat handwriting is a letter of recommendation," while their female counterparts rehearsed the ladies' epistolary with the likes of "A fine specimen of Ornamental penmanship is a speaking Picture."[1] The division of handwriting along gender lines was nothing new, of course. Nor was its split into practical and ornamental branches. But French's copy phrases deserve a second look, for they tell us much about the meaning of handwriting in nineteenth-century America.

We picture, first of all, a young man approaching the countinghouse in search of employment, penmanship specimen in hand. Businessmen did indeed regard good handwriting as a necessary qualification for office work, so we can take French's maxim literally. But the neatness of the young man's hand recommended the lad to his employer as more than a skillful copier. It spoke to the young man's trustworthiness, his industry, and his self-discipline —in other words, what Victorians called character. And indeed, Victorian writing instructors represented writing as a process of character formation, both in the literal sense of making letters and in the figurative sense of constructing a self. As conceptualized, learning to write required the triumph of the student's will over his body; as practiced, it often entailed unprecedentedly stringent external controls. All told, penmanship pedagogy promised a good deal more than training in a particular skill. Its real product was not handwriting but men, men of a type compatible with a new economic and social order.

Women, however, were excluded from this agenda. They were not to form characters, in either sense of the word. Whereas a man's pen produced a written product—in French's copybook, a letter of recommendation—women's best efforts at handwriting paradoxically generated not a single character. Instead, what their pens produced was a "speaking picture," audible as the spoken word, visible as a drawing. And if nineteenth-century penmanship pedagogy represented women as incapable of producing the written word, it was because they were doing precisely that as never before. Female levels of writing literacy now matched male levels, and women used their writing skills not just for the boudoir epistles envisioned by French but in new and threatening ways, as novelists and later in the century as office workers. Small wonder that writing in Victorian America was charged with tensions generated by changing gender roles as well as by a changing social and economic order. These tensions resonated in the circumstances under which writing skills were acquired, in the underlying philosophy of penmanship instruction, and in the very scripts themselves.

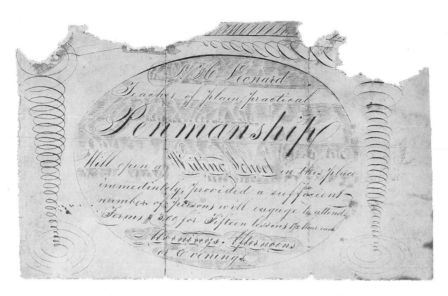

13. Handbill for an itinerant writing school, early nineteenth century.

THE NEW WRITING MASTERS—AND MISTRESSES

In colonial America, the dominant figure in penmanship pedagogy was the writing master—centered in the port cities, trained in multiple scripts, possessed of expensive English copybooks, equipped with a penknife. The writing master did not disappear in the nineteenth century, but he survived as a greatly changed character, largely because the technical skills involved in the job declined precipitously. The dozens of American copybooks that appeared from the years of the early republic usually featured instruction in at most three hands: an oversized round hand for beginners; a business script for boys, variously known as a running or current hand; and a ladies' epistolary, a reduced-scale and minimally modified version of the basic running hand. Almost entirely gone were the many Gothic scripts and print hands of the colonial era. As a result, the teaching of penmanship no longer required a lengthy apprenticeship.[2]

Under these circumstances the venerable figure of an Abiah Holbrook or a Henry Dean gave way to such characters as James Guild, a traveling peddler, tinker, portrait painter, and writing master from Turnbridge, Vermont. Itinerants like Guild acquired a rough competency in penmanship and then peddled their skills in back-country towns and villages, posting handbills or otherwise scaring up business with the offer of brief but concentrated courses of instruction (figs. 13, 14). Of one such enterprise, Guild wrote: "This was a bold attempt to go into so popular a place as this as a professor of penman

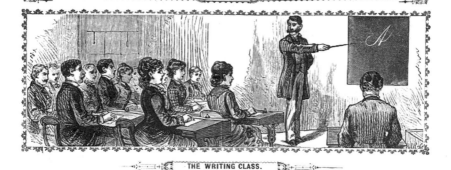

HOW TO ORGANIZE AND CONDUCT WRITING SCHOOLS.

THE WRITING CLASS.

14. A Gilded Age itinerant writing school for ladies and gentlemen.

ship when I had had only 30 hours instruction, but I thought if I could get a school started, I would run the risk, and in first place I got me a room, and then went round the Village and told them I was going to teach writing, and if they would send, if they was not satisfied, nothing to pay."[3]

Guild did get pupils, eleven the first day, sixteen by the second, "an from that to 20 & now then I was in great business." Guild kept one step ahead of his pupils, teaching by day and improving his own skills by night. When challenged by students who came upon a specimen of his unimproved writing, Guild penned them a response "in the most elegant stile." When later challenged by skeptical townsmen, he presented several penmanship manuals of the day, which "furnished me with a bold face when I was assaulted," as he explained. "I could look them in the face and ask and explain the Rules of writing which they could not, and by this means I could stop their mouths." He continued to meet with dissatisfaction, though, because he offered instruction in only the elementary "corse hand," and it was a business hand that was in demand. Ever the man of the moment, Guild worked up a system whereby he claimed to "learn Schollars to write a good running hand in 12 days." As proof of his newly acquired skill, he offered "a countifit bill on Auburn Bank." With that, he wrote, "my fame began to rise. . . . My School continued 3 month and I had the respectable number of 115 Schollars."[4]

Not all nineteenth-century writing masters were incompetent, however, nor were all itinerant. Many a writing master offered private courses of instruction in well-established urban areas, by the 1840s, often in the context of a full-fledged "business college." A number achieved even wider fame by publishing erudite penmanship manuals and copybooks. Dozens of writing masters published scores of works on penmanship, many of them in multiple editions.[5] Ironically, these instruction manuals spelled the death of their authors, for they made it possible to transfer the responsibility of penmanship pedagogy into less skilled hands.

By the 1830s the focus of penmanship education had shifted from the specialized, mercantile courses of instruction to the common school.[6] It is at this point that the skill of writing moved from the older trio of commercial skills that included arithmetic and accounting to the three R's of public elementary education. The penmanship instructor was rarely a writing master; his specialized, advanced skills were no longer required. Proficiency in multiple hands was unnecessary. Nor, with the increasing use of factory-made steel pens, was the skill of making and mending a proper nib. Most important, by mid-century, mass-produced copy-slips and copybooks were available to provide such manual expertise as was necessary. Instead of imitating the skilled hand of the writing master, students imitated the engraved models in their schoolbooks.

Of course, many rural schools kept to the slate-and-chalk, quill-and-blank-paper practices throughout the century, generally for lack of funds, so many teachers continued to set copy and mend pens much as they always had. But such schools had never employed writing masters, nor could they be bothered to adhere to a penmanship program that required any level of sophistication. In rural New Hampshire, for example, the primary concern was how to keep the ink from freezing in the wintertime.[7] It was in the urban schools that the de-skilling of penmanship pedagogy had the greatest impact, for here writing masters were indeed displaced by classroom teachers—often female—armed with mass-produced copybooks and manuals. Some large urban school systems employed a well-paid male specialist in handwriting (the penmanship supervisor), but he engaged in no actual instruction. His work was supervisory and administrative in nature.[8] Thus disappeared the art, mystery, and trade of the colonial writing master.

MIND, BODY, AND CHARACTER FORMATION

In place of the traditional writing master came not only a new breed of instructor but also a new representation of the process and product of handwriting. Open a copybook of the eighteenth century and you will find model alphabets, words, and copy phrases. Aside from fairly brief paragraphs on ink making, paper preparation, and writing position, there is little commentary. The content of a nineteenth-century penmanship manual is very different. Lengthy catechisms on the theory of penmanship and whole chapters on hand and body position dwarf the visual models for imitation. The roles that mind and body played in the execution of script had been entirely rethought.

Penmanship manuals had long stressed that the process of writing involved both a physical and a mental component. Before one can take pen to paper, they insisted, one must have an idea of the letter form. Good penmanship, explained the English writing master John Clark in 1714, requires the writer "to get an *exact notion,* or *idea* of a good *Letter* which may be done by frequent and nice Observation of a Correct Copy." Clark's manuals, like others of his century, aimed to do little more than present "a Correct Copy," that is, they consisted largely of model alphabets and copy sentences created according to such fashionable aesthetic principles as symmetry, regularity, and variety. Aesthetic considerations continued to figure prominently in the works of Victorian writing masters, but by the second third of the nineteenth century, the achievement of a beautiful hand was no longer represented as a passive process of mental imitation.[9] Instead, it was regarded as an active process in which the soul was uplifted and the body disciplined. Victorians were to form their letters as they formed themselves, through moral self-elevation and physical self-control.

Critical to the representation of penmanship as self-elevation was the reduction of the alphabet into a small number of constituent handwriting "elements" or "principles," a novel aspect of penmanship instruction that dated from the last decade of the eighteenth century. Instead of learning their ABC's, penmanship pupils began with bits of letters—ovals, inverse curves, and so on—that were understood as the aesthetic building blocks of the alphabet. Moreover, they were expected to grasp these elements intellectually before they could execute them physically. Much of a pupil's penmanship education consisted of oral analysis of letters; the student called upon to comment on the letter q would be expected to answer "the parts of *q* are Element IV., Fourth Principle, and Elements I., II., IV." So complex were these oral exercises that even a penman who represented himself as simplifying the process could imagine a reformed penmanship lesson as consisting of the following dialogue: "TEACHER. The length of the q below the base line is what part of the length of the g below the base line? IDA. It is three-fourths as long. TEACHER. Give rule 4. CLAUDE. In the f, l, b, h, k, cross one space above the base line." Such were the rules of penmanship with which James Guild armed himself and that teachers' manuals included as the theory of penmanship until the 1890s.[10]

Most penmanship manuals of the 1800s presented some variant of this technique, but the approach became a recognized school of penmanship only in the late 1840s, when Platt Rogers Spencer first advanced his system (fig. 15). Spencer was by far the most successful Victorian writing master, so much so that handwriting of his era was and still is denoted Spencerian. Spencer was part business tycoon, part philosopher, and this combination

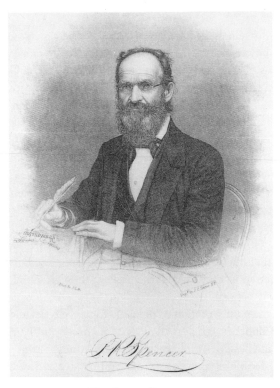

15. Platt Rogers Spencer, 1869.

clinched his almost complete dominance of penmanship education in post-bellum America.

Born of New England stock in Dutchess County, New York, in 1800, Spencer moved with his family to northern Ohio in 1810. After brief stints in the mercantile world as store clerk and supercargo, Spencer established himself as a writing master by the age of fifteen. In 1848 Spencer published a set of copy-slips in collaboration with Victor M. Rice, an organizer of business colleges and normal (teacher-training) schools who ultimately became superintendent of public instruction for New York State. It was probably this association that launched the Spencerian empire, an empire that embraced public and private penmanship education at every level, from primary schools to mercantile colleges. If anything, the dominance of Spencerian penmanship became greater after Spencer's death, in 1864. A small army of "Spencerian authors," at one point including no fewer than thirty-eight relatives and miscellaneous associates, issued complete textbook series, marketing them successfully among school administrators in forty-two states. Meanwhile, the chain of Spencerian business colleges expanded to encompass dozens of institutions throughout the United States. There were rival systems, of course, but the Spencerians were not wrong when they branded their competitors mere imitators.[11]

Spencer's success owed something to the business acumen and energy of his associates but even more to his unique presentation of the art of penmanship. Like almost every other nineteenth-century penman, he reduced the alphabet to a few elemental principles, but he also grounded his approach in a moral and aesthetic philosophy. Spencer did not represent handwriting elements as mere bits of letters; instead, he identified them with natural forms. Should the pupil "seek the origin of those forms and combinations which he is called upon to analyze and reproduce in his practice," stated the *Spencerian Key to Practical Penmanship,* "he will be led immediately to the study of Nature. . . . There the elements of all the letters, in ways without number, enter into the composition of countless objects fitted to delight the eyes of the beholder." The straight line could be seen in sunbeams, the curve in waves and clouds, the oval in "leaf, bud and flower, in the wave-washed pebble, and in shells that lie scattered upon the shore." The "true imagery of writing is culled then from the sublime and beautiful in nature."[12]

It followed that training in Spencerian script entailed contemplation of ideal forms based in nature. The penman would begin with those ideals in his mind, then reproduce them with his hand. Such an approach pleased professional writing masters for, in Spencer's words, it "takes Penmanship quite out of the circle of arts merely mechanical," providing it with "dignity as an intellectual pursuit." More critical, it allowed writing masters to claim moral benefits for penmanship. Because it entails the contemplation of natural forms, argued the Spencerian authors, penmanship "is a noble and refining art." "The study of penmanship," seconded writing master Fielding Schofield, "refines our tastes, assists in cultivating our judgment, and thereby makes us better men." (Schofield was one to know. He had started life as "a ragged urchin in the City of Poughkeepsie, N.Y. where he sold newspapers on the street." In his new calling, he was highly regarded as "a gentleman of integrity and character.") Penman Paul Pastnor argued that, through penmanship instruction, the "uncultivated masses . . . attain such a love for beautiful forms and such a facility in producing them as to really elevate and ennoble their thoughts and lives." Uriah McKee made this reform program concrete when he took as his paradigm "the young man who is accustomed to spend his evening on the streets or in debauch in the bar-room." If, "by chance," this youth "becomes interested in the study of the beautiful"—and by this, McKee meant the "study of artistic penmanship"—then "very soon vulgar stories, bar-room scandals and billiard halls begin to lose their attraction."[13] It is doubtful that most Victorian Americans credited penmanship with such transformative powers, but they did believe in the moral benefits of contemplating nature, and Platt Rogers Spencer offered them the opportunity to do so while sitting at a schoolroom desk or entering transactions in a ledger book. If professional penmen seized on the Spencerian paradigm as a way to raise the status of their skill, the writing public seized on Spencerian script as a system of moral and spiritual uplift.

In the early part of the century, there is no doubt that writing masters gave priority to the mental component of penmanship. Intellectual apprehension of form was both the first step in learning to write and the most important one. In 1791, in the first writing manual published in America, *The Art of Writing,* John Jenkins insisted that if the pupil could impress elemental forms on his mind, the pen would easily follow the mind's commands. Simon Ray Greene, a penmanship student, left us twelve full pages of this sentiment in his copybook of 1801: "Observe the copy and write better if you can." In 1818 the poetically inclined Francis McCready captured this same philosophy in a couplet: "Impress the mind, with analytic forms, / The eye receives them, and the hand performs." [14]

By the second third of the century, however, such views were distinctly old-fashioned. Victorian penmen represented the mental component of penmanship as a means of self-elevation, but they increasingly paid their greatest attention to penmanship as a physical act. The key word now was *muscularity*—the "Muscular Disciplinarian" of George Winchester's copybooks, William Davison's "Muscular Guide" to penmanship—and the most pressing need was to exert control over the body of the penmanship pupil. Thus Williams and Packard characterized the teacher's knowledge of penmanship form as secondary, especially in the age of preset copybooks. Of "the first importance," they insisted, was "that the class should be utterly under the teacher's control, and that everything be done promptly and in order." [15]

Victorian manuals spelled out methods whereby extreme levels of physical control might be maintained over pupils. Teachers distributed writing materials in numbered, standardized steps ("Position," "Open books," "Monitors about face,") marked by predetermined signals. They counted out loud or barked commands ("up," "down," "left curve," "quick,") as pupils performed their handwriting exercises; some manuals recommended the use of a metronome. By such means, commented the Spencerian authors with pride, "entire classes may soon be trained to work in concert, all the pupils beginning to write at the same moment, and executing the same letter, and portion of a letter simultaneously." Thus will the penmanship class proceed "with all the order, promptness and precision of a military drill." Spencer was not alone in his use of the military metaphor. The penman S. A. Potter likened the classroom drill to "the military training of a squad of men moving at one impulse," while Thompson and Bowlers compared the "steady, uniform movement" of the pen in writing "to the movements of the feet in military drill."[16]

Surviving student copybooks suggest that opportunities for subverting the penmanship regimen did exist, at least in the small homogeneous towns and villages of antebellum New England. In 1795, for example, Alce Arnold of East Greenwich, Rhode Island, worked out a problem dealing with wine measurements in her copybook. Her solution: "He was to receive . . . gal 28 140/292 in Wine Alce arnold come drink some." Sometime in the 1810s Melissa Wilson Holmes of New Braintree, Massachusetts, found time to daydream about her marital choices in penmanship class, experimenting with different versions of her future name as a married woman. In 1833 Reuben Commins of Charlton, Massachusetts, dutifully copied "Remember sinful youth you must die you must die" down the page until he reached the bottom, where he wrote: "Remember sinful youth you must go"—and the remainder of the sentence, which we can only speculate read "to hell," was carefully scissored out. Lincoln Varney's irreverence has survived. In his copybook of 1847, the lad from Brunswick, Maine, copied a poem about a drunken farmer, organized the "Watchman Association . . . to investigate truth, pursue inquiry, and peep into back windows," and in flourished script, listed the "School Regulations in Maine" as "No snapping apple seeds at the master" and "No kissing the girls in the entry." Such deviations were rare, and most students dutifully practiced their letter elements, alphabets, words, and maxims down the page, but diversions appear with sufficient frequency to suggest that restive pupils in country schoolhouses found ways around the regimen.[17]

In urban schools, however, especially in the postbellum era, the program appears to have been strictly enforced. The Boston school committee, for example, informed its teachers that "every pupil must sit in the right position," that they all must write "the same copy at the same time," and that instructors must "require an exact copy of a copy."[18] There are a number of practical reasons for this discrepancy. The blank, often homemade, practice books of the early part of the century left some leeway for inserting original words, whereas the standardized, ruled, pre-engraved copybooks purchased by city school systems after the Civil War were more constricting. Then too, rural teachers had their hands full during penmanship practice, making and mending pens, setting copies, mixing ink. They had no time to maintain strict control over their classes, unlike teachers in those urban schools that provided steel pens, commercially published copybooks, and bottled ink.

More critical, however, urban schools had different problems. One of the primary functions of the common school was to transform its pupils into reliable citizens and obedient workers, and nowhere did this task appear more daunting to Victorian Americans than in their cities. With industrialization, immigration, and northward migration of African-Americans, urban school populations reached unprecedented levels of diversity, comprising not just native-born Protestant whites of middling circumstances, but also foreign-born, Catholic, black, and poor pupils. In the minds of many school officials and the middle-class constituency they represented, these latter groups would pose a real threat to American morality and stability unless means could be found to civilize and control them.[19] Penmanship training did not present the only pedagogical opportunity to exercise those means and achieve those goals, but it offered a prime one. Given the conception of handwriting as copying, rather than composing, instruction in penmanship served as a lesson in conformity. And given the conception of handwriting as something that required extreme levels of physical discipline, penmanship pedagogy had an obvious utility in regulating the "student body" of America.

There was more to handwriting instruction than neutralizing the threat of pluralism, however, or imposing social control on a potentially unruly and dangerous population. Although classroom discipline certainly reached new highs under the penman's regime, the ultimate goal of Victorian penmanship pedagogy was not so much the direct imposition of control as the instillation of habits of self-control. Through self-mastery, characters would be formed: both the letters of the alphabet and that sturdy core of self that Victorians prized so highly. Contemporaries well appreciated the congruence of the two processes. When the educator William Alcott argued that high standards should be set for boys to imitate in forming their characters, he began with a penmanship lesson. "The *more* perfect the copy you place before the child," he insisted in *The Young Man's Guide*, the more perfect is the child's handwriting. "So in human conduct, generally," for "it is a part of the divine economy to place before his rational creatures a perfect standard of action, and to make it their duty to come up to it." Not coincidentally, Alcott was the author not only of character manuals as that term is usually understood, but also of a treatise *On Teaching Penmanship*.[20]

It is small wonder that the language with which Victorians described the execution of script and the construction of character should be so similar. To begin with, like character, handwriting functioned as a form of self-presentation in nineteenth-century America. In the colonial era, as we have seen, self-presentation involved the external display of one's social identity. Victorians, on the other hand, expected their handwriting to reveal something more interior, namely, the solidity and integrity of the writer's character—or lack thereof. Employers, asserted writing masters vociferously, look for masterly and methodical hands and steer clear of hesitantly or sloppily executed hands as indicative of analogous character types. Nothing, remarked

J. S. Montgomery, "so distinctly bespeaks a cultivated taste and a disciplined imagination, as correct and elegant chirography." One penman went so far as to put a price on a good hand; it was worth, he claimed, five hundred, even a thousand, dollars per year. Conversely, a poor hand betrays "an ill-formed mind" as well as "an ill-trained hand" and, in the words of another professional penman, smacks of "vulgarity and negligence." Indeed, concurred a Boston school principal, "to write illegibly or badly is almost to forfeit one's respectability."[21]

Moreover, if proper handwriting created an impression of respectability, it was because the acquisition of penmanship skills—and of character—was understood as a process of self-development. The key role in the process of character formation—in both senses of the term—was assigned to the will, a mental but not strictly intellectual attribute such as Jenkins or McCready had addressed, and an attribute whose object of discipline was the body. In their extended discussions of writing posture, hand position, and physical movement, Victorian manuals portrayed the will and body locked in struggle, with the victorious penman ultimately able to master the latter by means of the former.[22] "Those muscles which are chiefly concerned in the production of written forms," read the *Spencerian Key to Practical Penmanship*, "are well known to be under the direction of the will. They are capable, therefore, of being trained." And trained they would be! The body, stipulated the Spencerian authors, "must always be in a position nearly erect—near to, but never leaning upon or touching the desk." Feet must be parallel to the slant of the letters, the left heel "opposite from the hollow of the right foot, and distant from it two or three inches"; the right arm must be parallel to the edge of the desk, resting just below the elbow; hands must be at right angles to one another, with the right hand resting "upon the nails of the third and fourth fingers." To hold the pen, continued the Spencerian authors: "Take the pen between the thumb and first and second fingers, and let the holder cross the first finger just forward of the knuckle joint. The end of the second finger should drop below the first, so that the pen may cross it at the root of the nail, and the end of the thumb should press upon the holder opposite the first joint of the first finger. The first and second fingers should touch each other as far as the first joint of the first finger; the third and fourth must be slightly curved and separate from the others at the middle joint, and rest upon the paper at the tips of the nails."[23]

Only now was the pupil ready to begin writing. "In first attempts at writing," read one Spencerian manual, "the muscles may not properly perform what the mind directs, but by frequent and careful practice they are rendered supple and obedient in the execution of every variety of form." Hence Victorian penmanship classes were devoted above all to copybook drills. "The

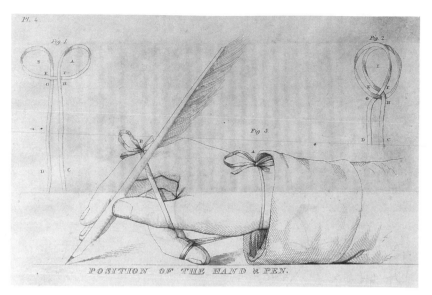

16. The talantograph, a Victorian device to encourage "freedom" in penmanship.

whole willforce must be brought to bear upon the nerve and muscle throughout the exercise," explained writing master Fielding Schofield. "That is what we mean by proper movement." In thus executing drills, read one manual, "the powers of the fingers, hand, and arm are developed and invigorated, and the muscles so trained that they become completely under the control of the will." Pupils would learn to harness the "power, and freedom of sweep of the fore-arm" in what penmen variously termed the combined, the fore-arm, or, most telling, the muscular movement and to practice the whole-arm movement, "the independent action of the entire arm from the shoulder," whereby bold capitals and flourishes were "struck" in a display of "command of hand."[24] If in their quasi-poetic treatment of handwriting elements, writing masters represented penmanship instruction as a process of self-cultivation, in their nuts-and-bolts discussion of how to put pen to paper, they represented it as a process of self-mastery.

Probably the ultimate symbol of this obsession with physical control was the so-called talantograph, a ligature used to tie the hand into proper writing position (fig. 16). Thus bound, it was impossible to rest the hand and arm as they executed long series of character-strengthening exercises. Victorians were drawn to binding as a solution to all manner of problems, from supporting the frail female body to preventing masturbation, as a literal rendering of their obsession with mastery of the body. Paradoxically, the ultimate end of physical binding was not constraint, but freedom. Corsets freed the body into its natural form, the prevention of self-abuse freed one from an unnatural vice, and the talantograph encouraged what was invariably described as natural freedom in penmanship. The promoter of the device promised that it would rid penmanship of any "stiff and formal appearance" and substitute "boldness" and "freedom." Similarly, Spencer's elaborate instructions were designed to produce "free and graceful Movement." "How justly bold," read a popular Victorian copy text, "when in some master's hand, / The pen at once joins freedom with command!"[25]

That Victorians regarded such restraint as not only compatible but ultimately synonymous with freedom parallels—indeed, it stems from—the paradox that lies at the heart of the Victorian concept of character. Autonomy came in the impulse to create one's self, restraint in the imperative to conform that self to an external model. The model was one of selflessness, an inner determination to fulfill one's moral duty, rather than of self-expression.[26] It was also a standard model, so that all men of character could be expected to be a good deal alike, sober and solid, just as, with their dark suits and dignified bearing, they looked alike. The model Victorian male might be an individual, then, but only in the sense of being a sovereign unit, not in the sense of being unique. Because writing was conceptualized as an act in which the will masters the body to conform to a standard prototype, penmanship was a natural for creating the model male self of Victorian America, the generic man of character.

That vision of the self-created, self-controlled American served important cultural functions. It served the needs of a producer society by encouraging moral self-restraint in an otherwise unregulated business world and economic self-restraint in the realms of consumption and leisure. In disciplining "deviant" populations, penmanship pedagogy responded to the alarm raised by pluralistic society, but even more fundamental, it aimed to shape all Americans into a single personality type congruent with a rapidly growing, liberal economy.[27]

GENDER TENSIONS IN VICTORIAN HANDWRITING

In 1787 the physician (and signer of the Declaration of Independence) Benjamin Rush argued that "pleasure and interest conspire to make the writing of a fair and legible hand a necessary branch of female education." In line with republican notions of womanhood that put a premium on utilitarian training for men and women alike, Rush envisioned female penmanship pedagogy as practical rather than decorative. "Italian and inverted hands," he continued, referring to ornamental hands usually reserved for women, "which are read with difficulty, are by no means accommodated to the active state of business in America or to the simplicity of the citizens of a republic." His advice did

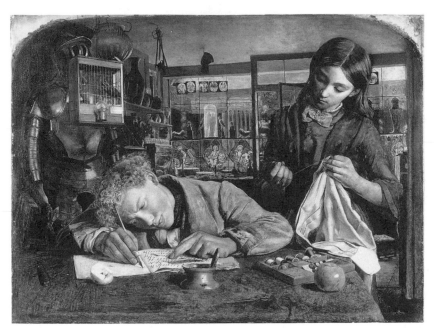

17. The boy writes, the girl sews.

not go entirely unheeded. Salem writing master Henry Dean, for example, did not believe in training his female pupils in the "effeminate habit peculiar to their sex" but instead tutored them in "a bold and masculine hand." At an exhibition of their labors in 1804, these same students were told to "reflect upon the opportunity which you now enjoy for silencing those illiberal insinuations respecting the versatility, caprice, and imbecility of the female mind."[28]

In the 1810s, however, the division of the penmanship curriculum into male and female spheres that had existed in the colonial era proceeded anew (fig. 17). Once again, boys and girls mastered the basics in common, but thereafter they ideally pursued separate penmanship curricula. Boys learned a fast and legible script, the mercantile running hand, suitable for business and public affairs, while girls advanced to the reduced-sized and painstakingly shaded ladies' epistolary, appropriate for private correspondence.[29] For boys, then, advanced penmanship instruction went hand in hand with an introduction to the business world, embodied in the ledger book entries and receipts found in their copybooks. For girls, penmanship training shaded into instruction in such social skills as proper letter writing and calling-card etiquette.

It is a good question whether most American children actually followed this bifurcated curriculum. Certainly not every common-school system could

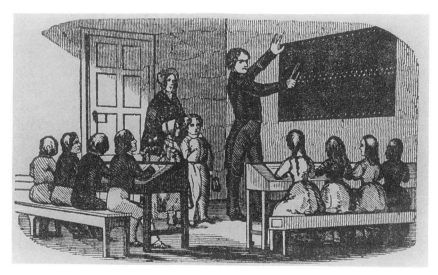

18. The separation of boys and girls in the schoolroom, from a mid-nineteenth-century copybook.

bother with such niceties as the art of polite correspondence; one doubts that the frigid schoolhouses of northern New Hampshire saw much training of this sort. Nevertheless, the divided curriculum was more than a paper fantasy (fig. 18). Private female academies offered instruction in women's hands, and business colleges, often established and operated by professional penmen, offered advanced training in mercantile penmanship to their male students. Private courses of penmanship instruction responded to a demand for practical business education for boys and polite accomplishments for girls. And such popular self-instruction manuals as *Gaskell's Compendium* also offered lessons in "business writing and Ladies' Fashionable writing."[30]

Most important, by the 1860s the most widely used textbook series were those that came in the elementary/business/ladies' sequence; these were national systems purchased by public schools by the gross. The Spencerian series, which set the standard and dominated the rest, followed this pattern. So too did its main rival, the Payson, Dunton, and Scribner copybooks, which included "invaluable business exercises for boys" and "a variety of bold, business styles of Capitals and Script" in its business series and promised to develop a "fine hand" and "an elegant epistolary style" in its ladies' series. Other series followed suit.[31] Clearly, many Americans were acquiring these skills. At the Philadelphia Centennial Exposition, for example, visitors could inspect prize specimens of ornamental penmanship submitted by schools from around the country. Outside the schoolroom, young women of the antebellum era copied maxims in their exercise books and transcribed poems into albums in ornamental and diminutive hands. Some of these hands required the ink painting of decorative elements; some were barely a millimeter high. We might expect such practices from eastern, urban school systems, with their penmanship supervisors, or among genteel New England ladies, but there is good evidence that they penetrated into remoter regions and humbler homes. Recalling his youth in a one-room schoolhouse in Oregon territory, for example, Clark Louis Barzee wrote: "We used the Spencerian system of writing exclusively. The copybooks were numbered from one to seven inclusive. Fifteen minutes daily were given to penmanship. When pupils finished this series, they were pretty good with their pens."[32]

But nineteenth-century penmanship pedagogy did more than separate women from men. It defined the act of handwriting as inherently male, thus excluding women from the process of writing altogether, at least on the symbolic level. Even in the colonial era the domain of handwriting had been a masculine one; the main uses of handwriting had been mercantile, and commerce was a man's world. The association between writing and the male world of work may have become even stronger in the nineteenth century as reading came to be associated with the female world of leisure.[33] But above all, it was the conceptualization of handwriting as an act of character formation that defined handwriting as masculine in this era. For Victorians, the formation of character, achieved by the mastery of the body by the will, was a specifically masculine process. Men, it was believed, were prey to base, physical appetites, but they possessed the mental strength to conquer them. Women, on the other hand, neither experienced the "lower" impulses associated with bodily needs and desires nor possessed the higher powers of will to conquer such impulses had they existed. While men actively forged their characters, women experienced a passive unfolding of their feminine natures. If character formation was an inherently male process, then, and if writing meant forming characters, then only men were truly capable of writing. The male gendering of handwriting in the nineteenth century thus functioned at a much deeper level than it had in the colonial period, for it suggested not merely that women do not usually write but that women in the profoundest sense *cannot* write.[34]

Accordingly, while children of both sexes learned the fundamentals of penmanship, boys alone received training in those aspects of handwriting that epitomized the inherently male process of physical self-mastery. Only they practiced the powerful, sweeping motions of the "muscular movement," for example, just as only they learned to execute penmanship with "command of hand." One writing master explained that in "the manner of its execution," the physical act of writing "demands direct decision, and masterly effort"; he entitled his essay the "Manliness of Penmanship."[35] One suspects that the very masculinity of the muscular movement depended at least in part on the contrast with the delicate execution of the ladies' epistolary. More important, somewhere in the language of manly vigor and the philosophy of masculine character formation, female writers simply disappeared.

If the philosophy of male character formation erased women from the written record, it may have been precisely because nineteenth-century women were wielding the pen in growing numbers. Literacy was relatively widespread in the colonies in the eighteenth century, and many scholars believe that by 1800 young New Englanders of both sexes were fully literate.[36] But there is more to America than New England. Immigrants, free blacks, and slaves—groups in which high rates of illiteracy persisted through the nineteenth century—were concentrated in the mid-Atlantic and southern states. More important for this discussion, outside of New England, many women of the postrevolutionary generation never learned to read or write. In their examination of mid-nineteenth-century census data, the historians Joel Perlmann and Dennis Shirley found that virtually all elderly New England women (women born between 1765 and 1795) were fully literate, but comparable data for southern women revealed that over a third were illiterate, almost double the rate for southern men. In other words, at the end of the eighteenth century, there were still large numbers of Americans who could not read or write, and far more of these were female than male. If, then, by 1860 census figures indicate that well over 90 percent of the white population in America could both read and write, it becomes clear that a good deal of catching up had occurred, most especially among women.[37] Thus the rise in literacy was largely a rise of *female* literacy. We should recall here that many of the colonial females who left their marks—but not their signatures—were fully capable of reading, so what was new in the nineteenth century for many women was not so much learning how to read as learning how to write. The salient image of the new literacy of the nineteenth century is neither the boy with his McGuffey's reader nor the girl with hers, but the girl with pen in hand (fig. 19).

Female writing had long presented a cultural problem. In the seventeenth and eighteenth centuries, when penmanship was associated so closely with the mercantile world, writing was by definition a male activity. That gendering of handwriting held especially true for the handwritten manuscript processed for public consumption—in other words, published writing. To some extent, as we have seen, the anomaly of female writing was solved by the confinement of women's writing to the private world of diaries and correspondence, by the publication of female-authored manuscripts in handwritten form, and by the use of scripts that identified penmanship as female and therefore less authoritative. But when colonial women did publish their writings in print for a public audience, these solutions were no longer avail-

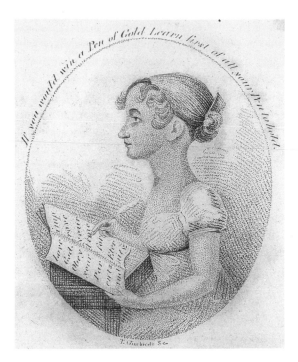

19. A young woman writing, symbol of the new literacy in
the early republic.

able, and the problem reasserted itself. "This, Sir," wrote one contributor to
the *South Carolina Gazette* in 1732, "I doubt not, but you'll think, comes awkwardly from a Female Pen."[38]

In the nineteenth century, the "female pen" continued to produce private
writings, again, often in female scripts. If anything, this sort of writing grew
in popularity. "Fair scribblerinas," wrote one antebellum commentator with
an edge of ridicule, "collect 'copies of verses'" and "keep albums." They indulge in "the refined enjoyments of sentimental, confidential, soul-breathing
correspondence with some Angelina, Seraphina, or Laura Matilda," composing "beautiful little notes, with long-tailed letters, upon vellum paper with
pink margins sealed with sweet mottoes and dainty devices, the whole deliciously perfumed with musk and attar of roses." Such "female scribes," he
continued, "must enjoy the 'feast of reason, and the flow of soul,' and they
must write—Ye gods! how they *do* write!"[39]

Given the inherent awkwardness of the female pen, however, what was
far more troubling than these boudoir practices was the new phenomenon of
female authorship. Female authors were not unknown before the nineteenth
century, but they were rare. From about 1820, when the novel assumed an

increasingly dominant position in the universe of reading matter, that situation changed dramatically. Many, perhaps most, novel readers were women, but more critical for our purposes, so were most novel writers, and a number achieved both fame and fortune from their books.[40] When these authors learned to write, then, they not only acquired a traditionally male skill, they also assumed a traditionally male prerogative, namely, the ability to appear in print. That power had all sorts of subversive implications. Unlike the handwritten letter, with its telltale script, paper, even scent, the printed page was genderless and therefore powerless to keep women in their proper place. Appearing in print did in fact permit women to move beyond the female sphere of private influence, allowing them to reach and shape a public readership. Indeed, as novels crowded out other, male-authored forms of reading matter, women writers threatened to wrest the powers of authorship away from men entirely.

Because they represented such a cultural challenge, many women novelists approached writing with some degree of trepidation. Most often, they published anonymously or under a pseudonym. Even then, authorship proved a source of anxiety. "I have a *perfect horror* at appearing in print," wrote Catharine Maria Sedgwick shortly before the publication of her first novel, "and feel as you have seen me when I have been trying to make up my mind to have a tooth out." Recalling the day she first heard of the publication of her literary efforts, Caroline Howard Gilman wrote that "I cried half the night with a kind of shame." It was "as if I had been detected in man's apparel."[41]

As female novelists made a bid for the traditionally male powers of print publication, the female pen became something more than a mere abnormality. It became a challenge, even a threat. The crisis created by female literacy and authorship was resolved at least in part by the conceptual conventions of Victorian penmanship pedagogy. Representing handwriting as a male process of character formation erased women from the written record, much as the practice of anonymous and pseudonymous publication achieved the same result. "Out of the loop" of character formation, women writers— we must now picture them as handwriters—were rendered culturally illegible. Perhaps this is why they were so often described as scribblers.[42]

The anomaly represented by the female pen and the typically Victorian manner of resolving it are epitomized by Fenella, a character (although one hesitates to use precisely that term) in one of Walter Scott's popular Waverley novels, *Peveril of the Peak.* Fenella is a woman of "many little accomplishments": embroidery, sketching, and, most especially, "the art of ornamental writing." It is noteworthy that Scott classified female writing as a visual art rather than a literacy skill. Even more telling is his depiction of Fenella as a "little creature . . . the least and slightest of womankind," whose face resembled "a most beautiful miniature." If she were any smaller, poor Fenella might actually disappear, and indeed Scott further diminished her presence by casting her as a mute, who communicated not in her writing but through a system of visual signs. Even when angry and most desperate to make her feelings known, Fenella resorts to "tones, contortions, and gestures."[43] Oddly enough, then, for all her skill with the pen, she is unable to express herself. But Fenella's muteness is no accident. The cultural logic of the Victorian era dictated that she be struck dumb in compensation for her superior ability to write.

One might be able to leave it at that were it not for the many indications that the "scribblers" had indeed left their mark, and in the very script that appeared to define them out of social legibility. Let us go back to the Spencerian hand. Let us go back, in fact, to Spencer himself. Here is how he was eulogized upon his death: "He seems to have been expressly created for the high commission which he was called upon to execute; for his organization was almost femininely fine and subtle, his temperament was strongly poetic, his love for the beautiful, whether in Nature or Art, amounted to an ecstatic passion, and his whole nature was emotional and sympathetic." Spencer was further described as a "sweet and gentle spirit," and penmanship as "his darling . . . which he so devoutly desired to serve." Future president James Garfield, himself a former writing master, recalled the "pathetic tenderness of his spirit."[44] Surely no one could have sounded more like the ideal of true womanhood than this creator of the character-building Victorian business hand.

And if we look at the hand itself, we see the same evidence of feminization. Contemporaries described its "graceful lines, and curves" as "pure and chaste and beautiful."[45] This was the grace and beauty of Nature. Spencer, as we have seen, claimed to receive inspiration for his letter forms from waves and clouds, pebbles and shells, sunbeams and flower petals. When we look at Spencerian, we too can note the loops and curlicues, the lush roundness of the letter forms and the ornateness of the capitals. By comparison with the spare, linear strokes of the eighteenth- and early nineteenth-century running hand, Spencer's creation looks positively—feminine (figs. 20, 21).

It should not be surprising, then, that one Victorian penman used the classically female plotline of innocence and corruption, nature and fashion, to describe what he considered the degradation of the original Spencerian hand. Like a "country girl, once the child of nature, full of beauty, life, and freedom," wrote "A.H.H." in 1877, the Spencerian hand "is brought to the city and trained to look more graceful and beautiful." There "her movements now must be of the greatest care, her waist is squeezed into the tightest corsets, her hair piled upon her head, liable to fall with any unguarded move-

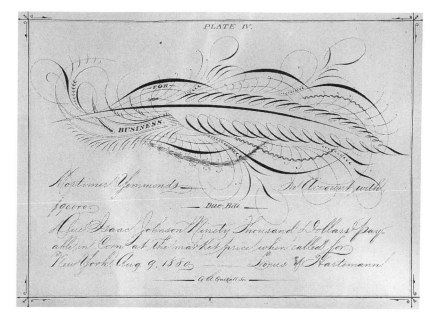

20. The feminine aesthetic of Spencerian script.

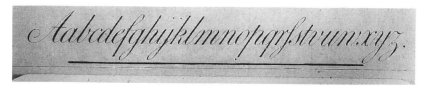

21. The countinghouse aesthetic of eighteenth-century script.

ment, her feet, once giving her a firm footing, are pinched into narrow shoes, till deprived of all that gave her freedom, she is transformed into a delicate and beautiful pet, almost wholly unfitted for anything useful."[46]

The feminization of script was probably most obvious in the Victorian branch of handwriting known as ornamental penwork or artistic penmanship. By mid-century, it had become common to exhibit one's skill and taste by executing ink drawings in the graceful style of Spencerian script. Such pen art was nothing new; in the seventeenth century, Edward Cocker was famous for his fanciful flying fish and knights in armor executed in ink. But these were different. The most popular subjects for such drawings were natural ones, most particularly, graceful and delicate animals—birds, swans, deer. They might grace a copybook, a wall, or, mass-produced for pleasure or profit, a set of visiting cards (fig. 22).

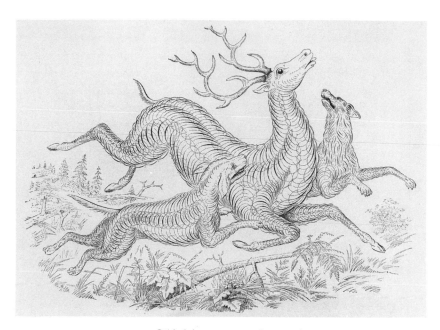

22. Gilded Age ornamental penwork.

Pen artists, it should be stressed, were not exclusively or even primarily female. No Victorian woman achieved fame for her ornamental penmanship. Conversely, the most famous penmen of the postbellum period, the men who ran private business academies, published penmanship books, and edited penmanship journals, certified their skill with penwork of this kind.[47] One such writing master was E. F. Richardson, penmanship instructor at the Southern Normal School and Business College and editor of the *Southern Penman*. In the editorial content of his journal, Richardson repeatedly stressed the acquisition of a good business hand as the key to a young man's rise in the world. But interspersed with these discussions of male script and male success were Richardson's advertisements for visiting cards—"Elk bounding over a landscape, etc., \$3"—along with testimonials to his skill. "The pack of cards you sent me I think are too nice to give away to my friends," wrote Clara Bush, a poet, "and I will keep them as a memento of the giver. The large design—deer bounding over a brook, with the swan striking at it—cannot be excelled by any one."[48] Even more breathless in his admiration was one D. T. Smith:

> The penwork of E. F. Richardson
> Can hardly be excelled,
> In neatness of his writing,

And drawing work as well.
For true and honest drawing,
He makes it up so plain,
That one can very easily see
On a horse's head the veins.

In making of an elephant
He can even make the snout,
The weapon the elephant will use
To knock the boys about.
He makes with his pen
The picture of anything,
And never starts to do a work
And let it end in vain.

Where'er his work has been on exhibition,
The prize it has taken,
It will always please inspectors' taste
And his eyes awaken.
Now may the God of Heaven
Give to him great success,
And take his soul to glory
And all his people caress.[49]

Let us hope that Richardson was a better penman than Smith a poet.

Virtuosi performances in pen art fit in well with the professional agenda of Victorian writing masters. As "Scribo" explained, business penmanship was a mechanical skill, but ornamental work placed penmanship within the realm of the fine arts; it was the same as portrait or landscape painting. Elsewhere pen art was identified as one of those aspects of penmanship that elevated the mind and might even purify the debauched.[50]

Most critical, pen art provided one more link between the ostensibly male sphere of handwriting and a feminine sphere of ornamental pastimes and aesthetic concerns. Scribo's opinion notwithstanding, delicately detailed renderings of swans are less reminiscent of such fine arts as oil painting, practiced professionally by men, than they are of such female ornamental arts and crafts as hair art, painting on velvet, and the making of small, decorative objects out of papier-maché, feathers, wax, and beads.[51] Beyond its specific associations with such female pastimes, ornamental penwork partook more generally of the sentimental female sphere of refinement and morality. In their delicate renderings of nature's beauties, penwork designs were expected to elevate the mind and uplift the moral sense, much as women themselves performed the same service.

The rhetoric of penmanship pedagogy had indeed erased any overt female presence from the page. Excluded from the process of forming characters, women were confined to a private world of letters and hence written out of what counted as writing literacy. Women made up the bulk of the newly literate, but as a subordinate group, it was culturally unacceptable for them to be visibly associated with a set of skills that was equated with worldly power and success. Similarly, the newly dominant form of written matter, the novel, was in many ways a female form, often written for and by women, but again such private uses of the pen could not be employed to define the cultural meaning of handwriting. The female presence was hidden, but nonetheless real. When Victorian men took pen in hand, theirs may have been a performance in muscularity, an exercise in character formation, a form of masculine self-presentation, but their hand was a feminized one. The scribblers, it would seem, had a script after all.

As its frontispiece, the *Theory of Spencerian Penmanship* included an engraving of two children at the beach (fig. 23). The boy kneels, seemingly unaware of the girl who stands in his shadow behind him. It is he who traces letters in the sand, but it is not his name that he writes. It is hers.

THE PALMER METHOD AND THE REASSERTION OF MASCULINITY

In 1878 an advertisement appeared in the "situations wanted" section of the *Penman's Art Journal.* "A teacher of penmanship wants a situation in some business college," read the notice, "willing to work cheap first year. Has first-class framed specimens, his own work, of business and ornamental. Can do any kind of pen-work. Address A. N. PALMER, Manchester, N.H." Austin Norman Palmer moved on from this obscurity to edit a penmanship journal and conduct a penmanship lecture circuit; to own and operate a three-campus business college based in Cedar Rapids, Iowa; to offer correspondence courses that attracted half a million customers from around the country; to sell a full line of penmanship supplies, from copy cards to pens to paper; and to publish a series of penmanship manuals, beginning with his *Palmer's Guide to Business Writing* in 1894. Developed in the 1880s, by the 1890s the Palmer method had begun to displace the decades-old Spencerian. By the second decade of the new century, it reigned supreme.[52] Rivals existed, but these were merely Palmer by another name, much as all systems of the second half of the 1800s were ultimately Spencerian.[53] How had Palmer so thoroughly eclipsed Spencer?

Palmer himself was clear on the shortcomings of Spencerian scripts. What

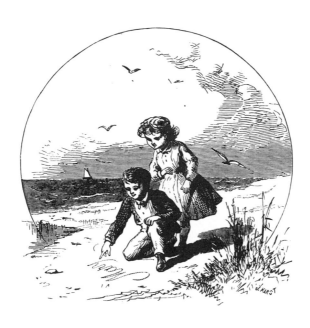

23. The woman behind the penman, from *Theory of Spencerian Penmanship*, 1874.

he described as copybook writing is very pretty, but, he added, that's all. With its ornate forms, which often required extensive lifting of the pen, and meticulous shading, which entailed the reworking of letters, copybook script was more akin to painting than to writing. It was far too slow, insisted Palmer. Speed it up, and the arm not only tires quickly, but the script becomes illegible. What America wanted and needed, argued Palmer, was a "plain and rapid style" adapted to "the rush of business." School systems that adopted the Palmer method echoed this critique. In 1910, for example, the penmanship supervisor for the Cincinnati schools characterized his Victorian predecessors as solely concerned that "the page of carefully drawn work be 'pretty.'" By contrast, he offered "real, live, usable, legible, and salable penmanship" and assured school officials that "no attempt is made to make the penmanship more beautiful than is consistent with utility."[54]

To meet these goals meant scrapping both the old letter forms and the technique of executing them. By comparison to Spencer's letters, Palmer's were spare—unshaded, sheared of superfluous lines, almost bereft of ornament (fig. 24). But what Palmer stressed even more than form, and what graduates of the Palmer method recall most readily today, was movement. Spencerians had styled their approach muscular, but in reality, it was muscu-

24. Penmanship remasculinized; the Palmer method alphabet.

lar only in the sense that the body was the object of the mind's control. "As the hand is only the instrument of the mind," wrote one Spencerian penman, "it can not acquire skill to execute beyond the power of the mind to conceive and direct. . . . The letters should be analyzed and studied until the pupil can shut his eyes and see a perfectly formed letter on his eye-lids."[55]

Palmer dismissed this sort of abstract, intellectual work. "If the movement is right, and its application right," he wrote, "the letter will take care of itself, and good letters must be the result." In place of intellectual analyses of letters, he substituted exercises in "ovals" and "push-pulls." Furthermore, he rejected the use of the fingers to form letters in favor of what he called muscular movement: sweeping motions of the arm from the shoulder powered by a "driving force" that was both "positive and assertive." The endless drills were designed "to realize the dormant movement power" of the muscles and to make this kind of motion second nature. So too was the stipulation that during drill work, the arm was to remain in perpetual motion, looping in space before ("applied preparatory motion"), in between, and after the execution of letter forms. "Put energy and life into the work," Palmer urged.[56]

So thoroughly did considerations of movement dominate those of form that Palmer recommended that small children, who as yet lacked the physical coordination necessary for cursive, might spend a preliminary year or two getting the muscular movement down pat. In line with Palmer's emphasis on movement, penmanship supervisors discarded the copybook method's preoccupation with "accurate formation of each letter" for a new focus on "the way the pupil does his work," even if "crude letters" were the result of maintaining Palmerian levels of speed and Palmerian methods of execution. Nor would advanced pupils be permitted to forget the primacy of movement over form. The most accomplished students, Palmer insisted, should begin their practice periods with movement drills, for they are to the penman "what the gymnasium exercises are to the athlete."[57]

For Palmer, there were no shortcuts. "There is no philosophical line of thought whereby one can argue himself into a good handwriting," he wrote. "There are no occult powers of the mind, which, touched by a master will power, can be made to vibrate along the muscles of the arm like magic. . . . There is no subtle line of argument that will, when carefully adhered to, en-able the recipient to become a good writer without that most necessary of all elements, persistent personal effort." What at first sounds like the work ethic Victorians lived by is in fact something quite different, a new, distinctly un-Victorian understanding of the relation between and the relative rankings of mind and body. Spencer and his ilk had depicted the act of writing as a triumph of the will over the body, a process of mental training and physical self-mastery; hence the complex oral exercises in letter analysis and the fetish with body and hand position. But Palmer rejected conscious mental effort—the "philosophical line of thought," the "occult powers of the mind," the "master will power"—as the driving force behind handwriting. For conscious will he substituted unconscious habit. Penmanship drill was essential not to build character or discipline the body but to imprint the memory of motion into the muscles.[58]

Palmer thus represented the skill of penmanship as a form of athleticism, commended muscularity for its own sake, and sanctioned a physicality unencumbered by mental masters. As we shall see, such a conception of the writing process incorporated the latest ideas emerging from the field of psychology and served the cultural agenda of progressive-era schools. Here we may note that the Palmer method joins the many phenomena, from the cycling craze to Sousa marches, identified by the historian John Higham as symptomatic of the 1890s mania for masculine vigor and activity. That mania has in turn been linked with a crisis of gender identity that first arose in the same decade. Faced with a loss of autonomy in an age of business and cultural incorporation, faced too with the New Woman of the Gilded Age, many men felt that masculinity itself was under siege. They rejected the feminized culture of Victorian America, its worship of the beauties of nature, its sentimental novels, its declawed theology, and strove to reassert their manliness in fantasies or acts of physical bravery and prowess.[59] It is not difficult to see how the Palmer method, too, stood as a rejection of a feminized culture, represented in this instance by Spencerian script, that for all its alleged muscularity and suitability for the business world smacked more of feminine grace and natural beauty than of male vigor or practical utility.

But was the world of business, the world that had long defined writing as a masculine activity, still unambiguously male? In fact not. For one, growing numbers of men experienced the new corporate and bureaucratic workplace as hostile to masculine autonomy and initiative. The male clerk, once a youth on the rise, became a permanent underling in the workplace hierarchy, a mere penpusher, or, to use contemporary terminology, a "quill driver." As early as 1873 one commentator described a government clerk as a man with "no independence while in office, no manhood," for he "must openly avow his implicit faith in all his superiors, in pain of dismissal, and must cringe and fawn upon them." As the new century drew near and the corporate, bureaucratic structure became ever-more prevalent, it became increasingly difficult to equate wielding the pen with wielding power.[60]

There is another wrinkle to this story: the penmanship equivalent of the New Woman. It was bad enough that new corporate structures threatened the manliness of clerical work, but to make matters worse, women moved into the office. They were not there to run the place, of course, although they quickly disposed of the traditional office cuspidor. They were there to type and take shorthand—in other words, to displace much of the need for penmanship—and, as bookkeepers and secretaries, to assume the responsibility of whatever handwriting did remain. By the 1880s private business colleges attracted large numbers of female students. Whereas in 1870 these colleges enrolled 5,824 students, almost all of them male, by 1900 they counted some 91,549 students, over a third of them female. Similarly, girls comprised between one-half and two-thirds of the pupils in public high school commercial courses. By 1920 women comprised 92 percent of stenographers and typists and 49 percent of bookkeepers.[61]

The business world had long defined handwriting as a quintessentially male activity; from the days of John Ayres, the mercantile hand was restricted to and expressive of an exclusively masculine domain. But the new business environment was different, populated by emasculated men and modern women. When the business world—and business penmanship—lost its gender exclusivity, it took on a gender ambiguity. It was one thing for women to write polite letters in the privacy of their boudoirs, even to pen a novel or two, but quite another for them to seize the pen that had long defined handwriting as part of the male domain. How could that pen be taken back, even if only symbolically? Enter Austin Norman Palmer. Palmer's muscularity displaced Spencerian beauty not just because a metaphysical female presence loomed in the curiously feminized script of the Victorian countinghouse but because the countinghouse, or rather its turn-of-the-century successor, the office, was no longer unambiguously male. The Palmer method reasserted the masculinity of penmanship, even as male and female arms alike pushed and pulled and ovalled in its name.

The political, cultural, social, and economic transformations that took place in the nineteenth century demanded new sorts of people. It was imperative that America's citizens not threaten the established order of things—the republican system of self-government, the evangelical system of morals, the social system of autonomous men on the make, and the capitalist system of economic competition and industrial growth. In fact, it was up to the citizenry to make that order work. If the native and foreign-born Bowery

"B'hoys" and "Gals" of America's cities threatened the stability and morality of the republic, they would have to be controlled, and Victorians knew of no better way to control people than to control their bodies. But even the less menacing characters of nineteenth-century America, sturdy mechanics, respectable gentlemen, and ambitious farm boys, had the power to foul things up if they did not keep their lower impulses in check and stick to hard work and thrifty ways. For such Americans as these, the answer was self-control, the triumph of the will over the body.

Because of its unique properties, handwriting played a role in assuring the control of the naturally unruly and the self-control of the potentially way-ward. As handwriting had been associated with the self since colonial times, handwriting pedagogy could be used to structure the right kind of selves for the nineteenth century. It used its own special vocabulary of individuality and conformity, mind and body, to do just that. Driving an Irish-born lad to practice his Spencerian to the beat of a metronome was forcing his body to conform to rules and comply with authority. Instructing the native-born youth to form characters with his hand according to the dictates of his will was training him to join the ranks of identical, self-disciplined producers.

Indeed, the conceptual vocabulary of handwriting was so germane to the task of shaping the Victorian self that we actually run into the problem of overlapping terminology; hence, the double meaning of *character formation*. As cultural work goes, this task was a natural for handwriting. But dealing with the problem of female writers was something else altogether. Nothing in the way nineteenth-century Americans understood the ability to write, either to pen or to compose, prepared them to deal with women's intrusion into the worlds of literacy and authorship. Nor was there anything in the way handwriting was understood that could help them. In fact, given the colonial association of penmanship with male mercantile activity, the opposite was true. The only solution seemed to be to dip the female pen in invisible ink, to define women out of the world of writing altogether. Yet they were not written out so easily. We see them ghostwriting in a Spencerian hand, only to be exorcised at the end of the century by Austin Norman Palmer, the high priest of manliness.

CHAPTER THREE

The Romance and Science of Individuality

"On the subject of penmanship there are two theories," explained a writer for the *National Magazine* in 1855, "each diametrically opposed to the other." The first "declares, dogmatically, that anybody can write any hand he chooses" because "the forming of a letter with a pen or pencil is a mere imitative mechanical process." Thus, "with a good eye and the necessary practice any one who has common-sense may imitate any shape or form set before him." We are reminded here of Lord Chesterfield's admonition to his son that "it is in every man's power to write what hand he pleases; and, consequently, that he ought to write a good one." We recall as well the nineteenth-century writing masters who insisted that with hard work everyone could achieve an admirable—and an admirably identical—hand.[1]

There was a second hypothesis, though, "yet in its infancy," but sufficiently established to have many advocates and a number of active practitioners. "It is this:—not only is it a wise provision of Providence that the hand-writing of every man should be different from that of every other, but a man's penmanship is an unfailing index of his character, moral and mental, and a criterion by which to judge of his peculiarities of taste and sentiments."[2] This is the theory of handwriting analysis, or graphology as it came to be called by the 1870s, and it embodies two basic postulates, uniqueness and correspondence. Taken together, these propositions commented as much on the nature of the self as on the nature of handwriting, for they asserted not only that each person's handwriting is different and reflects his or her character but also that each person is characterologically unique. In counterpoint to the writing master's generic man of character, then, the graphologist proposed the distinctive individual. Not just two theories of penmanship were diametrically opposed to each other; so also were two theories of the self.

Just what those who perceived every person's handwriting as unique made of human individuality, how they described it and accounted for it, and why they were drawn to it is no simple story. In the first half of the century, the distinctive individual with the distinctive hand was regarded as a rare specimen, to be approached all the more reverentially for his (or occasionally her) rarity. Only these few, it seemed, had escaped the homogenizing forces of contemporary life. This was the attitude assumed by what can be termed the handwriting romantics: the first proponents of handwriting analysis and their more numerous, more popular kindred spirits, the autograph collectors. By the postbellum era, graphologists characterized all human beings and their scripts as unique, but this universal individuality was a convenient scientific fact, not a cause for veneration. It provided a useful means of determining the true identity of crafty men and women in disguise. Opportunities for deception, it seemed, flourished in an urban world of strangers and in a society peopled by self-constructed characters. Thus, while writing masters created copy after copy of characters appropriate to the new social and economic order, handwriting readers and collectors celebrated the individuality that order threatened and used it to expose the deception that order fostered.

In the mid-1770s the Swiss pastor Johann Kaspar Lavater published his *Essays on Physiognomy*, which set forth the art of reading character in the human visage. The face, explained Lavater, can be divided into three layers of features, each of which is an index of certain categories of traits. The brow and eyes are clues to intellectual qualities, the nose and cheeks to the subject's emotional makeup, and the mouth and chin reveal physical characteristics. Every face is unique because every individual is unique, and the face is but the external manifestation of the individual's distinctive character makeup.

Lavater devoted almost the entire work to an elaboration in text and illustrations of his physiognomical theory, but in a later edition, he included as well a brief and somewhat tentative chapter on handwriting as an index of character. Here he would assert only that it was "highly probable, that each of us has his own hand-writing, individual and inimitable," asking rhetorically: "And is it possible, that this incontestable diversity of writing should not be founded on the real difference of moral character?"[3] The first statement, that every hand is distinctive, was not, as we have seen, terribly new, but the second suggestion, that hands differ because they reflect the characterological makeup unique to each individual, was novel. It is this assertion that underpins the practice of handwriting analysis and makes possible the reading of handwriting as an index of character and aptitude. Over the course of the nineteenth and twentieth centuries, the theory and methods of handwriting analysis changed repeatedly, but in Lavater we can detect the concepts—uniqueness, character, correspondence—that never varied.

In his few pages devoted to handwriting, Lavater did little more than lay out the principal arguments for the analysis of handwriting and to illustrate his approach with ten specimen signatures. His was a mere suggestion. It was not until 1812 that this suggestion was expanded into the first full-length work on handwriting analysis, a brief treatise entitled *The Art of Judging the Mind and Character of Men and Women from Their Handwriting*, by the Frenchman Edouard Auguste Patrice Hocquart. A second, expanded edition of this work followed in 1816.[4]

Hocquart was an obscure character in his own day, and he remains so; just why he should have taken an interest in handwriting analysis is not certain. He made clear in his own writings that he admired the works of Lavater; he published a French translation of the Swiss pastor's work in 1808 and later in his life, he published his own *Physiognomies of Political Men of the Day*. As a bookseller, publisher, author, and engraver, Hocquart may have been able to conceptualize writing as a continuum from the mental to the physical in a way that encouraged the perception of handwriting as an index to character.[5] At any rate, he was willing to assert the still-novel idea that handwriting revealed not only the qualities of mind attributable to the writer's sex and nationality but also those unique to each individual. In the second edition of his book, Hocquart grouped these individual qualities of mind around two variables that allegedly determined character type, namely, energy and imagination. Here Hocquart's aim was to replace Lavater's four temperaments—the age-old melancholic, bilious, sanguine, and choleric humors—with a schema he considered more exact.[6] In both editions Hocquart demonstrated his new art of judging character by analyzing at some length the signatures, reproduced in facsimile, of twenty-four famous men and women.

The Swiss theologian had set some Englishmen to thinking, too. In his "Characteristic Signatures" of 1823, Thomas Byerley, a minor member of the English literati, argued that it is possible to "discover in the mere character of a man's hand-writing, a speedier insight into the character of his mind, than by any other possible means." He demonstrated his convictions with facsimile signatures and corresponding character analyses of famous men and women. Another English man of letters, Isaac Disraeli, argued in an essay "On Autographs" that "assuredly Nature would prompt every individual to have a distinct sort of writing, as she had given a peculiar countenance—a voice—and a manner." That distinctiveness of hand he linked to distinctiveness of character, and he proceeded to interpret the *"physiognomy of writing"* in the scripts of English monarchs, although these were merely described, not reproduced. No doubt Disraeli would have preferred to illustrate them. He recommended Hocquart's "small volume which I met with at Paris" as "curious for its illustrations, consisting of *twenty-four plates, exhibiting fac-similes of the writing of eminent and other persons,* correctly taken from the original autographs."[7]

Precisely what handwriting styles might indicate about individual writers attracted the attention of Americans as well during this period. By 1787 Benjamin Rush could report that he had "once heard of a man who professed to discover the temper and disposition of persons by looking at their handwriting." Rush was disinclined to inquire "into the probability of this story" and related it primarily to assert the "one thing in which all mankind agree upon this subject," namely, that poor writing was "rude" and "illiberal," the unambiguous "mark of a vulgar education." In his diary of 1806, however, the architect Benjamin Henry Latrobe displayed more curiosity. He wondered at the similarities in handwriting that existed among family members. For Latrobe, such likenesses were clearly remarkable, not just the expected uniformity that resulted from training in a standard hand. He noted that Aaron

Burr, whose father had died when the boy was an infant and who had never seen his father's handwriting until long past the age of maturity, nevertheless wrote a hand identical to his father's. The same could be said of his own daughter Lydia, whose adult "Scrawl" resembled her mother's, although she had lost her mother at an early age, had had no opportunity to examine her handwriting, and had been trained to write a beautiful hand while in school. "But of what use to quote a hundred instances," wrote Latrobe in his diary, "when the question extends over the whole human race, past, present and to come."[8]

It was not until the late 1830s, however, that Americans publicly recorded their assessment of how well the new handwriting analysis answered Latrobe's question. Writing for New York's *Knickerbocker* magazine in 1838, R. C. Sands conceded that such "accidental properties of a person" as gender, age, nationality, and profession could be detected "in a majority of instances, from his chirograph," but he stressed the frequency of exceptions and insisted that these correspondences could be attributed to such external circumstances as penmanship training. If one could identify a script as French, for instance, it was only because French writing masters trained their pupils after handwriting models that were not used elsewhere, not because the French were fundamentally different in character. Similarly, if male and female scripts could be distinguished from each other, or the clerk's hand from the lawyer's, it was only because men and women, merchants and attorneys, were given different models of handwriting to acquire. Extending this line of analysis to individual peculiarities took one far afield, both from the truth and from pretense to intellectual respectability. To believe that "the bent of natural inclination, or the predominance or deficiency of any intellectual quality" can be detected in handwriting, wrote Sands, would be to believe in a system of "divination" that "cannot be proved by any process of reasoning from first principles."[9]

But writing in the same year as Sands, the Reverend Samuel Gilman suggested that it would be "more philosophical to credit such pretensions, than to ridicule or distrust them." For if, he continued,

> a *nation* has its peculiar style of writing, so that a French manuscript is as easily discernible from an English one as are the respective dialects of two countries; . . . if the chirographies of the two sexes are almost immediately distinguishable, so that a brother and sister, educated under the same circumstances, and taught by the same writing-master, shall yet unavoidably reveal their respective styles; and if, lastly, different *classes* of persons shall be known by

their different hand-writings, so that a mere child could
pronounce which is the mercantile clerk's, which the lawyer's, and which the leisurely gentleman's, let us beware
how we rashly discredit the experienced inspector of autographs, who deduces from the signature of an *individual*
the qualities of his mind.[10]

Even when referring to those distinctions frequently accepted as genuine—
the difference between male and female penmanship, for example—Gilman
did not credit them to external circumstances completely unrelated to the
writer's character. Sands would probably have explained the difference between a brother's and a sister's hands by noting that the brother had been
trained in the male running hand and the sister in a ladies' epistolary, but
Gilman made a point of noting that the siblings had received identical training, rendering the dissimilarities of script contingent on character, not cir-
cumstance. For Gilman, it required no great conceptual leap to suppose that
handwriting could reveal the qualities of mind unique to each individual.

Neither Sands nor Gilman, the first with his scornful dismissal of handwriting analysis, the second with his reasoned argument in favor of it, appears
to have made much of an impression on the American public. Far more influ-
ential was the presentation of these new ideas in connection with actual autographs and in the form of celebrity gossip. In 1836 and 1841–42, Edgar Allan
Poe published chatty, occasionally backbiting, analyses of literary autographs,
reproduced in facsimile, in two issues of the *Southern Literary Messenger* and
then, at greater length, in three of *Graham's Magazine*.[11] Poe described his
aim in the second series as threefold: "First, to give the Autograph signature—that is, a fac-simile in woodcut—of each of our most distinguished literati; second, to maintain that the character is, to a certain extent, indicated
by the chirography; and thirdly, to embody, under each Autograph, some literary gossip about the individual, with a brief critical comment on his writings." The analyses were not without distortion. Poe publicly admitted that
in the first series, "qualities were often attributed to individuals, which were
not so much indicated by their handwriting as suggested by the spleen of the
commentator," and he privately admitted to having been pressured, in the
second series, into modifying his opinions, compromising his "critical impar-
tiality" by praising "ninnies" of the literary world. Nevertheless, he insisted
in his "Chapter on Autography," that the notion that "a strong analogy does
generally and naturally exist between every man's chirography and character
will be denied by none but the unreflecting."[12]

Many remained unreflecting. A reviewer for the *Saturday Visitor* insisted
that "the notion of character being denoted in the scratchings of an author"

was of doubtful merit and represented Poe as "carried away with an innocent belief of the science of autography." But the facsimile signatures were a big hit; nothing like them had been seen before in America. Poe reported that the *Graham's* articles had enjoyed "a great run—have done wonders for the Journal," while newspaper reviewers hailed them as "most capital," "food for merriment," a "literary treat," and a "chapter of wonders . . . served . . . up with vinegar and sweet sauce."[13]

HANDWRITING, INDIVIDUALITY, AND THE UNCONSCIOUS

Lavater and those who elaborated on his ideas were positing something new about the nature of human beings. They maintained that the distinctiveness of an individual's hand derived from the uniqueness of his or her character. In this assertion, it is not difficult to detect what has often been termed a modern conception of the self. If in the colonial period there had been no expectation that handwriting would reflect an individual's unique qualities of mind, it was not so much because handwriting was considered to be an especially murky medium of character, as because the modern concept of the individual did not yet exist. Furthermore, early handwriting analysis drew on a recognizably romantic version of the modern self. What romantics celebrated in humankind was not the individual as he achieved some universal ideal but as he was unlike any other individual. Idiosyncrasy, eccentricity, singularity, originality—these were the qualities romantics celebrated in humanity and admired in individual human beings. For them, the unhindered expression and progressive unfolding of this uniqueness was the work of life.[14]

Of course, most romantics perceived distinctiveness as a relatively rare quality, not a universal characteristic of humanity. Singular individuals, men and women distinguished by rare talents and temperaments, stood out precisely because the masses were so undifferentiated. Indeed, romanticism can be understood as a reaction against larger social and cultural forces that threatened individuality and turned human beings into copies of one another. Among these forces can be counted the mechanization of work, the development of the factory system, the increasing impersonality of urban life, and the frantic and dehumanizing pace of the marketplace. These developments occurred in Europe before they did in the United States, but by the 1820s and 1830s commerce, manufacturing, and urbanization had changed the timbre of American life as well.

Romantics latched onto whatever countered these forces. They celebrated the eccentric genius who resisted the homogenizing pressures of contemporary life. They subscribed to a vitalist metaphysics that championed the integrity of the organism against a reductionist and dehumanizing mechanism.

Early handwriting analysis can be counted among the romantic phenomena that partook of these intellectual inclinations. Thus, it differentiated between the meaningless scripts of the masses and the exceptional handwritings that revealed extraordinary characters. It celebrated those rare examples as specimens of distinctiveness in a world hostile to the survival of individuality. And it did not try to dissect them, for not only would that violate the sacred but it would also destroy their vital essence, hence their meaning. But what lent handwriting analysis its greatest conceptual power was the role it assigned to the unconscious. It was the unconscious mind, not the conscious will, from which handwriting originated, and it was this same unconscious that provided safe haven for the individuality revealed in script.

The starting point for the early proponents of handwriting analysis was the admission that most people's scripts are meaningless because most people lack distinctive characters. "The great mass of people in the world," wrote Thomas Byerley, "may be said to consist of mere negatives; of persons who act as they are desired, think as they are taught, and *write after the copies set before them;* and the utmost that you can expect to discover from the handwriting of such persons is, that they have no individual character at all." Hence Byerley skipped over a number of kings and queens, since, as he explained, "common-placed character . . . is as rife in palaces as elsewhere," so that not all royal autographs rated as "characteristic signatures."[15]

Much as Byerley used characterless hands to debunk members of the royalty, Poe used literary autographs to expose alleged geniuses of the literary world. According to Poe, scripts that did not deviate from writing masters' models indicated nothing more than a complete lack of character. Thus he remarked of William Cullen Bryant's handwriting that it was "one of the most commonplace clerk's hands which we ever encountered, and has no character about it beyond that of the day-book and ledger." What was "deficient in his chirography," commented Poe wryly, was deficient as well "in his poetical productions." Viewing the autograph of yet another "feeble and commonplace writer of poetry," Poe was not surprised to find it executed in a "clerk's hand," a "hand which no man of talent ever did or could indite." If hands that evoked the countinghouse betrayed male literati, those that bespoke the ladies' seminary gave away their female counterparts. Thus the signature of poet Rebecca S. Nichols was "formed somewhat too much upon the ordinary boarding-school model to afford any indication of character." Conversely, he described the handwriting of another female author as evincing "a strong disposition to fly off at a tangent from the old formulae of the Boarding Academies," and the woman herself as "not destitute of originality—that rarest of all qualities in a woman."[16]

But some hands—some *people*—were not innately "mere negatives"; the modern world had made them so. Poe ruled out the handwriting of men immersed in the worlds of law and business as meaningless because it had been disturbed "by those adventitious events which distort the natural disposition of the man of the world, preventing his real nature from manifesting itself in his manuscript." Poe praised the dramatic works of David Paul Brown, but claimed that his signature revealed nothing. Why? Because Brown was both playwright and attorney, and, Poe noted, "no one can expect a lawyer in full practice to give in his manuscript any true indication of his intellect or character." (The same point was often made with respect to Walter Scott.)[17] Literary editors met the same fate. Forced to keep up with the rapid pace of the modern, urban world, their hands soon lost all character. Poe thus attached the greatest significance to the handwriting of people sequestered from the modern world, the farther the better. "In the case of literary men, generally, we may expect some decisive token of the mental influence upon the manuscript," he wrote, and "we may look with especial certainty for such token" in scholars far removed from contemporary affairs. Thus of the nearly hundred signatures he analyzed for character, Poe singled out as the most revealing that of Professor Charles Anthon, "the most erudite of our classical scholars."[18]

Like Poe, Isaac Disraeli dismissed most scripts as lacking in individuality and pointed to the circumstances of contemporary life by way of explanation. Adherence to school models indicated this lack of distinctiveness. But Disraeli also implied that handwriting had *once* revealed character, and that individuality had been lost as society changed. For Disraeli, as for many romantics, the threat came from the machine. "Regulated as the pen is now too often by a mechanical process," he wrote, referring to copperplate copybooks, ". . . the true physiognomy of writing will be lost among our rising generation." He blamed the writing masters who trained their pupils to conform to standardized models, forcing them into "automatic motions, as if acted on by the pressure of a steam-engine," so as to produce "fac-similes of each other . . . , all appearing to have come from the same rolling-press." Under the influence of mechanization, it was not only writing but the writers themselves that were in danger of becoming standardized. Indeed, this was the real point. "Our hand-writings," rued Disraeli, have become "as monotonous as our characters in the present habits of society."[19]

Like many romantics, Disraeli and Poe perceived individuality as threatened by the alienating and stultifying circumstances of contemporary life. Most people could not maintain their individuality under such conditions; nor, therefore, could their handwriting. But a few could. These were the men and women whose scripts became talismans of individuality in an age perceived as hostile to individuality. Hence, students of handwriting ignored that of ordinary men and women, concentrating their efforts instead on the autographs of the famous, most especially kings and queens, statesmen and warriors, artists, composers, poets, and writers. By the same token, analysis of these scripts was never meant to yield a comprehensive portrait of character. Certain characteristics, not coincidentally those revolving around Hocquart's variables of energy and imagination, attracted the most interest. Taken as a whole, the adjectives usually applied to the analysis of hands—*bold, forceful, dashing, picturesque, deliberate,* and so on—constituted a composite portrait of romantic "genius." About the only variation came in the description of a hand that lacked the qualities of genius.

Genius, as every romantic knew, could not be apprehended through dissection. To subject the individual to the same process of rationalization and standardization that had destroyed the uniqueness of his fellows would be nothing short of desecration. Furthermore, it would be futile, for what endowed an individual with genius, like what endowed an organism with life, could not be analyzed into its constituent parts without disappearing altogether. And finally, invasive techniques were not perceived as necessary. Individuals who had escaped the corrosive effects of modernity radiated their genius. Romantic readers of handwriting therefore sized up the script as a whole, then provided a pithy but sweeping characterization of the writer in question. Of the handwriting of Henry VIII, for example, Disraeli wrote "bold, hasty, and commanding." Poe's analyses were equally impressionistic: "dashing, free, and not ungraceful, but is sadly deficient in force and picturesqueness" (writer Nathaniel P. Willis); "indicates, in the most striking manner, the unpretending simplicity, directness, and especially the *indefatigability,* of his mental character" (reformer Orestes Brownson); "a certain calm, broad deliberateness, which constitutes *force* in its highest character, and approaches to majesty" (clergyman William Ellery Channing).[20]

What these readings consisted of was less an analysis of handwriting than an intuitive apprehension of the essence of another human being. Interpretation of handwriting involved an almost mystical encounter between the writer of the hand and the reader of the hand, an intimate rendezvous of one soul with another. Indeed, this was a process that seemed to require as much genius as it grasped. As Thomas Byerley argued, just as it was not "every one to whom [handwriting analysis] has any sensible application," so is it true that "it is not every man who understands this sort of criterion." Not all were endowed with what romantics described as the ability to intuit transcendent truths from particulars and to experience the power of sympathy, that intimate identification with another soul that allows for true understanding. Nathaniel Hawthorne clarified just what sort of person Byerley had in mind when he wrote that "there are said to be temperaments endowed with sympathies so exquisite, that, by merely handling an autograph, they can detect the writer's character with unerring accuracy, and read his inmost heart as easily as a less-gifted eye would peruse the written page." And the author of an article on the "Peculiarities of Handwriting" gave an example of one such sympathetic soul when he wrote of one author that she "possesses the gift of being able to read a person's character by his handwriting."[21]

Among those who subscribed to the tenets of early handwriting analysis were such romantic figures as Friedrich Schleiermacher, Walter Scott, Elizabeth Barrett Browning, and Charlotte Brontë.[22] Although early handwriting analysis clearly drew on a romantic notion of the self as a unique individual, it is not immediately obvious why romantics should perceive handwriting in particular as capable of embodying that distinctiveness. Great works of literature, art, and music might betoken singularity of mind, as might an eccentric style of living or even dressing, but why should script be counted on to do the same? Certainly, most people did not share that expectation, nor had they ever. In the eighteenth century, script had functioned as a studied presentation of social identity, and it had been judged according to the same neoclassical aesthetic principles as painting or poetry; that is, it was good insofar as it reproduced faithfully a timeless, universal model of excellence. In the nineteenth century, handwriting was perceived as an equally standardized product, and penmanship pedagogues exploited the social utility of this premise; for them, copybooks offered just such a model for imitation, just such a guide for character formation. To perceive handwriting as an index of individual character, then, required not just a new conception of the self but also a new conception of script.

Before we explore the basis for that new idea of script, it is worth noting that romantic reconstructions of handwriting and the self should be thought of not as parallel phenomena but as a single development. Romantics conceptualized script and self in terms of each other. The process is most apparent in Lavater's passages on handwriting and in kindred commentary on handwriting analysis, but it is present as well in the language used by romantics in their general discussions of originality and imagination. *"Imitators,"* wrote the poet Edward Young in 1759, "only give us a sort of Duplicates of what we had," but "the pen of an *Original* Writer, like Armida's wand, out of a barren waste calls a blooming spring." Fifteen years later, the philosopher Alexander Gerard argued that the imaginative man presents "ideas, not as copies, but as originals," so that "all genuine productions in the arts, are marked with strong signatures of a bright and lively imagination."[23] In Young's and Gerard's phrases, we see the romantic self depicted, just as, intriguingly, we see it delineated in terms of duplicates and originals, pens and signatures—

in short, in the vocabulary not so much of literature or authorship in general but of handwriting in particular.

Part of the reconceptualization of handwriting was aesthetic. Romantic aesthetics jettisoned both the mimetic and the universal ideal in favor of an ideal that valued in human productions precisely what was prized in individuals: originality and imagination, particularity and uniqueness. According to this system, distinctive handwriting would be the most valued, and its peculiarities would hold special interest. But more fundamental, if romantics were able to count handwriting among those human productions capable of distinctiveness, it was because they traced the provenance of script to a far deeper level of being than the conscious will, to what they regarded as the seat of individual identity and uniqueness, the unconscious mind. Instead of perceiving the individual's handwriting style as somehow deliberate, a conscious choice dictated by one's social role or a willed effort at self-mastery, they saw it as an involuntary emanation from the soul. Escaping from the deep, it bore the distinctive markings of the writer.

Critical to this association of script with soul was the perception of handwriting as gesture. As we have seen, interest in the physical process of producing script was hardly new. When eighteenth-century writing masters urged a bold hand on their mercantile students, it was so that the finished product of the pen might recall the bold movements of the writer's arm and, by extension, the boldness of the mercantile character. Their successors in the next century also focused as much on the process as the product of writing, whether that meant training boys in muscular penmanship or girls in delicacy of motion. For both sets of pedagogues, however, the physical motions involved in writing, like all gestures, were in some way deliberate. They were calculated to achieve certain effects while avoiding others, through the studied imitation of models and through bodily self-command, in order to present the writer in a consciously chosen role. It is easy to recall Chesterfield's advice that one stage one's posture, carriage, and facial expressions, but even those who argued for the innate sincerity of gesture met their match in the many manuals that coached readers in the methods of appearing sincere through prescribed modes of bodily performance.[24]

Handwriting romantics, by contrast, regarded gestures as involuntary acts that by definition could not be contrived. What a person *says* is no guide to character, explained Hocquart, for "when we speak, it is almost always under the influence of the will." Gesture, on the other hand, "escapes us" involuntarily, "carrying the imprint of truth," and of all these gestures, "there are none that carry the imprint of the individual more than his manner of writing." Hartley Coleridge, nephew of the celebrated poet and a literary figure in his own right, concurred. "Into every habitual act, which is performed unconsciously, earnestly, or naturally . . . ," he wrote, "something of the predominant habit of the mind, unavoidably passes." Of all such acts, there was none "into which the character enters more fully than that of writing: for it is generally performed alone or unobserved; seldom, in adults, is the object of conscious attention, and takes place while the thoughts, and the natural current of feeling, are in full operation." For Thomas Byerley, gesture alone betrayed "gleams of character"—thus he went so far as to reject Lavater's physiognomy—and like Hocquart and Coleridge, he placed the gesture of handwriting above all others. "In using his pen," he argued, "a man acts unconsciously, as the current of his blood impels him; and there, at all times, nature flows unrestrained and free."[25]

For handwriting romantics, the gesture of handwriting was a revelation, even a betrayal of the innermost self. Handwriting was not a conscious component of the public self or a triumph of the will over the body in forming character. Indeed, the will neither created nor liberated the self; it served only to contrive surface appearances. It played no essential role in handwriting. For the traces of authentic selfhood, among which they counted handwriting, romantics looked instead to the unconscious. From here emanates character, in the sense of intellectual makeup and emotional temperament. From here too emanates the written character, bearing the imprint of the individual who holds the pen. Thus character, in the medium of handwriting, originates in the unconscious, then escapes us (Hocquart), starts forth (Byerley), or, in the words of Samuel Gilman, "unavoidably" reveals whence it came, making it possible to deduce "from the signature of an *individual* the qualities of his mind."[26]

The concept of the unconscious has a substantial pre-Freudian history—these references are not unusual—but what is noteworthy is the identification of the unconscious with an individualized self.[27] Here lay the core of the romantic agenda. Romantics feared the effects of what Disraeli called the present habits of society on individuality, and they looked to the unconscious as its only refuge. The solution, wrote Thomas Carlyle, lay in withdrawing from the "thin and barren domain of the Conscious or Mechanical" into the "inner sanctuaries" of the mind, "that domain of the Unconscious, by nature infinite and inexhaustible" whence "all wonders . . . rise like exhalations from the Deep."[28] The theory and practice of handwriting analysis appealed to romantics because it posited just such a sanctuary for threatened individuality and represented handwriting as just such a wondrous exhalation. To account for the correspondence between an individual's handwriting and his or her character by representing handwriting as an unconscious act was to relocate the source of individuality to a part of the mind that was inaccessible to external control and impervious to self-control. No writing master could obliterate true distinctiveness by forcing his gifted pupils into the common mold of character. Nor could writers themselves, at least those rare individuals able to withstand the corrosive effects of the nineteenth century, help but reveal their authentic selves.

The cultural meaning of romantic handwriting analysis comes into further focus when we examine such ostensibly kindred sciences of character as physiognomy and phrenology. There was no actual conflict; many who believed character could be read in a person's script also believed it could be read in a person's face or head. But while handwriting analysis focused on men and women who had somehow managed to differentiate themselves from the norm, phrenology, the most popular of the nineteenth-century pseudosciences, concentrated on ordinary people. True, phrenological readings of famous men and women made for good magazine and lecture material, but most of those who took an interest in phrenology wanted their own heads examined. They might visit a phrenological parlor for that purpose or wait for an itinerant skull-reader to come to town, purchase one of the many do-it-yourself manuals, or send in a dollar and a daguerreotype for mail-order analysis. However accomplished, they wanted a comprehensive and detailed portrait of their strengths and weaknesses, the better to capitalize on the former and reform the latter. Most of those who sought phrenological aid were either respectably middle class or hoping to be so. They wanted to be successful not by standing out but by fitting in.[29]

Thus, despite superficial similarities, the contrast between handwriting analysis and phrenological analysis was substantial. The key difference lay in how skulls and scripts were imagined to reveal character. Phrenologists posited a fortuitous but otherwise opaque correspondence between mental traits and physical features. Proponents of handwriting analysis, on the other hand, proposed a deep-seated repository of characterological uniqueness (the unconscious) and a mechanism of transmission (the unconscious gesture). Thus the impulse that lay behind handwriting analysis—the vicarious celebration of individuality—could have no place in phrenology. There was no hushed reverence before genius in Orson Fowler's consulting rooms; phrenologists took on the bumps of all comers. There was no sympathetic apprehension of the unconscious, only the methodical exploitation of an empirically derived relation between mental and physical characteristics. Nor did phrenologists limit their analyses to those aspects of character that signified individuality; they pursued a full range of traits, including the most quotidian. And they claimed no genius of their own; all that was required was the cash to buy a phrenological self-instruction manual. Above all, phrenologists and their clients believed that there was an ideal set of character traits that could act as a universal model for self-reformation. Proponents of handwriting analysis, by contrast, celebrated those individuals who had managed to resist and transcend those norms and whose individuality lay beyond the reach of manipulation. Genius, in its unfettered glory, radiated from their scripts. It could certainly be apprehended by kindred spirits; indeed, it might even illumine those watching in awe from the shadows.

AUTOGRAPH COLLECTING

In Sands's disparagement of handwriting analysis and Gilman's apologetic endorsement of it, we can sense that the dominant attitude toward such a notion, at least among well-educated audiences, was one of skepticism, if not derision. But one curious cultural phenomenon of the Victorian era suggests that the concepts underlying romantic handwriting analysis—the uniqueness of human character, its emanation from the unconscious, its governing influence on penmanship style—might have lurked or even loomed somewhere in popular consciousness. This was the growing popularity of the new hobby of autograph collecting.

The cult of the autograph, as one historian of the phenomenon in England termed it, dates only to the end of the eighteenth century, not so coincidentally the era of Lavater. Even then, it was limited largely to "antiquaries in their nonage and dilettanti men of parts." By the early nineteenth century, American antiquaries and dilettanti had taken up autograph collecting too. In Albany, the Reverend William B. Sprague began his collection in 1815, eventually amassing no fewer than 100,000 specimens. Israel Tefft's collection, also begun in 1815, grew from some 5,000 autographs in 1838 to some 30,000 at his death in 1861. When sold at auction, the catalogue of the sale numbered 260 pages, and the collection was disposed of in 2,630 lots.[30]

But as the new century wore on, interest in autographs turned from the rich or rarefied to the truly popular. It now became customary for signatures of famous men and women to adorn their portraits. In Europe, shops, catalogues, and auctions specializing in autograph material catered to ever-growing numbers of collectors. All these made their appearance in America by the 1850s. Autograph facsimile albums, at first expensive folios, were available by mid-century in cheap editions. Indeed, the publication of Poe's autography articles made a sensation mainly because they provided readers with reproductions. By the 1830s autograph collecting had become a popular hobby in America, one no longer limited to the wealthy or scholarly, and famous people found themselves increasingly bombarded with requests from autograph collectors—"musquitoes of literature," as Washington Irving was reported to have labeled these nuisances.[31]

As a practical matter, there was considerable overlap between those who analyzed and those who collected autographs. To read autographs often meant to acquire them, especially in the case of living personages. Collectors, on the other hand, looked for signs of character in the autographs they obtained. Thus, collector Frederick Netherclift expected his autograph facsimile albums to appeal "to those who believe that there exists an analogy between the hand-writing and the character of an individual."[32]

More significant, in gathering autographs, collectors were guided by many of the same notions adhered to by the early practitioners of handwriting analysis. They too focused their efforts on the signatures of those people who, in the words of one collector, had "risen above the common herd." They too regarded the unconscious as the medium through which character was expressed in handwriting. Thus collectors especially prized signatures that had been composed without any forethought or deliberation, deeming them unconscious and therefore authentic products of the writer's innermost self. "There is something furtive about a true autograph," wrote one commentator. "We should come by it obliquely, and not by direct attack. A name written at the request of a stranger is only about as valuable as the same name stamped by machinery. To have any character, it should have been written in a careless or confidential moment." Hence, autograph collectors preferred to obtain the signatures of living personages by ruse rather than request or purchase. These "autographic harpies" resorted to all manner of unscrupulous methods, soliciting signatures from authors on the pretense of petitioning Congress on their behalf, for example, or plying a man like the Duke of Wellington with "letters of inquiry as to the characters of . . . imaginary privates of fictitious regiments."[33]

Again like the early proponents of handwriting analysis, autograph collectors engaged in an almost mystical encounter with their subjects, savoring the greatness that emanated from the handwriting of remarkable individuals. One newspaper writer described the collector as having "much of the mystery of human nature breathing through his pursuit." If anything, however, the experience of collecting autographs was even more profound than the experience of reading them, for physical contact with the actual *stuff* of individuality seemed alive with magical possibilities.[34] When writer and editor Sarah Josepha Hale endorsed the plan of constructing an autographic quilt, each patch signed by a celebrity, a fellow journalist commented sardonically that "no doubt some mystic influence would charm the sleeper under such a spread." In fact, many autograph collectors ascribed just such magical properties to ink. "The characters of most men are commonly assumed to ooze out at their finger tips," wrote one, "else whence this pleasing hope, this fond desire, this longing after—an autograph?" Another went so far as to confound the self as a pathway of genius, with the pen as a conduit of fluid; he equated the emanation of individuality with the production of script, mixing blood with ink. "Their ambition," he wrote of autograph collectors, "is to drink inspiration from original fountains, from the streams of thought in the channel through which it first flowed from the author's pen."[35]

If we follow this metaphor, we might give the nineteenth-century autograph collector, denounced by contemporaries as an autographic mosquito, harpy, and fiend, a new epithet: the autographic vampire. Judging by the reaction autograph seekers provoked, this would not be too extreme a term. No doubt, in an era when men and women took every pain to compose themselves into public personae that suggested private virtue, it was as distressing an experience to be caught unawares by an autograph seeker as to have one's visitors penetrate beyond the parlor to the boudoir or for an amateur photographer to snap one's candid picture.[36] But given the reification of self in script, even a straightforward request for an autograph could be experienced as not merely an irritation or embarrassment but a violation of the most intimate and threatening kind. It was, in the increasingly suggestive words of one writer whose autograph was frequently solicited, an unwilling "exhibition of one's private personality," the surreptitious snipping of "a lock of one's mental and moral hair," a "subtraction from our potency."[37] Thus autographs were talismans of individuality in more than a symbolic sense. Their individuality endowed them with real powers, found in magical substances from amulets to rhinoceros horns, and they were sought after—and withheld—because of them.

THE LEGAL MYSTIFICATION OF HANDWRITING

If we look at handwriting that purports to have been executed by a particular individual, how can we be certain it is in fact that person's hand? "The test of genuineness," wrote Coleridge in 1836, "ought to be the resemblance, not to the formation of the letters in some other specimen or specimens, but to the general character of writing, which is impressed on it as the involuntary and unconscious result of constitution, habit, or other permanent cause, and is therefore itself permanent. And we best acquire a knowledge of this character, by seeing the individual write at times when his manner of writing is not in question, or by engaging with him in correspondence; either supposition giving reason to believe that he writes at the time, not constrainedly, but in his natural manner."[38] The writing style is a bit stiff for Coleridge, but the content is what we might expect from a poet of romantic persuasion. Here is handwriting as an emanation of the unconscious; here too is the impressionistic analysis of script and the rejection of minute analytical techniques as a violation of character.

In truth, though, the author of these lines was not Samuel Taylor Coleridge but his nephew, Justice John Taylor Coleridge of the English bench, who was presenting his opinion in the case of *Doe v. Suckermore*.[39] As we have seen, seventeenth-century Anglo-American courts had rejected as unreliable, even meaningless, testimony regarding the aesthetic appearance of handwriting. Then, tentatively and haltingly in the 1700s, decisively in the early nineteenth century, it became legally acceptable for witnesses to testify with regard to the genuineness of a handwritten document based on their previous familiarity with the alleged writer's script.[40] What underlay this change of heart was the novel conviction, first put forward by the legal scholar Geoffrey Gilbert in 1726, that the differences among hands, like differences among faces, actually testified to the uniqueness of each one, making recognition of a script tantamount to identification of the writer.[41] Coleridge's opinion in *Doe v. Suckermore* held a special place in this judicial shift. It acted as the capstone to the rulings initiated by Gilbert's treatise; and throughout the nineteenth century Coleridge's words were cited, both in England and America, as the ultimate authority on the judicial treatment of disputed documents.[42]

Was the learned judge a spiritual brother to Lavater and Hocquart, Disraeli and Byerley, Gilman and Poe? Hardly. Although he subscribed to the notion that every man's handwriting is as distinctive as his face, he never suggested that either reflected his character. Nevertheless, at the same time that the handwriting romantics celebrated autographs as quasi-mystical exhalations of genius, the stolid legal minds of the era engaged in some curious mystification of their own. Like the early proponents of handwriting analysis and the autograph collectors, they too recognized the silent encounter between the reader and writer of a script as intensely significant, and they resisted the dissection of handwriting into component parts. These notions shaped their interpretation of just how the genuineness of a disputed document could be established or disproved.

Once comparison of hands became judicially acceptable, witnesses familiar with a man's script might testify as to whether he had written a particular document, but strict rules limited the definition of familiarity. Legal exceptions notwithstanding, as a practical matter, the only allowable witness was a person who had actually seen the writer in question engaged in the physical act of writing—not, as in the seventeenth century, penning the specific document at issue, but writing *something*. Secondhand familiarity with a person's script—having received a personal letter from him, for example, or having perused documents attributed to him—did not count from a legal standpoint. The rationale for this rule was that the person comparing the style of handwriting in the disputed document with the memory of a script in his head must be certain that his mental impression was based on a genuine specimen.[43]

What strikes us as odd today is the concomitant assumption that the original encounter with handwriting, however fleeting or distant, created a meaningful impression of individual identity. In *Garrels v. Alexander*, the witness had seen the defendant write only once; Lord Kenyon ruled the evidence admissible. In another case, one attorney, frustrated in his attempts to find admissible witnesses, swore "to a knowledge of the writing of the opposite party from having once looked over his shoulder when writing a letter at an alehouse." In an English case of 1803 involving a contested will, a witness deposed that he had seen the dead man write just once seven years earlier, and then only his signature, but he thought that "he should know the deceased's signature again." A generation later in Louisiana, a witness who could neither "well read hand-writing" nor "do much more than write his own name" testified about the handwriting of his mother, a woman who, because of advanced age, had not at the time of the trial written for years. And in a New York case of 1847, a witness who testified about the genuineness of a signature had seen neither the alleged signer nor his handwriting in sixty-three years. Thus what might seem the most incompetent of witnesses and compromising set of circumstances did not stand in the way of presenting testimony so long as the physical act of writing had been personally witnessed.[44]

Meanwhile, it was forbidden to draw any conclusions based on the concrete, visual juxtaposition of two documents, the first certifiably genuine and the second under dispute. With few exceptions, courts in the first half of the nineteenth century repeatedly refused to allow juries to compare documents or to allow the testimony of "expert" witnesses, usually postal inspectors or bank cashiers, who claimed that their professional knowledge of handwriting qualified them to make such determinations. Legal authorities justified these rulings by pointing out various practical considerations. How can we be sure that the document serving as a basis for comparison is truly genuine? How can we prevent a biased selection of such documents? And what if members of the jury cannot read?[45]

More critical, it was claimed that jury members and expert witnesses could not possibly have the necessary knowledge with which to form an accurate evaluation of handwriting. The uniqueness of a hand, legal authorities insisted, could only be grasped through an intuitive and unconscious apprehension of its totality. "The evidence of hand-writing arises from this," explained one of the attorneys in an 1803 English case. "That by nature and habit persons contract a mode of forming letters giving a character to their writing as distinct as that of the human face. One man knows the face of another; though he cannot describe the minute particulars, by which he knows it. So it is of hand-writing. . . . You see a man in the act of writing; but you do not observe the manner, in which he forms his letters. The impression however is general." Judge Coleridge concurred when he wrote that "the witness is supposed to have received into his mind an impression, not so much of the manner in which the writer has formed letters in the particular instances, as of the general character of his handwriting." Here is where jurymen and experts who were examining a person's handwriting for the first time would err. With no generalized mental impression embedded in their memory, they would mistakenly evaluate a script by inspecting its details.[46]

This legal wisdom was repeated in the American editions of English treatises on evidence, and its ramifications played out in American courts. An 1806 treatise published in Philadelphia, for example, explained that because "the process by which the mind arrives at the belief of hand writing" is "the recollection of the *general character*" of the script, not "the formation of *particular letters*," courts have not allowed people who were previously unfamiliar with the disputed handwriting to present testimony or, if they are jury members, to evaluate the genuineness of documents from personal examination. In 1839 the legal principle still held. In that year a treatise published in New York noted that "in every person's manner of writing there is a certain distinct prevailing character," and it is this that impresses the observer's memory and forms the basis of his court testimony.[47]

Although legal authorities of the first half of the nineteenth century never raised the possibility that handwriting might reveal character, they approached handwriting in a manner suggestive of the handwriting romantics. For both the proponents of handwriting analysis and the autograph collectors, handwriting was a token of individuality. Because legal minds never drew any links between the uniqueness of a script and the uniqueness of a personality, however, they did not make of that individuality what the romantics did. They did not celebrate it as evidence that an inspired few had escaped the homogenizing influences of urban, industrial civilization. Nevertheless, their insistence that the essence of handwriting is something more than the sum of its minute particulars partook of the romantics' rebellion against mechanism and championing of vitalism. A world explicable solely in terms of matter and motion left little room for the strivings of the human soul—or even the quirks of the human hand.[48] Thus handwriting romantics and legal authorities alike shrank from subjecting handwriting to microscopic dissection, the former so as not to defile the soul that had produced it, the latter so as not to destroy its organic essence.

And because they never considered the uniqueness of a script to represent the uniqueness of character, legal minds felt no compunction about recognizing every human being's handwriting as unique. To argue that everyone writes a distinctive script was not to say that every character was distinctive, every man and woman a repository of originality and genius. For Byerley and

Poe, the clarion of character trumpeted forth from the handwriting of but a few; for Judge Coleridge, each handwriting was different but mute. No one had as yet developed a school of handwriting analysis that posited both the uniqueness of each hand and its ability to serve as an index of character. But that was soon to change.

THE NEW SCIENCES OF DETECTION

In 1872 *The Mysteries of Handwriting: The Art of Judging Men from Their Autographs* was published in Paris. It was written by two men, Adolphe Desbarrolles and the Abbé Jean-Hippolyte Michon, the first looking backward and the second striking out on his own. Desbarrolles's opus included works on astrology, phrenology, and chiromancy (another term for palmistry).[49] He was thus allied with the tradition that categorized handwriting analysis with the pseudosciences and occult arts and that kept handwriting analysis on the margins of intellectual respectability. For several decades after Poe had published his autograph facsimile essays, the only published writings of any sort that gave more than passing notice to handwriting analysis in America appeared in phrenological journals.[50]

The tradition continued with what was probably the first full-length work on handwriting analysis to appear in the English language, *The Philosophy of Handwriting*, published by John Henry Ingram in 1879. Ingram, who for the occasion assumed the nom de plume Don Felix de Salamanca, followed the established romantic routine of reproducing famous signatures in facsimile and providing brief, impressionistic analyses of the extent to which they exhibited "the eccentricities of genius" and "the impress of individuality" on the one hand or the clerkly conventionality of "commonplace people" on the other. He departed from predecessors like Poe (whose biography he had written) in several ways: when he used the term *chiromancy* to denote handwriting analysis; when he described chiromancy as one of the "Asian mysteries"; and when he promised "to pry . . . into the abstruse mysteries of this occult science."[51]

By the time Ingram published his treatise, however, it was already outdated. Desbarrolles's coauthor, the Abbé Michon, had repudiated his earlier association with the mysteries of handwriting in favor of a rational system of analysis, transforming a heretofore romantic or occult interest in celebrity autographs into a special branch of the science of psychology. He called it graphology. During the 1870s Michon published his *System of Graphology* and his *Practical Method of Graphology*, founded the Société de la Graphologie, and edited the journal *Graphologie* until his death in 1881.[52] His work established the analytical framework within which graphologists on both sides of the Atlantic operated well into the twentieth century.

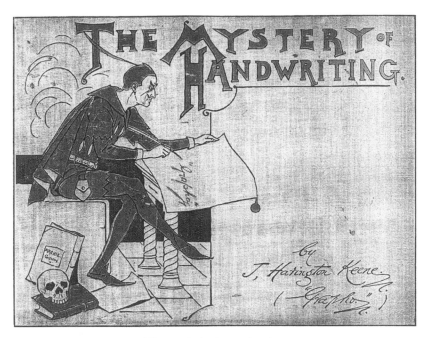

25. The graphologist as wizard, 1896.

Michon and his successors were anxious to place the study of character in handwriting on a sound scientific footing. They admitted that much remained to be done and that many conclusions would therefore have to remain tentative, but they insisted that their discipline be taken for what it was, a science in its infancy. Graphological facts are based on observation and deduction, wrote the American graphologist J. Harington Keene, and "what scientific mind will ask for more?"[53] In fact, however, science or the lack thereof was the least of what separated the old handwriting analysis from the new graphology. For starters, even many of those who argued the most strenuously for the scientific basis of graphology subscribed to such kindred methods of reading character as phrenology and palmistry, albeit with the insistence that these too were intellectually rigorous. Some published books on these arts; others organized their graphological works around the standard phrenological set of traits. Desbarrolles was not the only graphologist to study the "mysteries" of the universe. Keene, after all, titled his book *The Mystery of Handwriting*, and he claimed that while the "graphologist of useful grade" has "no supernatural power" and "his processes are not cabalistic or occult," the most gifted graphologists do in fact possess a "seer faculty" (fig. 25).[54]

More critical, what most fundamentally distinguished the old handwriting analysis from the new had little to do with their relative degrees of scientific legitimacy. Instead, the new graphology struck out on its own when it shifted the focus of analytical efforts, changed the nature of analytical techniques, and redefined just who could practice handwriting analysis. Romantics, as we have seen, concentrated their interest on the autographs of famous men and women. These signatures exuded a generalized but nonetheless powerful sense of genius. For kindred souls, endowed with the exquisite sensibility that was itself a sign of genius, reading character in an autograph meant engaging in a kind of spiritual communion with the writer; ordinary men and women, who might collect autographs, could feel the heat of genius even if they could not penetrate its fire with their own. Graphologists, by contrast, focused on the handwriting of commonplace souls, especially strangers. Reading character in these samples required a minute analysis of the writing's smallest, seemingly insignificant details. And anyone could undertake such an analysis; all that was needed was one of the many graphology manuals now being published for a general audience and an average amount of common sense.

For graphologists, scientific handwriting analysis was primarily useful as it revealed the hidden characters of potentially dangerous strangers. Here graphology was following the lead of physiognomy and to a lesser extent phrenology, which owed at least some of their popularity to the practical skill they offered to Victorians in exposing deception.[55] Some early proponents of handwriting analysis had in fact concerned themselves with the problem of deceptive appearances, in particular Edouard Hocquart and Thomas Byerley. Indeed, their interpretation of handwriting as gesture and their placing of handwriting above all other gestures must be understood in this context. "Nothing is more difficult to know as man," wrote Hocquart, "how to penetrate his thoughts, to recognize that which, having no material existence, cannot strike our senses." For Hocquart, as we have seen, a man's words offered unreliable evidence of character, for speech is a willed and therefore potentially duplicitous act, but a man's unconscious gestures, especially the act of writing, were a different story altogether. Byerley drew a similar distinction between artful appearances and the involuntary, and therefore profoundly authentic, acts of the body, and he too singled out the gesture of handwriting as the most authentic. "In all other actions . . . ," he wrote, "*some share* of guile and deception *may* lurk, which it requires penetration, experience, and skill to be able to detect," but handwriting, because it is an unconscious act, reveals the self for what it is.[56]

In antebellum America, however, proponents of handwriting analysis, unlike those of physiognomy and phrenology, did not address this set of concerns. The focus remained on famous men and women. Some of these might be exposed as humdrum personalities and talents, but the real interest was in savoring rather than debunking individuality. Romantic handwriting analysis, with its interest in physical gestures instead of physical traits, its interpretation of gestures as derived from the unconscious, and its portrayal of the unconscious as a haven for embattled individuality, was ideally suited to that cultural task. The same could not be said of either physiognomy or phrenology. When postbellum graphology turned its attention to the problem of deception, however, it did not jettison the link between the unconscious gesture and individuality. It simply redefined individuality, from something to be relished to something that could be stalked.

Turn-of-the-century graphology manuals brimmed with tales of prospective employees, business partners, and spouses who sought to deceive their way into positions of trust and advantage by an exterior show of virtue. Some of these stories ended luridly, with embezzlement, bankruptcy, and infidelity—"Oh Mr. von Hagen, had I only followed your advise! . . . Charlie is unfaithful to me, he drinks and gambles and I am so unhappy!"—but in others, the graphologist, perceiving the real character rotting beneath the cunningly contrived exterior, was able to warn his client in time to avert tragedy. "If we have an art by which the inner and motive character of our fellows can be estimated with more surety than any other index will afford," wrote J. Harington Keene, "how valuable that art must be to the everyday citizen who has ordinarily to learn the true character of his associates by laborious and often costly experience! A mere scrap of writing tells him the kind of man he is welcoming as the stranger within his gates to his family circle, to his purse, to his heart!"[57] No matter how hard an ill-intentioned stranger might try to conceal his character, the moment he put pen to paper, he unwittingly committed an act of self-betrayal, becoming an open book to the graphologist. Here the graphologist was said to have an advantage over the physiognomist and phrenologist, for a careful examination of the face and head required the presence and cooperation of the subject, not likely in the case of a person bent on deception. But with handwriting, pointed out graphologist John Rexford, we can "read the character of friend or foe, living or dead, with or without their permission."[58]

Keene, who in a mail-order practice that spanned the last three decades of the nineteenth century was said to have "prevented, graphologically, more than two thousand marriages that would have been disastrous,"[59] summarized the promise of graphology in a poem dedicated "To the Reader":

> Sweet lips that smile, and eyes that fondly beam,
> Are oft but shadows of the things they seem.
>
> Fair words that promise much are easily said;
> Warm clasp of friendly hands ere now has led

To pitfalls dark and deep the trusting feet
Of him who judged these signs the proof complete.

Herein a power lies, within the reach
Of all who study what it fain would teach;
Whereby the writer by his pen doth show
The inward self of those we outward know;
Describing to our vision, clear and sure,
The heart that fails, or strength that will endure.

Ours be the task to choose, while pass along
True hearts and brave from out the motley throng![60]

To sort out friend from foe entailed a painstaking and methodical analysis of the characteristics, major and minor, of the handwriting under review. The heart of Michon's work was the development and systematization of just such a science of graphic signs, each a key to some aspect of character (fig. 26), much as the details of cranial topography provided the phrenologist with characterological information. Graphologists were called upon to analyze such general attributes as the direction of a line of writing, the slope of the script, and the spacing between letters, as well as such specifics as the shape and orientation of letters, letter-parts, flourishes, and even punctuation. Some graphologists insisted on the use of a magnifying glass or even a microscope for such work. Every sign, large or small, represented a personality trait. Thus, for instance, ambition could be detected in writing that ascended from left to right; in a t-bar that followed the same inclination; and in a capital M in which the first point of the letter was higher than the second.[61]

Graphology manuals usually presented their information in one or both of two formats: an alphabetical arrangement of character traits (ambition, avarice . . . zeal) with their corresponding graphic signs or a discussion of general and letter-by-letter handwriting characteristics and the personality characteristics they indicated. Presumably the prospective employer could use the first technique to scan for such critical traits as honesty, while the second was more conducive to a comprehensive profile. Indeed, the graphological portrait that emerged from a painstaking analysis was said to equal a photograph in accuracy and detail.[62]

Graphologists offered no new theoretical explanation for the correlation of graphic signs with character traits. They continued to assume that the unconscious was the conduit between character and handwriting, but they could not pinpoint a more precise mechanism of transmission to explain the correlation between a specific graphic sign and a specific trait. What they

Explanatory of the signs of the 42 Faculties.

Amativeness.
Conjugality.
Friendship.
Inhabitiveness.
Philoprogenitiveness.

Acquisitiveness.
Alimentiveness.
Combativeness
Destructiveness —
Secretiveness.
Vitativeness,

Approbativeness

Cautiousness =

Concentrativeness.

Self Esteem.

Benevolence
Conscientiousness
Firmness —
Hope:
Spirituality.
Veneration.

Constructiveness.
Ideality.
Imitation.
Mirthfulness.

Sublimity.
Agreeableness.
Causality.
Comparison.
Eventuality =
Human Nature —
Calculation.
Colour.
FORM.
Individuality.
Language.
Locality

Order.
Size.
Time.
Tune
Weight.

26. The graphological signs of phrenological faculties, 1900.

termed scientific proof was really just empirical observation: experience had shown that these correlations existed, never mind exactly how they occurred. At root, the new science of signs was the latest, gussied-up version of the doctrine of correspondence, in which the external, material world was seen as parallel with and exactly analogous to a deeper reality. "The physical is but the materialisation of the mental," wrote the graphologist Richard Dimsdale Stocker, "which in turn is nothing but the manifestation of the spiritual." A rising line of script signified ambition, for example, because the writer hoped for his fortunes to rise in the same manner; an open lowercase "a" meant candor because the writer would freely open his heart and his mouth.[63]

But it was precisely this reliance on analogical reasoning that made graphology so accessible to a popular audience. Not everyone could have the occult powers of the chiromancer or the exquisite sensibility of the romantic genius, but everyone could follow a commonsense argument. The authors of graphology manuals made it clear that anyone could analyze handwriting with the aid of their books, much as the authors of phrenology manuals appealed to a mass audience, and since graphology served mainly to sniff out the tricksters who preyed on us all, everyone *needed* graphology too. Thus when Michon and his followers redefined the function of handwriting analysis and created a new methodology of interpretation, they opened up the practice of graphology to ordinary men and women.

There were many skeptics, of course. Critics alleged on the one hand that each person's hand varied from writing to writing, so that many scripts would correspond to a single character, and on the other that a whole class of students would simply copy the writing master's hand, so that many characters would correspond to a single script. Graphologists answered that an individual's script would naturally vary with mood or, over a longer span of time, with growth and maturity. As for that hypothetical class of penmanship pupils, people who doubted the truth of graphology should either take a closer look—variation did in fact exist—or take a second look once the pupils had graduated into adult life. Then, as the adult character took shape, so would the mature, distinctive hand.[64]

Critics also alleged that some hands were utterly without character and must therefore be meaningless. The usual example of a blank script was the clerk's perfect copperplate. Graphologists agreed that handwriting shows the mark of individual character as it deviates from the copybook norm and admitted as well that clerks indulged in precious little deviation, but they insisted that the disinclination to diverge was in itself a commentary on character. "The average clerk," explained graphologist Henry Frith, "writes a clear open hand, neat and orderly in appearance. Why? Because he is not greatly imaginative. He is doing routine work for which nature has moulded him, and because his character is plodding, steady, honest, and not imaginative." In other words, Frith concluded, "he is a clerk because he has these characteristics, he has not these characteristics of writing *because he is a clerk!*"[65]

Critics of graphology thought they had struck a fatal blow when they pointed out how easy it was to mask one's hand. Even if you graphologists are right, they argued, and character can be read in handwriting, then a person can conceal his true character by altering his natural script. But graphologists had an answer to this objection too. The person who consciously alters his handwriting, they argued, can change only what he is conscious of, namely such gross attributes as slope and size. What he cannot change—because he is not even aware of their existence—are the minute details that best distinguish his natural hand from all others. The trained graphologist seizes on these telltale signs and exposes the man for what he truly is.[66]

The figure of the deceiving stranger made its appearance in more than graphology manuals. Tricksters of all sorts, male and female, lurked in Victorian literature. "Things are seldom what they seem; skim milk masquerades as cream," sang the *H. M. S. Pinafore*'s Buttercup in what might have been the motto of the Victorian social imagination. Indeed, these deceivers lurked in copybooks; "A man may smile and smile and be a villain still," ran one copybook maxim.[67] The mistrust of surface appearances was not new to the nineteenth century, of course. That wariness dated back to the sixteenth and seventeenth centuries, when the emergence of a market economy and society injected elements of deception into human encounters. But the nineteenth century brought with it new conditions of life, first in Europe, then in the United States, that further sensitized men and women to the potential for duplicitous appearances. In these decades, more and more Americans left farms and villages to live in cities, and cities grew from relatively small centers of activity to huge metropolises. One never knew just who one's fellow city-dweller was, for he too had arrived only yesterday from parts unknown, for reasons that could not be determined. As the intimacy of the small town gave way to the anonymity of metropolitan life, one's neighbors were indeed strangers, part of what Keene had called the motley throng. In such an environment, it was believed, deception flourished, with tragic consequences for the unwary.

By itself, the urban world of strangers might well have generated an atmosphere of mistrust, but it was how inhabitants of that world conceived of the self that lent credence to their fears and an edge to their anxieties. Victorians regarded both masculine character and female virtue as generated from within but visible to others in the correct manner of self-presentation. Men and women of genuine worth would be naturally genteel in matters of speech, carriage, and dress. Furthermore, they were expected to cultivate and display their natures through such self-improving and refined activities as inspirational reading, church attendance, and the purchase of tasteful home furnishings. The problem with this system, of course, is that inner reality and outward appearance do not necessarily correspond, opening up the possibility of empty facades and concealed designs. Anyone could affect cultivated manners and pretend to live a life of genteel respectability. And all it took was cash to buy the right kinds of books, clothing, and furniture.[68]

Handwriting played more than an incidental role in this drama. Penmanship was one of those aspects of Victorian self-presentation that, it was hoped, could confirm the inner reality of character and virtue. But it was feared that it might instead create opportunities for duplicity. Writing masters might argue that a good hand could result only from an arduous process of male character training or a natural unfolding of female delicacy and virtue, yet in practice, correct penmanship often functioned as nothing more than a superficial display of refinement. "Good penmanship is as necessary for a lady or gentleman," read the *New York News*, "as a good style of talking or reading." Other observers equated tasteful handwriting with good taste in dress. All "who aspire to . . . getting a good name" were advised to "be mindful of such matters."[69]

Unfortunately, handwriting was subject to the same discontinuities between character and presentation as any other external accoutrement of social identity. Victorians knew as much. When the "owner of a large estate, with servants, money, and influence at his command," has a "mean, cramped or illiterate hand," commented a New York newspaper, we exclaim, " 'What! is this the production of So-and-so? It looks like a wretched scraping of some poor laborer with a scarcity of ink to boot!' " Others complained that the handwriting of a "well-taught boot-black" may be indistinguishable from that of a gentleman, while "the signature of a sage" may look "like the scrawl of an idiot."[70] The least-threatening consequence of this state of affairs would be for penmanship to serve merely as a superficial display of gentility or propriety and therefore an unreliable gauge of true worth. But at its worst, handwriting might serve to deceive, for who could tell when the bootblack might scheme to defraud the gentleman?

In the case of women, the greatest threat seemed to be that outward appearances, instead of reflecting the self, might actually displace it entirely. Even before mid-century, critics complained that the writing masters at female seminaries trained their charges in what one commentator termed "a very lady-like sort of dissimulation, intended, like the Chesterfieldian politeness of a courtier, to conceal the workings of thought and feeling—to substitute the cold, slippery, polished opacity of a frozen pool, for the ripple and transparency of a flowing brook."[71] In the Gilded Age the critique of fashionable female penmanship intensified as "young ladies of the so-called better class of society" tossed aside the Spencerian round hand for the tony English angular. Society women view the round hand as fit only for clerks and shopgirls, rued one observer of this "foolish mania," and regard "writing in an 'Englishy' way" as "one of those little accomplishments that betray the lady, like the selection of costumes or the use of perfumes." In casting aside the curved lines of nature found in Spencerian, these observers feared, women were forsaking the very wellspring of feminine character. In place of virtue, they substituted Dame Fashion.[72]

For men, an apparently blameless exterior might cloak the basest of characters, the most wicked of motives. The penmanship equivalent of the confidence man was the trickster who disguised his natural hand or, far more dramatic, the man who assumed the hand of another. In the popular literature of crime, the forger loomed as an object of horrified fascination (fig. 27). What made him so dangerous was his ability to counterfeit not only bank notes or documents but entire identities. A typical account portrayed the forger as a polished gentleman able to pass as a man of character. Forger Frederick Elliott, "polite and gentlemanly . . . , kept company with many of the most aristocratic young bloods around town." James Ralston lived the high life as a British financier, philanthropist, and member of Parliament. Robert Perreau "appeared in the station of a gentleman." It was because the forger looked "as much as anything like a suburban clergyman strayed from his pulpit," able to impress the unsuspecting as "a fine, genteel appearing man," that he was so uniquely effective—and threatening. The actual act of forgery was only the coup de grâce in this essentially social drama.[73]

There *were* people, of course, who specialized in detecting forgers, namely, handwriting experts. In the first half of the nineteenth century, resistance to this class of witnesses, typified by Justice Coleridge's 1836 opinion, kept most of them out of the courts, but increasingly over the course of the second half of the 1800s, handwriting experts took the witness stand.[74] These were not the experts of Coleridge's day, however. The older sort—writing masters, frank inspectors, bank officers, and engravers—had testified as men whose work entailed familiarity with handwriting; the new breed, first appearing in the 1850s, were professionals. They were not graphologists; they sought to establish the identity, not the character, of a writer. Their sole occupation was to examine disputed documents, and they claimed a body of exclusive scientific expertise that allowed them to do just that. They claimed the ability to establish whether a document was forged—and if it was, to identify the forger. They might offer evidence that the ostensible creator of a document could not have penned it. Even more spectacular, they might establish the identity of the penman by proving that both the questioned document and another penned by the suspect were the work of the same individual, although the two documents might appear very different to the untrained eye.[75]

Handwriting experts did not gain instant credibility. Often they were regarded as hired guns, testifying to whatever truth paid the best. When they disagreed among themselves, as occurred in several high-profile cases, they

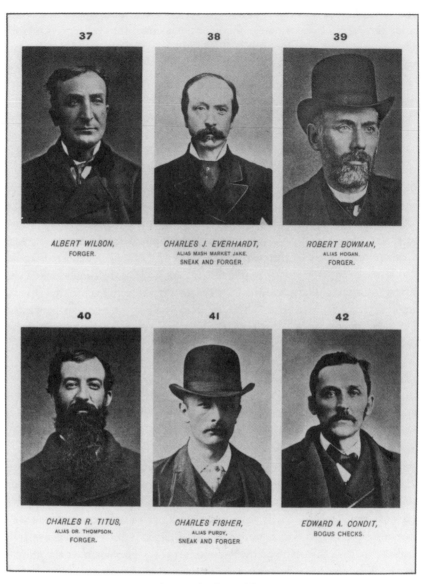

| 37 | 38 | 39 |

ALBERT WILSON,
FORGER.

CHARLES J. EVERHARDT,
ALIAS MASH MARKET JAKE.
SNEAK AND FORGER.

ROBERT BOWMAN,
ALIAS HOGAN.
FORGER.

| 40 | 41 | 42 |

CHARLES R. TITUS,
ALIAS DR. THOMPSON.
FORGER.

CHARLES FISHER,
ALIAS PURDY.
SNEAK AND FORGER.

EDWARD A. CONDIT,
BOGUS CHECKS.

27. A rogues' gallery of forgers.

came off as incompetent. But there were theoretical objections to their expertise as well. Many argued that an "adroit penman can so disguise his own writing, or so closely imitate another person's, as to deceive the very elect."[76] Graphologists faced this objection too, and, indeed, handwriting experts responded in much the same way as the followers of Michon. They insisted that they looked behind superficial appearances to the telltale elements peculiar to, and undisguisable by, each individual. "Every adult handwriting," explained the handwriting expert Daniel T. Ames, "possesses peculiar personal characteristics, unconsciously established through the force of habit, that became unavoidable, and which mark the identity of handwriting as conspicuously and certainly as does physiognomy the identity of the person." A person "can no more conceal" such subtle peculiarities—a characteristic t-bar or l-loop, for example—from a true handwriting expert, "than he could his personal identity by drawing up his nose, squinting his eyes, or walking with a limp." The expert's job is to "strip [forgers] of their disguise, and reveal their true identity as he would the person by removing a mask."[77]

The relation between handwriting experts and graphologists is a curious one, ranging from concordance to mild skepticism to antagonism. Some experts embraced graphology completely, going so far as to cite the works of Michon, Frith, and even the distinctly occult Rosa Baughan, whose opus included an examination of "the significance of the moles of the body astrologically considered."[78] Others rejected graphology entirely as the latest form of charlatanism. While they agreed with graphologists that the peculiarities of script amount to the undisguisable uniqueness of each individual, they perceived writing much as did master penman A. N. Palmer, as an entirely mechanical procedure, "independent of any mental operation," that could reveal nothing more significant than the fixed but utterly arbitrary habits of muscular movement stored in the unconscious (fig. 28). The individuality detectable in the telltale signs of script was interpreted as mere physiological idiosyncrasy, not, as the graphologist claimed, as distinctiveness of character.[79] Most handwriting experts took a middle road, accepting the general principles of graphology as practiced by its more sober-minded, scientific exponents, while dismissing the excesses of graphological "fakirs" as "silly stuff" inviting ridicule. They faced the difficult task of separating themselves from the charlatans in their *own* field, making any association with mystic arts doubly dangerous. Indeed, given their intense desire to be perceived as professionals, even scientists, it is surprising that they lent any degree of support to graphology.[80]

That they did points to a deeper kinship and a common agenda. Both handwriting experts and graphologists made the concept of individual uniqueness a cornerstone of their theory, and both used that concept toward the same end: the exposure of duplicity. Neither universalized romantic notions of individuality in order to celebrate the uniqueness of each man and woman. Instead both exploited the fact of individuality to unmask people. They were not alone in their methods and goals. The historian Carlo Ginzburg has pointed out that an epistemology of telltale signs took hold at

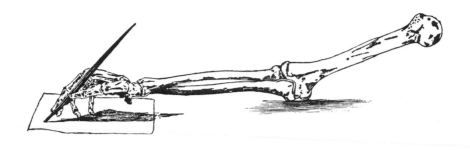

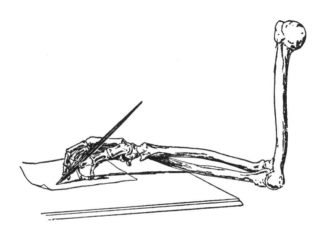

28. Handwriting as a physiological product, envisioned by a turn-of-the-century handwriting expert.

the end of the nineteenth century, embodied in Sherlock Holmes's methods of detection, Sigmund Freud's methods of psychoanalysis, and Giovanni Morelli's methods of art connoisseurship. These he links to the efforts of Alphonse Bertillon and Francis Galton to use such apparently trivial characteristics as ear shape and fingerprint pattern to identify individuals as individuals, information used to assist in police surveillance.[81] To Ginzburg's detectives, psychiatrists, and art historians, one could easily add Gilded Age graphologists and handwriting experts. (Indeed, Bertillon was also a handwriting expert.) They too used the telltale marks of the unconscious to identify individuals who would have preferred to remain lost in a generic crowd.

To some extent, their expertise in the matter of individuality was enlisted in the service of the American state, as it was in France and England. By the end of the nineteenth century, both the police and the courts made use of handwriting experts in apprehending and convicting criminals, and despite the questionable scientific credentials and ostensibly different goals of

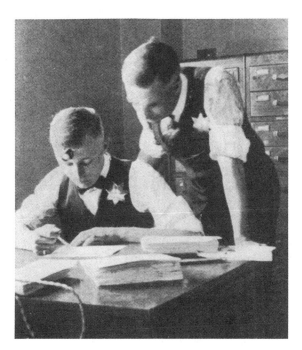

29. Handwriting as a means of identifying criminals:
Berkeley, California, police detectives, 1921.

graphology, they called on graphologists to help them do the same. From the 1920s and 1930s, a vastly expanded government apparatus embarked on the task of identifying individuals with a new intensity, epitomized by the FBI's use of handwriting experts (fig. 29).[82] But during the Gilded Age the impulse to locate and analyze individuals stemmed far more from private than from public needs—above all, the need for security and certainty amid the anonymity of urban life and the instability of industrial capitalism. Men and women for whom life in the faceless throng was a daily reality, and sudden, disastrous changes in fortune ever a possibility, pursued this strategy. For them, graphology could reveal which individuals might spell their ruin. It hardly mattered, then, whether occult arts or scientific knowledge was used to apprehend the culprits. All that was needed was for experts in individuality to be mobilized in surveillance and exposure.

Historians have characterized the Victorian era as an age in which an ideal of the self known as character held sway. In molding Americans into models of industry, thrift, and sobriety, that ideal suited the requirements and goals of a producer economy. In positing a correspondence between integrity and respectability, virtue and gentility, it met the needs of an increasingly urban and commercial society in which anonymous transactions, both social and economic, were fast becoming the norm. We have seen how that culture of character translated into the theory and practice of penmanship pedagogy, how the teaching of handwriting was expected to lead to the formation of character and to control those who were culturally unable or personally unwilling to reach that goal.

But the man of character was not the only model of the self in the Victorian era. In fact, this model seems to have bred its own opposite. In romantic handwriting analysis and autograph collecting, we see a contrary impulse, a reaction to those same forces that had dictated character as the ideal form of the self to begin with. Machines, cities, factories, commerce—all of these were imagined to function best when human beings patterned themselves according to generic models of character. By the same token, many Victorians would rue the day that machines, cities, factories, and commerce had turned them into indistinguishable copies of one another. They might hold out little hope for themselves, but they derived vicarious pleasure from the individuality of those few who had somehow managed to escape the homogenizing effects of nineteenth-century life. These utterly proper Victorians felt and did things that were completely "un-Victorian." In savoring individuality in the autographs of a Napoleon or Byron, they thrilled to the genius of a French despot and an English libertine. In pestering celebrities for their signatures, they deliberately intruded into the private realm. In collecting slivers of calling cards and running their fingers over autographs, they looked for magical powers.

We need to expand our understanding of Victorian America to accommodate such impulses. The culture of character, with its emphasis on conformity and rationality, did not flourish unchallenged. Alongside, perhaps underneath it, existed a counterculture of individuality that allowed for a vicarious and irrational thrilling to human idiosyncrasy. The relation between these two cultures cannot be determined easily or precisely, but it is worth noting that likely the same people who patterned their own handwriting after copybooks savored the distinctive scripts of people who seemed larger than life. It may be that meeting the demands imposed by the culture of character permitted—or even required—a restorative sip of the magic elixir of individuality to be, in the words of one Victorian who delighted in autographs, "rolled upon the tongue of the memory for no inconsiderable portion of time."[83]

Individuality itself, however, could be used in the services of what we usually think of as Victorian culture. That is precisely what occurred in the last decades of the nineteenth century. Graphologists and handwriting experts concurred with handwriting romantics in associating handwriting with the unconscious and equating both with individuality, but their agenda was decidedly different. They responded to the unreliability of appearances in a culture where character was just another method of selling or, worse yet, concealing character. Neither the handwriting expert nor the graphologist celebrated human individuality. Instead, both employed it as a means to ferret out duplicity. If in the early part of the century people had approached individuality with a certain amount of reverence, stealthily and gingerly, by the end of the century, individuality was there to trail, to dissect, to unmask, to exploit.

If we adhere to this schema too rigidly, however, and insist on some absolute separation between the antebellum era and the Gilded Age, we shall miss some of the ambiguities and continuities that existed within the nineteenth century and that hold significance for developments in the twentieth. We should recall, for example, that while Gilded Age graphologists argued for the scientific basis of their practices, few spurned the occult altogether. Nor, presumably, did the people who purchased their manuals. We should also note the scattered instances of Gilded Age handwriting analysts who looked and acted nothing like detectives: an unidentified man whose mail-order graphological services included the portrayal of his client's "spirit-bride," and the robed and turbaned characters who appeared at county fairs, offering to read handwriting specimens at two bits a head.[84] These are mere whispers heard amid the cries of duplicity and danger, but they suggest that even at the end of the nineteenth century, men and women were drawn to the fact of individual difference for purposes other than surveillance and exposure. As we shall see in the next chapter, these hints are straws in the wind, foretelling a further transformation of graphology in the early twentieth century.

Furthermore, the temporal divide between romantic and scientific approaches to handwriting masks some important continuities. There were distinct lines of philosophical agreement that extended over the course of the entire century and beyond. In approaching handwriting, nineteenth-century men and women conceptualized individuality according to two discrete models, one characterological, the other physiological. Romantic handwriting readers and Gilded Age graphologists alike subscribed to the first; for them the uniqueness of every person's handwriting reflected the uniqueness of every person's character. For judges and the handwriting experts who testified in their courts, the uniqueness of handwriting was solely the result of physiological idiosyncrasy. In the twentieth century these two models would define the lines along which cultural conflict operated. In their battles over the teaching and interpreting of handwriting, educators, psychologists, graphologists, and scientists once again arrayed themselves along the fault line of individuality.

CHAPTER FOUR

Yourself, as in a Mirror

Graphology in the Modern Age

In 1929 the graphologist Nadya Olyanova captured the essence of the early twentieth century in an analytical exercise she titled "Modernism Graphologized." She presented two capital M's, one from the gay nineties, the other representing the spirit of the day. "See the difference of *style* in the two letters," she wrote. "The one, ornamented, is indicative of the spirit of yesterday when hoop skirts, ornamentation, laces, petticoats and bustles were in style. The other, severe, simple, exact bespeaks the spirit of to-day—modernism."[1]

Olyanova's M's were not truly representative of handwriting practice in the 1890s and the 1920s, but she was clearly on to something. For it was during the time spanned by these decades that Americans found new meaning in handwriting and demanded that handwriting fulfill new purposes; above all, the conditions of modernity created these needs and desires. Romantic handwriting analysis and autograph collecting had offered vicarious satisfactions; Gilded Age graphology, security in a dangerous world; but graphology flourished as never before in the early twentieth century because it offered comfort and hope in its message of universal uniqueness to a culture troubled by the state of the self. Graphology assured its mass audience of self-consciously ordinary men and women that every human being is in some way exceptional and therefore capable of living an extraordinary life. Through graphology, men and women would burst the "laces" of Olyanova's not-so-gay nineties.

Graphology sent another message, however. In addition to the promise of liberation came a secondary notion that held a darker appeal. According to this message, the self-knowledge gained through handwriting analysis should be used to help one adjust to one's ordinariness. Here, too, however, graphology responded to contemporary anxieties about the self—in this case, not the longing for a more meaningful life but the even deeper fear that one's very being was nothing but show, hollow beneath the husk. In asserting the essential reality of the self, graphologists offered their clients a stable sense of identity, a service at once soothing and sobering.

In their reading of handwriting, graphologists and their followers did not stand unopposed. American scientists consistently and derisively rejected graphology as occult. To the extent that they recognized any significance in script style, it was only to suggest correlations between stylistic elements and the corporate characteristics of genetically defined groups. In particular, scientists fixated on sex differences in handwriting style as proof that characterological differences between men and women were genetic. If graphologists offered men and women unfettered potential, scientists sought to remind them of the biological restraints that necessarily constricted their lives. The New Woman, in particular, would be relaced, bound by the filaments of her female letters.

Well into the twentieth century, the belief in and practice of handwriting analysis assumed many of its nineteenth-century forms. Autograph collecting, for example, attracted an ever-broader spectrum of Americans. The "autograph fiend" continued to trick living celebrities into personal correspondence, and he was now joined by "the imp who prowls around hotel corridors with an autograph book in hand, in search of distinguished strangers." Less wily, but no less irritating to many whose autographs were sought, were collectors like the young Edward Bok, whose perseverance in obtaining what he called personality letters led Oliver Wendell Holmes to quip "Bok again!" Increasingly, however, collectors obtained autographs not by ruse or cheek but by purchase. Auction houses, retail shops, and mail-order catalogues specializing in autograph materials catered to an expanding and lucrative market. At the low end of the market were collectors of small means, who could afford only signatures, many of them razored out of letters or visiting cards and listed in the bargain section of autograph catalogues for a quarter. At the upper end were wealthy gentlemen like J. P. Morgan who acquired whole documents. Their activities, they insisted, had nothing in common with the vulgar and trifling purchases of the twenty-five-cent collectors. They aimed to preserve the past, thereby nourishing the "reverence and respect that is due to leaders in all the chief aims and ambitions of life" and sparking a "horror and detestation of those who have committed crimes against society, Church or State."[2]

What appealed to men of wealth, however, was no different from what drew the lowbrow collectors, namely, what one of the former termed insight into "the personality back of the autograph," the thrill of "divining personal character from an examination of handwriting." As in the mid-nineteenth century, it was the rare individual who could be expected to have a distinctive signature. One collector noted that "few, if any, graduates from business colleges, writers of the florid Spencerian . . . or servile followers of any of the copper plate models of the published 'copy-books,' ever secure representation in an autograph collection." Instead, the writing most admired by the autograph collector in his graphological wisdom was the "hand moving rapidly over a page in unconscious obedience to a mind that has far too much to write to bestow a thought upon the formation of a letter." Only great men and women—the standard poets and artists, statesmen and generals, now joined by captains of industry (many, not so coincidentally, collectors themselves)—had such busy minds and differentiated hands.[3] Into the 1900s, then, autograph collecting continued to define individuality as a scarce and therefore highly valuable and collectible commodity.

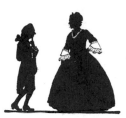

These two types would be very uncomfortable! They might marry

*no moral principle.
Our handwriting is a
thing imperishable.
By it "the living epistle
is not known and heard
of all men, but known
and read."*

(Specimen No. VII)

Peace-loving, peace-cultivating man

*but in order to explain clearly the idealism
of our movement, the hopes and aspirations of
its leaders, and how equal suffrage works
out where it is being tried. There exists a*

(Specimen No. VIII)

Woman of too much force

30. Marital incompatibility (in the form of the New Woman?), graphologized, 1912.

Meanwhile, graphology continued to concern itself with the evaluation of prospective spouses, employees, and business partners. By the 1910s, however, the emphasis had shifted from sniffing out unsavory characters in disguise to providing a scientific and efficient method of filling one's personal and professional needs (fig. 30). In his graphological practice George Beauchamp offered to determine "whether or not two persons are adapted to each other," not to unmask a gold-digger or gigolo, and to suggest the kind of "work to which one is adapted," rather than to expose the potential embezzler.[4]

Beauchamp catered to the man on the street, but by the teens and twenties, some graphologists actively sought out corporate clients. In setting themselves up as employment advisers, who lent their expertise in matters of hiring, promotion, and firing, graphologists took their place alongside other practitioners of the flourishing business of personnel science. Some of these were university-trained psychologists, who administered various standardized intelligence and aptitude tests. Others promoted pseudoscientific methods of character analysis. The Blackford Plan, purporting to assess character from such gross physical traits as hair color, was the most popular of these, but phrenology and physiognomy enjoyed a boomlet as well. Professional psychologists scoffed at these systems as groundless, but many took a somewhat more lenient attitude toward graphology, allowing that although it currently lacked a scientific basis, future research might show there was something to it after all.[5]

Graphologists, of course, were not waiting; nor, it would seem, were executives in major corporations and heads of small companies. All made use of graphological services to evaluate prospective business associates and, even more common, for assistance in hiring the best men and women, placing them in positions appropriate to their skills, and ferreting out those who needed to be fired. Executives appeared to mistrust their own judgment and gratefully accepted the graphologist's firm guidance. "I think many business men pride themselves on their ability to size up individuals at a glance," wrote Warren W. Colson, a business executive from Boston, but having read the "extraordinary" and "uncanny" character portraits provided by graphologist William Leslie French, Colson was "quite willing to admit that I should take Mr. French's delineation in preference to my own judgment." So too evidently did the well-satisfied clients of DeWitt B. Lucas, whose enthusiastic endorsements filled the pages of Lucas' *Handwriting Analysis in Business*. Lucas promised to "fortify the executive and make him secure in his position," to endow him with "unusual wisdom and sagacity in dealing with people near or far, known or unknown to him." He marketed perspicacity in a number of forms: a brief analysis, or "commercial cameo," for thirty to fifty cents; a three- to four-hundred-word profile for two dollars; a full analysis, some five hundred to a thousand words, for five dollars; an annual contract for unlimited graphological analyses at one fixed price; even reports by telephone or telegraph.[6]

Had the executive in Carolyn Wells's 1933 thriller *The Broken O* made use of Lucas' services, he might never have had to hire detective Fleming Stone to investigate the disappearance of several thousand dollars. For only when Stone consults a graphological manual and visits graphologist Miss Curry does he determine the identity of the employee/criminal. "What made you suspect him, Mr. Stone?" the detective is asked once the culprit is nabbed. "That o, with an opening at the bottom of it," replies the enlightened Stone, "means invariably a stealer of large sums of money."[7]

UNIVERSAL UNIQUENESS

When they entered the twentieth century Americans did not abandon their earlier interest in the script of the celebrated and the slippery. By the end of the nineteenth century, however, it had become increasingly clear that handwriting held a new meaning for many Americans. Autograph collectors had venerated individuality but attributed it to only a few; graphologists had regarded individuality as universal, but exploited it only for the information it provided. Then, tentatively in the 1870s, more confidently at the turn of the century, and with full conviction and energy by the 1910s, Americans perceived the individuality of handwriting in a new light, as something both universal and inspirational. It was not just the isolated genius who could claim a distinctive handwriting. Everyone could, even the most lackluster of individuals.

It is not surprising that many ordinary Americans of this era placed a premium on human individuality and the potential for shaping and controlling one's life it implied. So many situations they faced—work, play, school, even family—threatened to rob them of their distinctiveness and autonomy.[8] In the nineteenth century, most American workers had been self-employed, working as farmers, craftsmen, or small shopkeepers. Even factory workers tended to work in relatively small units, for bosses who owned, managed, and lived near their companies. By the turn of the century, however, industrial capitalism had taken its modern, corporate form, with salaried managers running tremendous industrial enterprises linked together in complex, national networks. For Americans of the early twentieth century, work meant becoming a blue-collar, white-collar, or pink-collar employee of a powerful and impersonal corporation. In those factories and offices, scientific managers and efficiency experts exerted ever-greater control over work processes, hoping to create a disciplined, docile, and productive corps of essentially interchangeable workers. And schools, with their packed classrooms and lockstep procedures, seemed designed to prepare children for this world of work to come.

Meanwhile, more and more Americans, both immigrants and migrants from small towns and farms, thronged America's growing cities. Many of these city dwellers, stuffed into tenements, trolley cars, and five-cent theaters, felt lost in, even trampled by, the vast and impersonal crowds of the modern metropolis. There was no shortage of experts to guide Americans through this new and often overwhelming world. Advertisers offered friendly "advice" on how to avoid social gaffes in the unfamiliar milieu of the modern city and how to maintain health in the unnatural, even noxious urban environment. Government bureaucrats and social workers tried to teach newcomers how to raise their children, how to run a household, even what to eat and how to cook it. Physicians and hospitals stepped in to supervise the process of childbirth. Relying on such advice and acceding to such authority increased the sense that control over one's life was not possible in mass society. Individuality, and with it autonomy, seemed to be a thing of the past.

It is also not surprising that Americans anxious to assert the reality of human individuality would do so in the meaning they assigned to handwriting. Since the spread of print, script had been linked with self, and in the tradition of handwriting analysis that dated back to the end of the eighteenth century, it was tied to the individualized self in particular. The introduction of the typewriter in the 1880s could only have strengthened that association.[9] Where the realm of handwriting had formerly included documents of both a private and a public nature—personal letters and diaries, as well as business papers and government records—most public documents were now typed, making handwriting almost synonymous with the private individual. Ordinary men and women of the late nineteenth and early twentieth centuries tapped into this reservoir of associations. They used the distinctiveness of handwriting to signify the stubborn persistence of individuality in the face of homogenizing pressures and the unsuspected existence of singular traits and talents that betokened extraordinary destinies.

A clear sign of the new meaning assigned to handwriting was the growing interest in the autographs of ordinary people. In the last three decades of the nineteenth century, Americans began to collect the signatures of friends and family members, and they purchased albums, emblazoned with the word *Autographs* on their covers, for that purpose. The very size and shape of these albums—they were small and horizontal—suggested the signatures within. It was the usual practice to accompany one's autograph with a clever saying or couplet. Those at a loss for words could consult compendia of "poetical selections" and "autograph-album verses" appropriate for inscription. But the signatures, often elegantly or ostentatiously executed, were clearly the focus of the page and the point of the album. They were hardly overshadowed, visually or substantively, by the accompanying ditty. For the first time, the signature of a school chum or cousin was of equal interest to that of a president or poet.[10]

Albums had existed before the Gilded Age, but they were so differently used and conceived as to represent another phenomenon altogether. For one, publishers had called these earlier albums just that—*Albums,* not *Autographs.* Furthermore, the earlier albums were sized and shaped like regular books, and they functioned like books. Inside could be found multiverse poems and essays, sometimes keyed to engraved or chromolithographed illustrations of landscapes or flowers, usually penned by the album owner's friends and family. Almost invariably, these entries dealt with such sentimental themes as the fragility of life, especially in the case of young women, and the sacredness of friendship. The albums seemed to fulfill a particular function for antebellum middle-class women, reminding them of the deep confidences of their girlhood and the bitter realities of distance and death. But they did not celebrate or even acknowledge the individuality of those who had contributed to the album. More often than not, contributors did not even sign their names in full. Instead, they penned in their first names or their initials, sometimes in tiny letters, the most diminutive statement of identity possible.[11] Clearly, these albums did not represent the same impulse as the later autograph albums.

The redefinition of individuality that lies behind the Gilded Age autograph album transpired as well in the everyday practice of handwriting. In the 1880s one commentator argued that despite "the pressure of life . . . so great in these latter times, . . . there still remain to influence handwriting, structural peculiarities that are largely mental!" Foremost among these was "the *Individuality* that a jostling, restless, circulating world threatens to eliminate." For a later commentator, the quintessentially modern confrontation between conformity and individuality was played out in a battle between print and script. The printing press, he argued, has undeniably narrowed the scope of personal expression, but even "with all its power to enforce uniformity," it "has been powerless to repress the national and individual character, which breaks out, and will continue to break out, in the domestic handwriting of the day. This assertion of character will last to the end, whatever mechanical influences may rise up to check its natural course."[12] Apparently by this time Americans were no longer satisfied with the vicarious pleasure in individuality offered by the celebrity autograph. They needed and wanted to assert their own individuality, and they knew that handwriting was the way to do so. Accordingly, ordinary people took pride in a distinctive hand as a kind of talisman of their own uniqueness. One Gilded Age penman argued, for example, that American men would never consent to adopt the English angular hand so fashionable among ladies because it sacrificed what men prized most in their handwriting—individuality.[13]

Some Americans deliberately adopted personal idiosyncrasies in their scripts to set their handwriting, and thus themselves, apart. A common strategy was appropriating the graphic mark of genius formerly reserved for statesmen and literati, namely, illegibility. Lawyers, university graduates, high school teachers, and professors were among those accused of cultivating the mannerism of "handwriting horrible" as a sign of their "ultra-mental development," while women of fashion scorned a "pretty hand" as a sign of commonness. "No doubt there comes a time in the life of nearly every student," wrote one penmanship supervisor in 1912, "when he feels there is a certain amount of prestige attached to the ability to create an indecipherable signature." Commented another educator: "What writer of exceptionally graceful hand but has been twitted by his friends with the byword that 'pretty' writing goes with a small mind?"[14]

Not all approved of such practices. In 1874 a writer for the *New York Mail* fulminated over the "gratuitous praise that has been awarded to those who write a 'characteristic hand.'" These penmanship reprobates "work out a standard purely their own, regardless of its fitness to universal requirements, and educate themselves up—or down—to it. Instead of seeking to reproduce forms already extensively in use," they ". . . endeavor to avoid such. In this—where originality is an injury—they seek to be original, and, unfortunately, are successful." That attitude had led to "an endless variety of styles" and a situation "in which individual taste is allowed too much scope." Resisting what he saw as the socially disruptive assertion of individuality, the author held up Germany, known for its uniformity of handwriting style, as a model worthy of imitation. Indeed, he recommended that "a National Bureau of Education" assume responsibility for "governmental supervision and consequent enforcement of a uniform system" of writing. One way or another, Americans simply must get over their persistent "desire to give undue prominence to individual peculiarities."[15] For this journalist, handwriting would be the arena for that discipline; other Americans knew handwriting as the arena for that desire.

Just how many Americans actually cultivated a distinctive hand is difficult to assess, but we can get some idea from the penmanship teachers whose students resisted conformity to standard models. As early as the 1870s, pedagogues acknowledged that many people wanted to develop a unique hand and hastened to reassure the public that handwriting instruction would not suppress individuality. In 1872 the Spencerian authors remarked that provided writers conformed to the aesthetic essentials of a script, they could "find scope for individual tastes and preferences" in the art of penmanship. In 1896 A. N. Palmer echoed that sentiment when he stated that "within certain well-defined boundaries I would not only permit, but would encourage pupils in catering to their individual tastes."[16] Such comments were comparatively rare in the nineteenth century, however. More critical, they suggested that variation in handwriting was a result of conscious choice rather than unconscious expression and that it reflected a personal aesthetic rather than a unique personality. But from the turn of the century penmanship authorities seem to have faced increasing pressure, and they were forced to address the issue of individuality in handwriting more frequently and profoundly.

"Time was," commented one contributor to the *Penman's Art Journal* in 1905, "when the teacher of writing who did not succeed in imparting his own style to his pupils, making them imitators, was considered a miserable failure. The most successful teacher of to-day, is the one who can develop the individuality in the pupil's handwriting, regardless of stereotyped forms." This announcement of the death of enforced uniformity was probably premature. Five years later, when one propagandist for the Palmer method reported that many female teachers believed and regretted that it destroyed individuality in writing, he pooh-poohed the women as sentimentalists. Nevertheless, he did feel called upon to answer them. Schoolchildren do not need, nor do they necessarily have, any marks of individuality in their script, he argued, nor should they deliberately cultivate them, as apparently some were wont to do. The idea was to conform, not to stand out. "The better the training and the abler the teachers," he quoted a handwriting expert as explaining, "the more uniform the writing will be. It is not the business of the teacher to develop individuality in handwriting."[17]

On the other hand, this Palmerian must have felt some obligation to reassure the "sentimentalists" among his reading (and writing) public, for he quickly added that it was not the business of the teacher to suppress individuality either. Indeed, he explained, it is impossible to do so. Adults invariably develop their own personal style, no matter how they have been trained in school. Trying to walk on both sides of the line at once, he concluded that the most revealing script is not the "complex, fanciful or freak handwriting" but the "simple, plain" hand of the Palmer method.[18]

In walking that fine line, supporters of muscular movement penmanship were increasingly willing to concede that the development of individuality in handwriting was inescapable and even desirable, although they never gave up on the necessity of a uniform standard. In an 1892 manual entitled *How to Teach Writing*, Lyman D. Smith maintained that "individuality is persistent, and will work its way into a standard hand" but that in so doing, "so much of the individuality as runs into idiosyncratic form will be and had better be sacrificed." In 1905 the author of *Writing in the Schools* also admitted to the inevitability of individual variation and similarly insisted that "notwithstanding these differences . . . , there is and there must be a common form toward which all legible hands approach." Within a few years, however, there seemed to be more pressure to deemphasize conformity as an endpoint and to reassure teachers and pupils that individuality in handwriting was not threatened. Palmer himself wrote in 1913 that although students must adhere to "the general style" of Palmerian script, they retained "the possibility of developing their own individuality" in handwriting. By 1921 normal-school pupils in Massachusetts were instructed that while "the style or kind of writing taught should be universal and formal rather than individual and peculiar," once that style had been mastered, "then character or individuality in style develops to suit individual needs." In 1924 the director of commercial education in the Pittsburgh public schools summarized the current status of the debate when he commented that "some of our educators stress the importance of teaching individuality in handwriting, while others contend that it develops sufficiently without being taught."[19] All these authorities placed

Grant S. Diamond Dime

Studying

Speeches in Chapel; Debating team

"Our manners are the mirror of the mind"

Esther Dickman Dickie

Singing Private secretary

Liberty Loan typist

"A flower of meekness on a stem of grace"

31. Tokens of individual identity (entries in a high school yearbook, 1919): nickname, hobby, quotation, signature.

the development of an individual style in a future beyond the pedagogical moment, preserving the enforcement of uniformity in the actual classroom. But they were facing a restive audience (fig. 31).

THE GRAPHOLOGICAL IMPULSE

The most explicit sign that handwriting was taking on new meanings and functions in this era was the transformation taking place in the practice of graphology. One indication of change was the feminization of the graphological workforce. The person most responsible for bringing about this transition was Louise Rice, a frustrated medical student whose outspoken feminism and early prominence in graphology—she was reaching a mass audience by 1912—encouraged other women to enter the field. Male graphologists continued to practice, but by the time the American Graphological Society was established in 1927, most of its members were female. That trend did not even let up with World War II, when a largely male influx of European graphologists arrived as refugees to America.[20]

The transformation in graphology is evident as well in the changing nature of its audience. Graphologists attracted an ever-growing and more popular following. On the eve of the Depression, one journalist reported that when it came to graphology, "one thing is certain: Everyone seems to be interested in it." In 1935 one practitioner described handwriting analysis as "a great American fad." Hardcover books that outlined the principles of graphology still found readers, but from the 1920s on, many of the how-to manuals were either inexpensive paperbacks or even cheaper pamphlets written and marketed for mass appeal. Laura Doremus' *Character in Handwriting*, for example, sold for twenty-five cents and appeared as part of Renard's Popular Topics Library. *Character Reading from Handwriting*, by "Grapho," cost thirty-five cents and took its place with paperbacks on astrology, jujitsu, and cocktail mixing in the Hobby Hand-Book series. Other pamphlets were issued as promotions for commercial products. William Leslie French wrote one for the Spencerian Pen company (fifteen cents, free penpoints included), and Vaseline and Mohawk Rugs followed suit.[21]

Meanwhile, the periodical press turned its attention to handwriting analysis. In the teens and twenties, popular journals like *Good Housekeeping, Woman's Home Companion, McClure's,* and the *Saturday Evening Post* carried articles by such prominent graphologists as French and Rice. Beginning in the twenties and catching fire in the thirties and forties, pulp magazines— *Real Romances, Motion Picture, Current Astrology,* and *Detective Story Magazine,* to name just a few—printed occasional stories and regular features on graphology.[22] Handwriting analysis achieved its greatest media exposure, however, in the graphological advice columns that appeared in major newspapers and pulp magazines. Readers sent in samples of their handwriting, along with details of their personal problems, which would be solved by graphological character analysis. Every week, the graphologist selected a few specimens for her column, analyzing them for prominent personality characteristics and providing relevant personal advice. Again, the pioneer here was Rice. Her first column appeared in the New York *Mail and Express* in 1912. By the early 1920s, Rice's weekly column, "What Handwriting Reveals," appeared in *Detective Story Magazine.* During the Depression and into the early postwar era, other graphologists ran similar columns in such publications as the New York Sunday *Mirror,* the New York Sunday *Daily News,* the Chicago edition of the New York *News,* and *Movieland* and *Astrology* magazines.[23]

The response to these columns was tremendous. When Rice ran her first column, her editor thought the whole idea silly, but he quickly changed his mind when a thousand letters came in after two days. So overwhelming was the reaction to Rice's column that she had to hire a half-dozen assistants, many of whom went on to become graphologists in their own right, to help with her mail. Even then, Rice reported working fourteen-hour days to keep up with the two to three thousand letters she received a week. When in the 1930s one of Rice's assistants, Shirley Spencer, started her own newspaper column, she received a similar volume of requests. Readers responded in such numbers partly because they knew that even if their handwriting was not analyzed in the newspaper, they would receive an analysis by mail. (Most newspapers specified that readers include a self-addressed, stamped envelope with their handwriting specimens, accompanied in some cases by ten cents as a "slight token of good faith.")[24]

Once businessmen recognized the popularity of handwriting analysis, they exploited its commercial possibilities. In the mid-1920s, purchasers of Eaton's stationery were entitled to a free graphological analysis by Rice. So too were the buyers of Eagle Pencils and, with the additional enclosure of a boxtop and an endorsement that read "I like Chipso for washing clothes because it makes them wear longer," the users of Chipso laundry detergent (fig. 32). In the 1940s, White Rose tea ("Your Character in Your T") and Kellogg's (the cure for "tired handwriting") hired graphologists to write advertising copy for their products.[25]

Meanwhile, graphologists did not seem to need corporate encouragement to market their services in the style of Madison Avenue, or even P. T. Barnum. Many carried on dignified practices in graphological consulting and training.[26] For others, however, no form of graphological work appeared too crass or trivial. Jane Lambe set up a booth on the Atlantic City boardwalk; George T. Foldes set up one at a wartime replacement depot in northern Africa, completing fifty-seven analyses in two hours. Others provided graphological entertainment at women's club meetings, Rotary luncheons, private "t parties," sorority gatherings, and even nightclubs. By the thirties, graphologists hosted radio shows; by the late forties, they appeared on television. And by the 1950s graphologists Glenn and Lucille Looker were on the road, traveling from the largest trailer court in the world in Bradenton, Florida, to the Gulf Oil refinery in New Orleans to the leper colony in Carville, Louisiana.[27]

Why all the gimmicks? We must rule out the explanation that graphology itself was just a gimmick, the latest way to make a fast buck. No doubt some readers of handwriting latched onto graphology with no more conviction and knowledge than was necessary to bring in paying customers. But most, even some of the tawdriest, practitioners believed implicitly in the intellectual seriousness and scientific legitimacy of their skill. They recognized the necessity of escaping from the charge of charlatanism and clearing graphology of "the aura of superstition" that clung to it. Regarding themselves as students of science, they studied the work of the most reputable European graphologists; Rice actually corresponded with Alphonse Bertillon for four years. For the most part, graphologists refused to descend intellectually to the level of fortune tellers.[28]

A more credible explanation is that graphologists, as members of a predominantly female occupation, had to worm their way into visibility any way they could. "She put up a big fight to get any kind of hearing," recalled Shirley Spencer of her mentor Rice. "In those days a woman had to be

32. The commercial appeal of graphology, 1935.

very brave, imaginative and ingenious to get newspaper space. . . . Women were trying to impress the editors with the fact that they could *think* as well as men and should have equal rights. Miss Rice did many startling things to get attention and, once she had it, would hold forth on her two favorite subjects, thus get[ting] space for graphology which otherwise no editor would give her. One should always judge Miss Rice's activities in graphology against the background of her early journalism." Indeed, many women may have taken to graphology in the first place precisely because it was perceived as intellectually marginal and therefore open to women. As a medical student in turn-of-the-century New York, Rice faced the reality that obstetrics was her only professional option. She left the study of medicine to study psychology at Columbia, a field equally hostile to women. From there Rice turned to graphology.[29] Excluded from the inner sanctum of science, then, many women had to be satisfied with working in the penumbra of scientific respectability, where, like it or not, they would have to keep company with palm readers and soothsayers.

When all is said and done, the crucial element in the transformation of graphology was neither the gender of its practitioners nor the degree of professionalism with which it was presented but the desires and needs it addressed. One basis for its widespread appeal was the promise it held out of popularity and success. According to some graphology manuals, these goals could be realized by analyzing the handwriting of one's personal acquaintances and business associates (fig. 33). In 1911 George Beauchamp informed his readers that "YOUR SUCCESS WILL BE ACCORDING TO YOUR ABILITY TO READ THE CHARACTER OF THOSE WITH WHOM YOU MAY HAVE DEALINGS, OR WITH WHOM YOU MAY HAVE TO LIVE." In 1926 the author of *Character Portrayed by Handwriting* argued that the knowledge of others gained through graphology gave one a competitive edge in the "battle of Life." A decade later, *Success through Handwriting* recommended graphology as a method of knowing others "because the people who like us are those whom we understand" and because rewards come to those who use their knowledge of others to cooperate with them.[30] As in the preceding century, the focus was on other people's handwriting, but now the goal was not merely to avoid threats to one's personal and financial stability but to marshal every available resource to attain a higher level of happiness and achievement.

Far more typically, however, graphologists represented the analysis of one's *own* handwriting as the key to popularity and success. Indeed, it is this focus on *self* analysis that most clearly distinguishes the practice of modern graphology from older forms of handwriting analysis. J. Harington Keene had analyzed the scripts of his mail-order and walk-in clients from the 1870s, but he was a rare practitioner in the nineteenth century. By the 1890s, how-

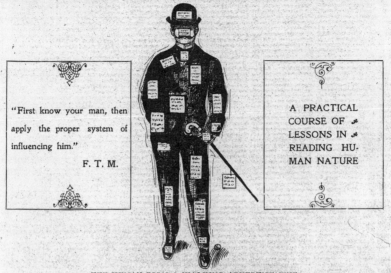

A CORRESPONDENCE COURSE IN

RADIAL CHARACTER READING

"First know your man, then apply the proper system of influencing him."

F. T. M.

A PRACTICAL COURSE OF LESSONS IN READING HUMAN NATURE

THE HUMAN FORM A WALKING ADVERTISEMENT.

**Concentration and Mind Force,
Quick Methods of Reading Character,
Reading the Characteristics of People at a Distance,
How Different Individuals Should be Approached and Influenced,
A Secret Method of Unveiling the Characters and Lives of Others,
Reading Between the Lines of Handwriting,
and Powess of the Human Mind**

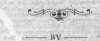

—— BY ——

F. T. McINTYRE, D. S. T.

33. "The Human Form a Walking Advertisement," from a character-reading manual of 1904, written by the "President of the Metropolitan Institute of Sciences, Inventor of the Celebrated Hypnotic Ball, the Suggesti-phone, etc.," and "Originator of the Complete Powerful Secret System of Personal Influence."

ever, demand for self-analysis was on the rise, as the *American Phrenological Journal* soon realized when, upon running an article on graphology, it received many requests from readers who wanted their own handwriting analyzed. By 1912 Rice's graphological advice column was up and running; when Beauchamp had argued a year earlier that "to know yourself is fine, but that is not enough," he was already fighting a losing battle. After all, his own clients wanted their own handwriting analyzed. "Are you successful, prosperous, happy?" read an advertisement for his services, printed in the back of his book. "If not let Professor Beauchamp read your character from your handwriting."[31]

By the mid-teens, graphological articles and books catered to the growing appeal of self-analysis. "In reading *your own character*," emphasized A. Henry Silver, "you will discover why you are not as successful as you should be, . . . whether your will power is strong or weak, and . . . whether you are in too great a hurry to achieve, or whether you are going too slowly through life." Louis Erskine argued that a graphological diagnosis of one's weaknesses would allow for their correction, enabling one to "acquire a lasting personality" that ensured personal and financial success. While some graphologists depicted handwriting analysis as a method of character development, the ultimate goal was not virtue through self-mastery but fulfillment through the manipulation of a portfolio of traits that had no inherent value. "Andrienne" drew on just this understanding of character when she claimed that handwriting analysis could help readers make their "strong points pay dividends." So too did Fritzi Remont when she argued that developing character simply involved guiding "misdirected" traits into positive channels and avoiding combinations of virtues that "become dangerous assets."[32]

In some ways, then, graphology shared much with the numerous approaches to self-improvement and self-development that emerged in this era. Like advertisers, for example, graphologists stepped in as confidantes and advisers to people unsure of themselves, offering formulas for success and popularity. Like self-help guides, graphology manuals portrayed the deployment of personal powers as the way to make both friends and money. Indeed, it is no coincidence that Welham Clarke's *Power and Force through the Application of Memory, the Reading of Character and Personality in Business and Social Life* should include a chapter on graphology, located between sections entitled "The Secret—Mental Gymnastics" and "Talking to Win."[33] Although the rhetoric of success and popularity can be found in graphological literature, however, even more pervasive and infused with much deeper levels of emotion was the rhetoric of ineradicable distinctiveness. Far more critical to the mass appeal of graphology in this era was the by-now long-standing identification of handwriting with individuality and the consequent use of graphology to assert uniqueness.

Everyone, wrote Clifford Howard in his *Graphology,* "has a style of writing peculiar to himself. What would cause these various distinguishing characteristics of penmanship if not the individuality of the writers themselves?" Readers attuned to the romantic cult of "celebrity" autographs were assured that the principle of distinctiveness applied as well to the janitor and housewife as to the general and the composer. "Never mind the collection of autographs of great men," wrote the graphologist Hugo von Hagen. "Handwritings of laborers or plain every-day men are for the graphologist of as much importance as those of bankers or merchants." And readers could rest assured that nothing could squelch this distinctiveness. "The individuality of the person is so strong that it colors all that he does," read *Talks on Graphology.* Wherever you went, "the same differences are to be seen: individuality still asserts itself."[34]

This message of a resilient and universal uniqueness encouraged men and women to turn to such advice columns as Rice's "What Handwriting Reveals." Every week Rice received thousands of letters, and she reported that fully two-thirds of her clients wrote her again and again, adding more details of their lives.[35] Most of these correspondents were native-born Americans; some, like Stella Matalino, Jesus Rosario, Valdimar Straunsky, and Chang, were recent immigrants. About half were men, half women. Most lived at the upper reaches of the working class and the lower levels of the middle class. They were factory operatives, tradesmen, clerical and service workers, low-level white-collar employees, homemakers, farmers, and farm wives. Most found themselves in situations they perceived as isolated or otherwise limiting, living on lonely farms, in backwater towns, or in poor urban neighborhoods, numbed by endless years of meaningless work, monotonous routines, and colorless lives. These were profoundly vulnerable men and women, saturated with a sense of ordinariness and insignificance, frustration and failure, sometimes even desperation. They felt excluded from the meaningful existence that they imagined others enjoyed, and graphology told them both why a better life was possible for them and where to find it. It lay within, in their individuality, in the hidden and dormant powers that were theirs alone.[36]

One category of letters was composed by women and, especially, men who were convinced that their ordinary lives did no justice to their extraordinary talents. Others presented themselves as possessing extraordinary personalities—doomed, evil, mysterious. Many more correspondents had no such conviction of their own distinctiveness but yearned instead for some escape from mediocrity. Typical of these were "Sam," who derided himself as "just a common scrub"; "Ruby," who dreamed of quitting her husband, children, and small-town existence for a life on the stage; "Perry," a farmer's wife who timidly inquired whether she was "good for anything or not"; and Michael K. Lynchburg, whose dreams of becoming an artist clashed with the reality of sixteen-hour days working in a restaurant. "Masterson, 34" accused fate of keeping him in a "miserable little job," while "Louise B." encapsulated her life in the phrase "Everything wrong and nothing to live for." As for "X," he knew only that life as a desk clerk, in which he never had to "speak to a person or move anything except the writing hand," was driving him to the brink of suicide. "A letter which has come to me so many times that I have come to look on it as all but a form sheet runs about as follows," wrote Rice in 1925: "I wish that you would tell me of some talent that I have, something that I can do to help the world," pleaded the mother of four, living on a farm miles from town. "I feel so unimportant."[37]

What these people looked for was to be told that they possessed some special talent or quality that offered a way out. "There," in your handwriting, promised Rice, "you will discover, perhaps, a you quite different from anything you have ever suspected, or that you in whom you have been afraid to believe, who is talented and unusual." Most graphologists held out the same hope. "A great many people with artistic talent are working in offices and factories to-day," read *What Does Your Handwriting Reveal?* "If they could be shown their potentialities and the road for which they have a natural bent pointed out to them, how much more happiness would be theirs. . . . Pick up your pen and stir the sleeping fire. You may have the potentialities of a Napoleon or a Paderewski. Your handwriting will tell you." Readers of an advertisement for Chipso detergent were asked, "Are you happy—if not, why not?" and urged to tell the Chipso graphologist "your discouragements . . . your hopes . . . your ambitions." Most significant, the promotion was also a contest; everyone would receive a reply, but a prize would be awarded for "the handwriting that shows the most INTERESTING PERSONALITY and CHARACTER." Three hundred thousand people responded.[38]

Often graphologists encouraged these frustrated souls, urging them to overcome barriers and make changes in line with their abilities and inclinations. Rice sent the overworked restaurant worker to art school, ordered the suicidal desk clerk to find an outdoor occupation, and advised another frustrated small-town dweller to "pull loose from your present condition" and "strike out definitely for a career of your own." She encouraged immigrant correspondents, many of whom felt despised for their foreignness and trapped by their meager education, to take advantage of the educational opportunities available in America to all. "Why vegetate between your fish stall and your furnished room," she asked "Fulton Market," "when there are boon companions, good talk, and new worlds, for the finding?" Rice had no patience for eugenicist theories of racial inferiority. "We can do with ourselves what we will," she wrote one Asian correspondent. "Ancestry may give us our blood and our bones and push our cheek bones and slant our eyes, but it has nothing whatever to do with our goodness or our badness." She similarly reassured those who were convinced that a family history of disease, insanity, or criminal behavior doomed them to an early death or a life of madness and crime. And she particularly encouraged women to fulfill their potential, urging them to ignore occupational barriers ("yes, indeed, there are numbers of professional women astronomers"), even if that entailed hiring a babysitter or insisting that the husband mind children and wash dishes. "I don't think that a woman is as inevitably born to housework as the sparks fly upward, you know," she insisted.[39]

Thus, to affirm their individuality and the power and possibility it implied, ordinary men and women purposefully cultivated idiosyncratic scripts, collected the autographs of their friends and relatives, and consulted graphologists. The story would end there were it not for the fact that graphologists did not always give people what they wanted. In the first place, they insisted that graphology was a science not an occult art, yet at least some of their clients seemed to be looking for something akin to magical self-transformation. How else to explain the popularity of those exotically costumed "fakirs" who appeared at country fairs, offering to identify a writer's age, sex, and station in life from a handwriting specimen? Or the packaging of graphological pamphlets in series that included works on astrology? Or the graphologists' impatience at having to explain yet one more time that they were not in the business of fortune telling?[40]

Even more telling, graphologists did not invariably reveal exceptional personalities to their clients. "How can you seriously ask if you are 'one of the great geniuses of the world?'" Rice asked "Myron." "Please bump your head into this sentence, following: You're a very ordinary chap, and unless you are careful your life will be a total failure, and you will be a laughingstock to every one who knows you." When "Stella" characterized most people as stupid and tiresome, while numbering herself among those "eccentric people" most likely to interest Rice, the graphologist replied tartly: "You bore me more than most persons do." She told "E.R.W" that he was not an enigma, "Faustus" that he possessed no dark destiny, "Polly X" that she was not wicked but "placid as a mill pool," and "Mephisto" that he was "no more a 'b-a-a-d' man than your own shadow."[41]

Furthermore, Rice counseled a good number of her correspondents to lower their horizons and be content with their mediocre talents and lackluster lives. Many who brashly claimed to be extraordinary received a dressing-down, but Rice also dashed the hopes of those who approached her timidly and anxiously, yearning to be revealed as something other than the ordinary people they appeared to be. She wrote "Luster" that he "needn't be discouraged because you have no one great talent. Few of us have. Most of us just go on through life trying to do some one thing as well as we can, and not wasting time in mourning because we are not especially gifted." To another would-be, she wrote that every girl goes through a stage when "she wants to be everything from a missionary to China to a circus rider," but such flights of fancy are unrealistic. To a bored hotel worker, she wrote: "You belong to the great big class that most of us do—the class which is not especially talented, but which can do all kinds of work, once we have made up our minds to win success and to be content in all the situations in which we find ourselves." She advised him to abandon his "feverish search for something that will meet a need which, when pressed," you "cannot define." To "M.E.R.," Rice stated bluntly: "Get it out of your head that you are unusual."[42]

Similar themes of mediocrity and limitation appeared in the advice offered by William Leslie French. Like Rice, French catered to a popular audience, composing upbeat articles on human potential for such middle-class magazines as *Good Housekeeping*. But, as we have seen, he also offered his graphological services to businesses, guiding them in personnel decisions. In the corporate context, graphology was useful not because it promised unbounded opportunity to every individual but because it matched individual abilities with available vocational slots. French was thus one of the many progressive-era experts whose job was to guarantee that corporate employment needs be met efficiently, with as little grousing on the part of the employees as possible. Grumbling could be minimized if workers understood that their goal in life should not be to realize some grand potential but simply to find a suitable niche and adjust to the life it entailed. French's sympathy with this corporate agenda colored even his popular writings; in 1913 he predicted in *McClure's* that in the near future, graphology would be used to help "men and women in finding themselves and in being placed in their proper environment," thus averting countless tragedies.[43]

Although delivered less in the social-science vocabulary of "adjustment" and more in the preacher's language of resignation, even predestination, Rice's message was essentially the same. Just why Rice adopted this stance cannot be known with any certainty. Perhaps her class background—her father was an Indiana physician—meant that she identified more naturally with people in power than those who were out. Then again, perhaps the vocational limitations she had experienced in her own life gave her a bitter appreciation of reality, lending her writings an edge of harshness. She herself hinted at a less biographical explanation when she characterized the modern

United States in much the same way that Alexis de Tocqueville had described antebellum America, as a society in which freedom and equality had produced mediocrity and conformity.

> In proportion as the age or the country allow individual freedom, the handwriting of individuals of that time will show increasing individual differences. But freedom is a word not lightly to be used, for the Individual has bloomed most luxuriantly, not in so-called free countries, but in centers of the completest civilization. Thus, the United States of America presents the greatest instances of very individual writing, but the great mass of its people use a much more commonplace "hand" than do the rank and file of countries in the Old World; and this corresponds exactly to our development, for while we produce rare individuals, our masses have little of that personal distinction which is often found in Europe, even among the humblest peasants.[44]

Apparently Rice sensed what her clients feared, that life in modern America, though free from the constraints associated with preindustrial life, was in some even more fundamental way uncivilized. Modernity threatened individuality.

What is still bewildering is what Rice's *audience* could find appealing in the dark side of her graphological message. If not the boundless potential for transformation promised by fortune telling, if not the consolation and hope provided by a glimpse of the Paderewski within, what else could graphology offer? A clue is offered by the request, often stipulated by correspondents to advice columns, that the response appear in print. Rice's readers faced the typical alternatives of a quick mail-order analysis or the opportunity to appear in the magazine itself. Every issue informed readers that if they chose this second option, they would have to move to the back of a line of more than a thousand persons. Clearly, those hundreds required public discussion of their handwriting.[45] But why?

THE GRAPHOLOGICAL MIRROR

"SHOW ME YOUR HANDWRITING AND I WILL TELL YOU WHO YOU ARE," Nadya Olyanova promised her readers. Americans in search of graphological help, it would seem, had no idea who they were. "There is no instinct so strong in the human heart," wrote Louise Rice, "as that one which yearns to get outside the envelop of flesh, and there, for the first time, really see what self looks like." But it is possible "to see yourself," she continued, "your innermost, most secret self, all set out, point by point" (fig. 34). In your own

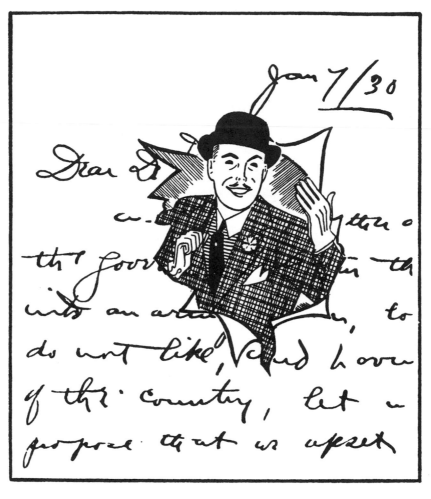

An ingenious, well-educated man of the high-pressure type, forging ahead so fast as to get past his point of destination. That is the picture a trained graphologist would visualize when he studied this letter.

34. The hidden self breaks through in handwriting, depicted in a popular graphology manual, 1936.

"familiar writing you may see the mirror which will reveal yourself to yourself."[46] Thus the crisis of identity went even deeper than the desire to be extraordinary. For many who turned to graphology, it was enough just to cast an image, any image, in the graphological mirror. Ideally, of course, one would discover hidden talents that promised an exciting life, but even if advised to make peace with one's limitations, appearing in print provided objective proof of one's existence.

Just what created these needs is of paramount interest here. The historian T. J. Jackson Lears has argued that for many well-to-do city-dwellers, the complexity and impersonality of modern life promoted a sense of insubstantiality, yet few correspondents to graphological columns were wealthy urbanites. Like many among the urban middle and upper classes of this era, these writers yearned for a more intense and meaningful life, but theirs was not a reaction against the airlessness and unreality of bourgeois existence. Their malaise originated in very different experiences—on the line, at a desk, in the crowd. Indeed, it may also have stemmed from a sense of isolation and exclusion from the same experiences—metropolitan life, executive positions, the latest technology—that sent the well-off on bootless searches for authentic experience. For these correspondents, the causes of mental anguish were very different from those of the bourgeoisie, and they called for different solutions: not the experience of vitality but the assertion of individuality.[47]

On the other hand, in their sense of insubstantiality, those who sought graphological help may have suffered from an ailment endemic to what historians have characterized as a culture of personality.[48] Character, a fixed nucleus of identity, had best served the interests of a society in which production was the imperative, but the shift to a consumer society demanded a new form of the self. That new self, personality, consisted of a series of carefully managed presentations, each designed to please a different audience. But as the ever-changing mask of personality displaced the solid core of character, some experienced the eerie sensation that their self had ceased to exist altogether. The novelist William Dean Howells expressed this sentiment for the middle and upper classes when he likened the human personality to an onion: "Nothing but hulls, that you keep peeling off, one after another, till you think you have got down to the heart at last, and then you have got down to nothing."[49] But graphologists, catering to an audience farther down the social scale, were also keenly aware of this malaise.

"The difference between the personality and the actual character is something which has done more to baffle the world than any other one thing," wrote Rice in 1925. In graphological terms, she explained, the signature, as the element of handwriting that was consciously composed and presented to an audience, represents personality, while the body of writing expresses character. The two often differ so markedly from each other, reported Rice, "that it is hard to believe the same person has written both," and in fact "the personality and the character are more often truly two than really one." Graphologist Anton Da Borcka concurred. For him, the signature disclosed only "our intentions in regard to our personality-impression," so that "to examine a signature without a specimen of script is like describing a person whose eyes alone are visible from behind a mask." What graphologists responded to was the fear that there was no face behind the mask. Under such conditions, individuals lost contact with who they were. "Some people," explained Rice, "impressed by the falseness of their own personalities, feel that they will never know themselves at all."[50] It was to these people that Rice and her fellow graphologists held up a mirror, one that reflected not the artifice of personality but the reality of character. Again, what the mirror revealed—exceptional talent or unexceptional ordinariness—was secondary. It was enough to confirm that one's existence was not a mirage or mask but solid and real and one's very own.

Given the close identification of script with self, graphology was uniquely poised to redefine and soothe the troubled selves of early twentieth-century America. It assured even the marginal characters who unburdened themselves to graphologists that they need not settle for lives of isolation and insignificance. Like the men and women living in the thick of urban glamour, the mainstream of a bracing modernity, they too were singular individuals capable of leading extraordinary lives. But modernity brought its own discontents. Deeper than the fear of an undifferentiated self lay the fear of no self at all. Graphology guaranteed the reality and solidity of the self but delivered an ambiguous message. Everyone would cast an image in the graphological looking glass, but the self revealed might be plain and colorless, consigned to a drab fate. If graphology might be used to assert uniqueness, and hence to rise out of a meaningless existence, it might also be used to counsel adjustment to that existence.

GRAPHOLOGY AND THE SCIENTIFIC ESTABLISHMENT

At the same time graphology caught the attention of the American masses, it achieved recognition in Europe as a theoretically sound if not fully mature science. In 1886 the Congress of the Sorbonne officially designated graphology a science and the Société de Graphologie was recognized as on par with analogous scientific organizations. One graphologist noted that on the eve of elections, *Le Figaro* had printed characterological analyses of leading candidates based on their handwriting. Following the death of Michon, the major figure in French graphology was Jules Crépieux-Jamin, a one-time dentist, whose 1896 study *L'Ecriture et le caractère* was cited as authoritative for decades.[51]

Graphology received the notice, and to some extent the blessing, of French experimental psychology in 1906 when none other than Alfred Binet, inventor of the I.Q. test, published the results of a series of graphological experiments. Binet did not regard these investigations as a whimsical detour from his serious scientific research in intelligence testing. He grouped the two together, along with his work in cephalometry (the measurement of cranial capacities) and the explorations being done by others in physiognomy and chiromancy. "These studies in graphology," he wrote, ". . . are a link in a chain; they are the fragment of a whole more vast, to which one could give the name: the exterior signs of intelligence."[52]

To test the validity of graphological claims, Binet asked Crépieux-Jamin, along with a number of other graphologists and several individuals with no graphological background, to analyze four sets of handwriting specimens, each for a different characteristic: sex, age, degree of intelligence, and level of morality. Crépieux-Jamin came off impressively. He was able to identify the sex of the writer 78.8 percent of the time and to distinguish geniuses from their intellectual opposites an astounding 91.6 percent of the time. His judgments with regard to age and moral status were less impressive, although not explicable as chance. The other graphologists did not achieve the same levels of accuracy, but they gave more correct answers than could be achieved by random guessing. But the results of the untrained readers could not be explained by chance alone, either, for they too exceeded 50 percent accuracy.

Binet interpreted his data cautiously. As a scientist, he criticized graphologists for their inattention to theoretical exploration and experimental verification. He was troubled by the imperfect link between sign and trait that, for example, caused the handwriting of most, but not all, geniuses to indicate high intelligence and that, on the other hand, allowed the handwriting of some mediocre people to exhibit the graphic sign for intellectual aptitude. He was bothered as well by the graphologists' vagueness, their varying rate of success, and the disagreements among them. Adding to the confusion was the fact that accurate graphological judgments did not seem to require graphological training; after all, amateurs had also beaten the odds. Nevertheless, Binet was impressed by the experimental results, especially those related to sex and intelligence. He concluded that accurate graphological readings were probably possible, at least theoretically, but that they necessarily involved an intuitive apprehension of the relations among graphic details. "In graphology," he concluded, "as in cephalometry, and probably also in chiromancy—there is something of the truth." Assimilation of graphology to "rational culture" would further reveal that truth. Until then, it remained "an art of the future."[53]

Meanwhile, what Binet looked for in France appeared to be happening in the German-speaking world. By the 1890s graphology had become the subject of German scholarly articles and monographs. Prominent investigators included such impressively credentialed scientists as William Preyer, professor of physiology at Jena; Georg Schneidemühl, professor of pathology at Kiel; the chemist and philosopher Ludwig Klages; and Max Pulver, who held a chair in graphology at the University of Zurich. The German graphologists certainly seemed a good deal more sophisticated than their French counterparts. For one, by and large they rejected graphology as a system of isolated graphic signs and character traits for a holistic apprehension of the subject's psychological profile. This moved graphology beyond the ken of the amateur with his do-it-yourself, step-by-step manual. They were also dissatisfied with the vague, empirical justifications provided by French graphologists and sought instead to establish the physiological mechanisms whereby character was transmitted to handwriting. And German graphology meshed with the latest in German psychology as well. Klages, for example, emphasized the operation of impulsion and inhibition in graphic patterns in a manner reminiscent of Sigmund Freud. Pulver, on the other hand, made use of Jung's introvert/extrovert duality in his graphology.[54]

In fact, German graphology sometimes approximated the metaphysical, even the occult. Klages located his graphology within the much larger construct of his metaphysics, a grand evolutionary passion play featuring such characters as the Archetype-Soul and the Substance-Soul that traced the development from Life to Thought to Will and ended with the death of the Soul at the hands of the Mind. For his part, Pulver argued that the uppermost layer of handwriting, the ascenders of constituent letters (the loops of cursive lowercase l or b, for example) reveal the writer's intellectual and spiritual qualities, the middle layer (such as lowercase a, c, and e) is the key to his emotional and social traits, and the descenders (like the loops of lowercase y and p) clue the graphologist in to physical and sexual characteristics. What we have here, of course, is Lavater's tripartite division of the face or, more broadly, the analogy presumed in many occult sciences to exist between microcosm and macrocosm.[55]

In the United States, however, the German graphologists were largely ignored by their American counterparts until after World War II.[56] A few popular graphologists made occasional reference to German graphological theories, but even they interpreted handwriting according to the science of signs that was first put forward by Michon. It is not difficult to understand why the Germans received such short shrift. For one, most of their works were never translated, and those that were appeared in English only in the 1930s. Then too, they put forth highly complex psychological and metaphysical concepts, and these simply would not do in a paperback do-it-yourself manual aimed at the masses.

It is also true, however, that American *scientists* never accepted the validity of German graphological theories, indeed, largely ignored them altogether. Even when Americans did acknowledge the existence of the Germans, it was only to dismiss them as continental metaphysicians. Having noted that graphology "has often been associated with physiognomy, chiromancy and magic," professors Clark L. Hull and Robert B. Montgomery of the University of Wisconsin allowed that Preyer and Schneidemühl "deserve special mention because of the positions they occupy in the field of the recognized sciences." But when all was said and done, argued the Americans, the German academics were no different from their popular counterparts. "While stoutly asserting the necessity of reducing graphology to the status of a true science," wrote Hull and Montgomery, "these writers show little less credulity than the pamphlet written on the same subject by William L. French and put out by a pen manufacturing company for advertising purposes."[57]

Only one thing gave Hull and Montgomery pause—Binet's experiments. "Such results and conclusions from a psychologist of Binet's repute," they conceded, "suggests that we may not without a previous scientific examination safely ignore the claims of graphologists, however extravagant and apparently unfounded they may seem."[58] Accordingly, Hull and Montgomery undertook just such an examination. Their subjects were seventeen members of a medical fraternity at the University of Wisconsin. The students submitted handwriting samples, subsequently assessed for the graphological signs (upward sloping lines of writing, long t-bars, etc.) commonly associated by graphologists with such character traits as ambition and perseverance. The students also evaluated one another's personalities for just those character traits; the researchers assumed that "the intimate personal relations obtaining in small semi-social fraternities" assured accurate character assessments.

The discussion of the experiment read like a parody of laboratory procedure, and one can well imagine Hull and Montgomery sharing a good laugh over their straight-faced presentation of such absurdities as using a microscope to measure t-bars to the nearest half-millimeter and calculating an "index of openness" for lowercase a's and o's. Of course, they made mincemeat of graphology. They concluded that there was no correlation between the specific graphic signs and character traits selected for study, and since these represented "a fair sampling of graphologists' claims as to the relations between handwriting and character," their results could "be taken with some assurance as typical of the whole." There was still the problem of Binet, but Hull and Montgomery disposed of him by suggesting that his graphologists had kept bad records and had previous familiarity with some of the specimens under analysis.[59]

For most American scientists, Hull and Montgomery were the last word on the claims of graphology. With the exception of the psychologist June Downey, to be discussed shortly, they were uninterested in correlating handwriting style with the personality of the individual writer. It is worth noting, however, that there were a few academics who tried to identify certain stylistic characteristics of handwriting as characteristic of particular groups or *genetic categories* of people. Some researchers, for example, investigated the similarities in the handwriting of twins or family members. Others tried to pinpoint the graphic signs of insanity or criminal behavior, conditions commonly understood to be genetic in origin. The same hereditary factors that created lunatics and psychopaths, it was assumed, would shape a peculiar style of handwriting. Accordingly, physicians, psychiatrists, and criminologists were urged to use handwriting as a diagnostic tool.[60]

Most often, scientists sought to correlate handwriting style with gender, and here they claimed their greatest success and achieved their greatest credibility. Binet in 1906 and Downey in 1910 were only the first among many to conclude that sex could indeed be determined from handwriting, if not infallibly then at least to a significant extent.[61] Intriguingly, while graphologists routinely claimed to detect the most minute details of character and talent from handwriting, they just as routinely insisted that sex could not be determined. "No particular style of handwriting is peculiar to either sex," wrote Henry Frith in 1890. "There are many ladies who write like men, and many men who write a 'ladylike' hand." Louise Rice agreed, noting that "many men of virility and power have feminine temperaments, and *vice versa,* so that temperament can be deduced, but not sex." Thus graphologists often stipulated that specimens be identified by sex before any interpretation could take place.[62]

How do we explain the fact that scientists accepted as present in handwriting the single trait of the writer that graphologists insisted could not be found? No doubt, at the heart of the disagreement lay a deeper ideological difference over the nature and meaning of individuality. If graphologists emphasized the uniqueness of every human being, scientists sought to reduce apparently individual differences to the characteristics of genetically defined groups. The first approach encouraged a sense of freedom and possibility; the second, a sense of mediocrity and limitation. But there was probably another source of conflict, which had to do with female freedom and possibility in particular.

Graphologists often explicitly linked the genderlessness of handwriting to the decline of the Victorian lady and the emergence of the New Woman. Commentators from Isaac Disraeli to writing masters of the Gilded Age had held that women, trained at female academies in the identical, fashionable female hand, lacked individuality in their handwriting. But from the 1890s on, the consensus seemed to be that as women's opportunities changed, so did their scripts. "When we consider that the occupations, the ideas, and the amusements of women very closely approximate to those of men, now-a-days," wrote Henry Frith in 1890, "we cannot be surprised to find that their writing reflects something, and in some cases a great deal, of the masculine element." In 1912 William Leslie French informed the readers of *Good Housekeeping* that "today, owing to the new conditions created by the higher education of women, it is much more difficult to determine sex from script. Every profession and line of work are affected by [women's] endeavors and influence, and in consequence, the leading traits of will power, judgment, and self-confidence appear in their strokes, to a far greater degree than heretofore." Archer Wall Douglas noted in 1924 that at the end of the last century, he had often been stymied in his graphological efforts by the "apparent lack of individuality" in female handwriting. "That I rarely encounter this difficulty now," wrote Douglas, "is, I believe, a mute testimony to the extent and rapidity of woman's emancipation in the last generation."[63]

Not every graphologist greeted these changes happily. Writing in 1896, J. Harington Keene made it clear that he was none too thrilled about "the so-called 'emancipation of women.'" In "aping the masculine pursuits and propensities," he noted, women "acquire the virile tone of character. In a similar way the 'dude' of the day becomes androgynous; and the result in one case is a masculine soul in a woman's shape, and in the other a feminine soul in the degraded form of the so-called 'dude.'" Keene was a decided exception, however, in a profession that within a matter of years would be largely populated by and would appeal to women. By the 1910s graphologists heartily approved of the changes in women's status. What the genderlessness of script shows us, wrote French in an article entitled "Her Handwriting," is that "equality of the sexes is not a vagary, a false claim." Rice concurred that "the old idea that we can tell the handwriting of a man from that of a woman is nonsense." Instead, she argued, "handwriting simply refuses to have anything to do with sex, since sex is merely an accident—something which does not materially affect the real you which lives in a body." Rice explicitly aimed this message at female readers who "altho brought up in a family which has persistently discouraged the idea, have always wanted to be an engineer or a blacksmith or an aviator, or anything else which has been thought impossible for women." Graphologists insisted that women could no longer be constrained or defined by their sex but must be free to unfold according to the unique pattern set by their individuality.[64]

If academic psychologists regendered handwriting, then, it might well have been because they were uncomfortable with this new female potential. One professional psychologist stood apart from her colleagues: June Downey, a professor of psychology at the University of Wyoming. Downey was the only American scientist working in the teens and twenties who agreed with Alfred Binet that there was probably something to graphology. She admitted that such "extravagant" graphological claims as the ability to determine "the color of a writer's eyes" or "the elasticity of his bank-account" from his handwriting did indeed "justify a healthy incredulity" but added that "the best graphologists" show "a caution and conservatism in interpretation that wins in a measure of the reader's confidence and a desire to hear what those of best repute have to say in defense of their art." Given the "intimate relationship between consciousness and motor expression," there was reason to believe that there might be some validity to graphology. Downey did not expect to find much of value in the English-language graphological literature, but the French and German treatises were another matter, "much more subtle, discriminating, and scholarly." She cited the work of Crépieux-Jamin and, even more enthusiastically, that of Preyer, Schneidemühl, and Klages.[65]

Downey conducted her own experiments, exploring potential correlations between graphic signs, mood, and temperament. There was no compromise of scientific method here, unlike the experiment cynically conducted by Hull and Montgomery, with its scant seventeen subjects and questionable methods of establishing personality traits. Downey took pains to correct for potential sources of bias and to document those that could not be factored out, to propose nongraphological explanations for her results, to raise all possible objections to her experimental techniques, data, and conclusions. She was not ready to "prove" the validity of all graphological claims, but she, like Binet, found it impossible to avoid concluding that there was probably some truth to graphology, certainly enough to merit further scientific research.[66]

What explains Downey's unique openness to the claims of graphology? Most likely, a number of factors came into play. To begin with, Downey's training came first in the fields of literature and philosophy and only later, under Edward Bradford Titchener at Cornell and James Rowland Angell at the University of Chicago, in experimental psychology. Her academic career, stretching from 1899 to her death in 1934, reflected both sets of concerns. It was the psychology of aesthetics, creativity, and emotion that captured her interest. Thus she published not only her graphological studies but also *Creative Imagination: Studies in the Psychology of Literature* and even a book of her own poetry.[67]

In addition, it seems inescapable that Downey's position as a woman in a male-dominated field played some role in her openness to graphology. That role is illuminated by Downey's own work on handwriting and gender. In 1910 Downey repeated Binet's graphological experiments on the determination of sex, with much the same results. The sex of the writer could, in fact, be identified from a handwriting specimen with a significant degree of accuracy. In interpreting her data, however, Downey focused on the experimental errors—in other words, on the cases where female scripts were judged to be male and male scripts judged to be female. Binet had noted what he termed "inversions of sex signs," but what he had failed to notice about them was that they occurred more frequently in the examination of women's handwriting than in that of men's. In general, Downey added, even when handwriting specimens are divided evenly between male and female, the readers of these specimens judge them to be predominantly male. "The reason for this excess of masculine judgments," Downey commented, "is evident from the statements of certain observers relative to what they considered to be the signs of masculinity and femininity in handwriting. Obviously, originality is held to characterize the man's hand; conventionality, the woman's. Consequently, masculine handwriting is thought to show a more extensive range of variability than does the woman's. . . . In the present case such a pressure of social judgment (if one may so express it) led to a constant error."[68]

Downey then went on to examine just what it was about the misidentified specimens that misled experiment participants. She found that the female hands ascribed to men were bold and individualistic; most had been executed by professional women. She also found that the male hands ascribed to women were conventional, small, and neat; many of the men were teachers. Downey reasoned that the facts "would apparently lead to a social rather than psycho-physiological interpretation of sex-differences in handwriting." In what may have been a veiled reference to homosexuality, she added that it was possible to argue that the misidentified scripts were misinterpreted for good reason, "that the inversion of sex signs in handwriting points to an inversion in other respects"—in other words, that the misread men really were feminine and the misread women really masculine in their "basal" natures. Nevertheless, she concluded with disingenuous dispassion that "the trend of my results makes me exceedingly doubtful of such an interpretation."[69]

Downey's academic credentials and career in effect typed her as one of Binet's "inverted sex signs," in her life if not her handwriting. She was certainly poised to respond positively to the graphological message that men could be and act like women and women, men, that gender was basic to neither personality nor potential. Rejecting the notion that membership in a genetically defined group—namely, one's sex—delimits self-development,

Downey opted instead for the liberating notion that each human being is a unique product of his or her gender-independent character traits and talents. Indeed, Downey's life reads like nothing so much as one of Louise Rice's graphological success stories. "Yes, June," we can easily imagine Rice writing, "indeed, there are numbers of professional women psychologists."

Graphology did not really leave its concern with celebrities and strangers behind when it entered the twentieth century. Devotees of handwriting analysis simply turned their gaze inward, to the genius and the mystery within. There they hoped to find the extraordinary personality or talent that would elevate them to the ranks of a Napoleon or Paderewski. Even those who were advised to be content with their own ordinariness were given to understand that the mediocrity of their lives was not an artifact of a superficial existence but the authentic expression of a core identity. It was reassuring to know there was something solid underneath the surface appearance, something genuinely one's own. Almost anything would do. The possibilities were thrilling, the need intense. After all, Americans were strangers to themselves.

The scientists who rejected graphology as groundless had a different agenda. In some ways, they seemed to belong to another era. When they asserted that men and women write characteristically distinct hands, they sounded like Victorian writing masters. A closer look, however, reveals that American scientists and graphologists were in fact engaged in a common conversation, and the topic of that conversation was distinctly modern. For twentieth-century scientists did not separate female from male scripts as they exhibited delicacy or boldness but as they conformed to or deviated from copybook models. Individuality was the meaningful variable in the scientists' analysis, just as it was the key to the graphologists' exactly opposite line of argument. If script is genderless, insisted the graphologists, it is precisely because the character of every man and woman is unique, unaffected by membership in the male or the female sex.

Individuality was the culturally sensitive, culturally operative issue in the early twentieth century; its use as both a category of analysis and a focus of struggle signals the modern age. It assumed this significance because of its close connection with power denied and power asserted by subordinate groups. Those who lived outside the charmed circles of wealth and status—factory operatives, office workers, small-town nobodies—experienced their lack of power largely as a lack of individuality. At the same time, the assertion of female potential depended on redefining women as individuals whose abilities were not predetermined by membership in a biological class but varied, as with men, from one person to the next. In affirming individuality in handwriting as universal, graphologists offered solace and inspiration to many who were seemingly fated by their class or gender to an ordinary, constricted existence. In denying it, scientists dashed, even ridiculed, such hopes. As we shall see, penmanship authorities of the progressive era added their own messages of restraint and limitation to the same conversation.

CHAPTER FIVE

Automatic Writing?

Learning to Write in the Twentieth Century

In 1889 William James published an article in the *Proceedings of the American Society for Psychical Research* entitled "Notes on Automatic Writing." There, James detailed the cases of a number of subjects, ranging from the clearly pathological to the irrefutably respectable, who produced words on a page without any conscious knowledge of their creation. Miss W., a nineteen-year-old girl diagnosed as suffering from "hystero-epilepsy," penned letters, poetry, even bills of fare, awake and asleep, completely unaware of her activities. "Ask her what she is writing, she replies, '*I* am not writing; that is "Stump" writing.'" Sidney Dean, a journalist, author, and former congressman, insisted on essentially the same point. "It is an intelligent *ego* who writes," Dean explained in a letter to James, ". . . It is not myself; of that I am conscious at every step of the process."[1]

It was not handwriting per se that interested James, of course, but the self that produces handwriting. "The great *theoretic* interest of these automatic performances," he explained, ". . . consists in the questions they awaken as to the boundaries of our individuality."[2] Apparently the self was not necessarily unitary, visible, or impermeable. There might be multiple selves, hidden layers of the self, or access to other selves, dead or alive, through some wider consciousness.

It is not surprising that when James chose to explore the nature of the self, he should do so through the phenomenon of automatic handwriting. After all, in their own ways, nineteenth-century penmanship pedagogues, graphologists, autograph collectors, and handwriting experts had each assumed an intimate association between handwriting and the self. Indeed, that relation had existed since the rise of print. The motley crew of psychologists, physicians, spiritual mediums, and psychic researchers who took an interest in automatic writing simply worked from the same assumption. "Handwriting is, in many ways, a summary expression of a man's being," wrote F. W. H. Myers, an English classical scholar whose research in psychic phenomena was cited by James as laying the groundwork for his own. It "obeys limitations of idiosyncrasy as well as of will. . . . Handwriting, that is to say, is a deep-seated thing. It is likely to have secrets to tell us."[3]

James's interest in automatic writing petered out in the 1890s, but the whole concept of automatic writing acquired new life over the next decades, when penmanship pedagogues gave it a new meaning. From the 1890s through the 1920s they characterized handwriting as an automatic act, using the vocabulary of the new psychology: involuntary movement, reflex action, motor habit. The authors of *How to Teach Handwriting*, for example, might easily have been talking about Miss W. and her "Stump" when, in a section titled "Automatization," they wrote: "When the writing habit has been completely formed, it is automatic; that is, the writer executes without paying much attention to the position, to the details of movement, or to the letters."[4] For penmanship pedagogues, the automatism of writing was neither pathological nor unusual. Nor did they regard handwriting as a "deep-seated thing" that had "secrets to tell." As conceptualized by penmanship pedagogues, the automatism of handwriting acted as a substitute for, rather than an expression of, consciousness.

This understanding of penmanship suited the broader agenda of progressive-era schools. Penmanship training, like all education, entailed handing over mental functions to what James termed (and A. N. Palmer quoted) "the effortless custody of automatism."[5] By redefining learning as an essentially physiological process and human beings as bundles of neuromuscular connections, educators deemphasized conscious will and identified the training of the body as the way to get results, and not just narrowly academic ones. Victorians had placed their hopes in the will as the ultimate source of social order, but consciousness of any sort had a way of getting out of hand, of working toward ends other than those envisioned by educators. The new conception of the learning process, steeped in the new psychology of the early twentieth century, either ignored consciousness or denied its existence. Educators now called for bodies to be disciplined, nowhere more so than in handwriting instruction. Thus educators claimed that the penmanship regimen, in asserting control over the "student body," would yield important social benefits. It would reform delinquents, assimilate foreigners, and shape a workforce.

At the same time, the recasting of handwriting as a form of motor automatism tacitly refuted the graphological agenda. Penmanship educators were well aware of the mass interest in graphology and the consequent popular identification of handwriting with individuality. Indeed, graphological propositions provided the implicit context in which pedagogical theory and practice would be read, so that there was no escaping a commentary on human individuality. When pedagogues defined handwriting as the automatic workings of nerves and muscles, they were dismissing as futile the graphological search for temperament and talent in script. And when they attributed the distinctiveness of each person's handwriting to mere physiological idiosyncrasy, they rejected the graphological vision of characterological uniqueness as chimerical.

Automatism was where penmanship authorities of the early twentieth century agreed. Much of the literature they themselves generated speaks more to the rift that divided them, into commercial penmen led by Palmer on the one hand and academic experts in the fields of education and psychology on the other. In many ways the two groups represented different cultures: the business culture of corporate America and the expert culture of progressive reform. Palmer and the academics squared off on many a pedagogical point: the optimum handwriting movement, the proper way to teach young children, the acceptability of left-handedness, and the most useful methods of measuring and rewarding progress. In the pages of pedagogical journals and school superintendents' annual reports, the conflict over these questions looms the largest; yet because these topics engaged the larger cultural issues of conformity and control, a more fundamental consensus existed.

ACADEMIC EXPERTS AND THE CRITIQUE OF
THE PALMER METHOD

When A. N. Palmer and his followers muscled their way into the twentieth century, they thought they had displaced the ornate script of the Victorian age for good and spoken the last word on penmanship. King Spencer was dead; long live King Palmer. There was, however, a second group of penmanship pedagogues who disdained the Palmer method and its look-alike competitors as no better than their predecessors and as untouched by the light of modern knowledge. These were the academics. Based in university departments of psychology and graduate schools of education, the academic experts sought to wrest control of handwriting instruction away from unqualified amateurs and to redirect the discipline along the lines of the modern natural and social sciences.

"Tradition has dominated the teaching of handwriting as it has no other school study," read professor Frank Freeman's *Teaching of Handwriting* (1914), a landmark in the movement for a scientific penmanship pedagogy. "It has been the last of the so-called formal subjects to be influenced by the newer educational thought." Unfortunately, such innovations as did occur in the teaching of penmanship had been "introduced by those whose prime interest in the matter was commercial rather than professional." Ordinary classroom teachers, lacking the ability to conduct "expert psychological analysis" and "careful pedagogical experimentation," were ill prepared to assess the claims of commercial penmen or to arrive at more scientific conclusions of their own.[6]

In the first quarter of the twentieth century, academics offered their help. Their efforts led them into three related areas of inquiry: how best to write, how best to teach writing, and how to measure the results of that instruction. Should all students use Palmer's "whole-arm movement," or were there more efficient ways of writing? Might these methods vary from individual to individual? What about left-handedness? Did Palmer's ovals and push-pulls (arm-movement drills), or any kind of drill, make pedagogical sense? And finally, how could educators test pupils to evaluate their levels of handwriting achievement?

When educational psychologists first took up the issue of handwriting at the beginning of the twentieth century, the Palmer method was not yet in wide use, and most classroom teachers were focusing on getting their students to reproduce copybook models as accurately as possible. The hottest issue in penmanship instruction concerned the proper slope of handwriting: whether students should execute a vertical script, as was the short-lived vogue of the 1890s, or the traditional, slanted script.[7] Academic investigators like Cloyd N. McAllister and Charles H. Judd of Yale and Frank Freeman of the University of Chicago, shifted the emphasis from correct form to correct movement. Learning to write, they explained, involved developing efficient neural pathways to the appropriate muscles, an evolutionary process achieved by the unconscious selection of efficient motions and the weeding out of inefficient motions. There could be no shortcuts to this process, for selection necessarily involved repetition, but once it had taken place, writing became an unconscious motor habit, a muscular automatism.[8]

With the process of learning to write understood from a theoretical standpoint, the next item on the academic agenda was the experimental determination of the parameters of an efficient handwriting movement. Academics recognized the existence of physiological variations among individuals—this, after all, was a premise of evolutionary thinking—and so they understood that some variation in writing techniques would naturally and legitimately exist. Nevertheless, as a matter of laboratory practice, they tended to focus on eliminating certain techniques as inherently inefficient and endorsing others as generally advisable. Their research convinced them that school practice, whether the straight up-and-down motion of vertical writing or the whole-arm movement of the Palmer method, was all wrong. In 1899, when McAllister hooked up volunteer subjects (including the laboratory janitor) to electrodes and recorded the direction of their hand movements as they wrote, he concluded that the optimum slope for handwriting was about 75 degrees. So much for vertical writing. In 1903, when Judd strapped his experimental subjects to an even more complex apparatus, he concluded that movements of the fingers, hand, wrist, and arm were all necessary for good writing (fig. 35).[9] So much for the Palmer method.

By far the most thorough and sophisticated investigations into the handwriting movement were undertaken in the 1910s by Freeman. Some of his experimental techniques and instruments were borrowed from McAllister and Judd, but he also made use of the tools of scientific management: Frederick W. Taylor's stopwatch and Frank Gilbreth's movie camera. With these techniques Freeman searched for the "one best movement." Armed with his data, Freeman took dead aim at Palmer, by then the dominant figure in

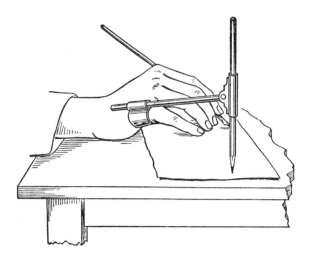

35. Laboratory analysis of the handwriting movement, 1903.

penmanship pedagogy. Like Judd, Freeman discredited Palmer's insistence
on the exclusivity of arm motion, asserting that a combined motion of arm,
hand, and fingers was superior. He also argued that efficient writing proceeded according to a particular rhythm, not the rhythm of the schoolroom
metronome or Palmer's endlessly repeated push-pulls but one that was ex-
perimentally determined to be unique to each letter of the alphabet.[10]

When it came to translating their research on the physical act of handwriting into concrete pedagogical reforms, academics shifted subtly from their
emphasis on universally efficient movement to a recognition of the individualized needs and characteristics of penmanship pupils. Here too they took
issue with Palmer. One of Palmer's greatest errors, they argued, was his ex-
trapolation of techniques used to train adults in business colleges for children
in elementary schools. The briefest introduction to developmental psychology showed that young children had not yet acquired mature levels of neuromuscular coordination and therefore could not achieve the level of motor skill
attained by older children or adults.[11]

Accordingly, the academics recommended new pedagogical techniques to
replace those they considered misguided. Instead of struggling with pen and
ink, small children should work at the blackboard or with pencil and special
wide-ruled paper. Instead of the push-pull and oval movement drills, students should practice the alphabet as the teacher counted out the rhythm
unique to each letter. Standards of achievement should take the child's age
into account; copybook models raised unrealistic expectations. It might even

make sense to postpone penmanship education until perhaps the age of ten, when the child would reach the level of physiological maturity necessary for handwriting.[12]

Furthermore, once children began writing in earnest, a too-rigid insistence on a single penmanship technique violated the laws of the human organism. Because of the physiological variation that naturally exists in any human population—in the anatomy of the hand, for example, or in the nuances of the nervous system—each individual could be expected to "evolve" as a writer in slightly different ways according to what was "fittest" for his or her unique physical constitution. There were limits to these variations, of course, but minor variations in posture, way of holding the pen, and manner of execution would legitimately exist. It was the teacher's job to guide the child through this individualized process of adaptation, steering him clear of momentary fancies, leading him to discover the neural pathways and muscular movements best suited to his unique psycho-physiological makeup.[13]

In their tolerance for individual variation, academics most deviated from handwriting orthodoxy over the issue of handedness. Amazingly enough, except for an occasional reference in penmanship journals, the possibility that some people might write with their left hands was not raised in the pedagogical literature of the nineteenth century, although in practice teachers were aware of left-handedness and did what they could to thwart it.[14] Indeed, the fact of handedness made its appearance in scientific literature only at the end of the 1800s, and well into the twentieth century scientists argued over whether handedness was a hereditary or an acquired characteristic and whether it represented a peculiarity of the hand or the brain.[15]

From the 1910s, academics like Freeman, Lewis Terman, Mary Dougherty, and Mary Thompson dealt squarely with the fact of left-handed schoolchildren, arguing that, contrary to usual school practice, these pupils should be allowed to follow their natural inclinations. They argued that right-handed writing performed by sinistrals would be of poor quality and, even more critical, that forced left-to-right transfer often created a stuttering problem. "Penmanship teachers may still be unwilling to surrender their traditional practices in dealing with left-handers . . . ," summarized one professor of education, "but that will only be a continuance of a bad tradition. There is clearly but one thing to do with the born left-hander, and that is to see that he uses his left hand."[16]

Academic authorities thus brought their expertise to bear on how best to write and how best to teach. A third item on their agenda was how to measure the success of both. The development of quantitative handwriting scales began in 1909, when E. L. Thorndike, professor of educational psychology at Teachers College, Columbia University, developed a method of assigning numerical ratings to handwriting samples. In the absence of such a scale, Thorndike asserted, penmanship pedagogues were in the position of students of temperature before the invention of the thermometer. With it, they graduated into the company of scientific educators. Within eight years academics had developed nine additional scales, including one by Freeman, but only the scale composed by Leonard Ayres of the Russell Sage Foundation joined the Thorndike scale in common usage.[17]

The penmanship scales developed by Thorndike, Ayres, and Freeman were part of a much larger trend to measure intellectual potential and academic achievement. The intelligence quotient or I.Q. tests developed by Alfred Binet in 1905 and modified by Lewis Terman in 1913 and the Army alpha and beta tests produced during World War I and widely used in the 1920s are the best known of these. These tests were designed to measure general, innate ability.[18] More obscure but as widely used were the quantitative tests and corresponding scales designed to measure actual achievement in specific school subjects. By 1918 academics had developed no fewer than 109 standardized tests in subjects ranging from reading, writing, and arithmetic to history, geography, and even drawing. Three years later, Thorndike estimated that although at least a million boys and girls had been tested for general intelligence during the previous year, over two million had been tested for achievement in specific school subjects. By 1922 more than three hundred such achievement tests existed; by 1929, closer to four hundred.[19] Thorndike, Ayres, and Freeman were leaders in this voracious impulse to measure, a trend referred to by contemporaries as "the scientific movement in education."[20]

Academic experts foresaw many uses for handwriting scales. They argued that standardized tests would motivate students to improve their penmanship. If a competitive spirit took over, so much the better. The scale could also be used to establish quantitative standards of achievement. Pupils would have to take note of minimum standards for satisfactory completion of a grade level, while teachers would need to ensure that their students as a whole met standards for classroom-wide averages. Meanwhile, quantitative comparisons of one class with another or one school with another could be used to figure out what methods were most effective or, by the same token, which individual instructors and schools were substandard. Tests tested pupils, but they also tested teachers.[21]

HANDWRITING INSTRUCTION IN THE CLASSROOM

Both Palmer and his academic critics designed programs of handwriting instruction to be implemented in schoolrooms across the nation. But what looked good in theory was not always workable in practice. Penmanship supervisors, grade norms, graded textbooks—none of these made sense in one-room schoolhouses. In isolated, impoverished regions of the country, schools could hardly afford the full line of Palmer paraphernalia or a set of testing materials. Nor were undertrained and underpaid teachers likely to keep up with the latest in pedagogical scholarship or to take the correspondence courses required by Palmer as a prerequisite for using the Palmer method in a particular school system.[22]

Indeed, poverty ruled out any but the most rudimentary kind of instruction. "It is obvious that proper training in handwriting cannot be provided in schools where pens, ink, and suitable paper are lacking," read the report of an educational survey of Virginia undertaken by northern experts in 1920, "or where the pupils have no smooth desk surface on which to write." Investigators found that in many Virginia schools, the only source of ink was "a five-cent bottle on the teacher's desk"; that "pens and paper which could receive writing in ink were more conspicuous by their absence than by their presence"; and that "five per cent of the white schools and forty-five per cent of the colored schools visited had desks which should long since have been consigned to the wood pile."[23]

In urban and suburban school systems, however, administrators were confronted with a genuine choice of pedagogical approaches and they had to make decisions. In actual practice, the schools appear to have been less consistent and rigorous in their application of either Palmer's or the academics' methods than either might have wished. School officials picked and chose, diluted and modified. Most adopted Palmer's insistence on muscular movement, at least ostensibly. They might make concessions to young pupils but rarely to left-handed ones. And by the late teens and twenties, most metropolitan school systems made some provision for standardized testing.

Freeman's experimental results were quickly incorporated into official educational orthodoxy, but ousting Palmer from real, live classrooms proved more difficult. "It is a bold school man who dares to stem the tide of systematically organized pedagogical opinion on arm-movement in penmanship," editorialized the *Elementary School Journal* in 1923, while Freeman himself grimly conceded that the "arm movement dogma" continued to reign supreme.[24] In Long Beach, California, handwriting supervisor Leta Severance Hiles flunked students who used finger movement to write. In St. Louis, students who successfully avoided using their fingers to form letters earned prize certificates, even when their handwriting was illegible. In Massachusetts, normal-school students were instructed to discourage their future students from using finger movement in writing. By 1928 an estimated three-quarters of American children were being trained in the Palmer method (fig. 36).[25]

Nevertheless, the application of the Palmer method was apparently neither as consistent nor as strict as either Palmer insisted or his opponents rued. To

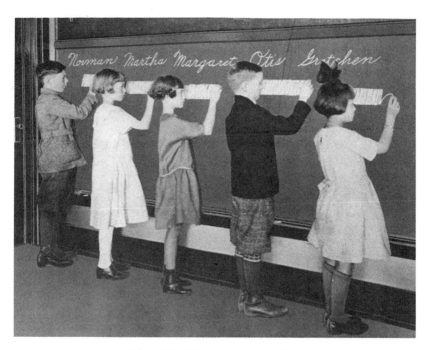

36. Practicing Palmerian push-pulls, 1912.

some extent, school administrators and teachers mixed Palmer's and Freeman's approaches because they did not really attend to or perhaps even understand the differences between them. In Colorado Springs, for example, the standard textbook was *The Palmer Method of Business Writing* and the penmanship supervisor insisted on muscular movement, even as she quoted Frank Freeman (out of context) on the same topic.[26]

But the real problem seems to have been that, as one educational administrator admitted, "the pupils cordially hate" Palmerian penmanship instruction, and "the teacher usually dislikes" it. The Palmer method simply did not work the way it was supposed to. Try as he might to approximate the "mysterious 'gliding' movement," recalled one survivor of "the rigid and inflexible system of torture known as the Palmer Method," no "words flowed out magically from somewhere up near the elbow." The challenge then became to beat the system: perhaps to "make the push-pull and then carefully erase the parts which slopped over the upper and lower lines," or, as one classmate did, to convince the family doctor "that she had contracted rheumatism in her arm and would no longer be able to attend penmanship class." According to both friends and foes of the Palmer method, most students used whole-arm movement only under duress in penmanship class and then abandoned it for the rest of the day.[27]

Meanwhile, from Buffalo, New York, to Vancouver, Washington, teachers complained that beginning Palmer pupils might write illegibly for several years before good form kicked in. Even the staunchest of Palmerians, like penmanship supervisor Walker of St. Louis, had to admit that "progress in accurate writing is, at first, slower in muscular movement writing than in finger movement writing." He expressed confidence that in time a practiced and mature movement would produce legible results, and reported that more and more teachers, disabused of their unfortunate copybook obsession with "accurately formed letters," were coming around to his more enlightened view. Still, some people—parents, teachers, even school principals— must have remained in the dark, for Walker was ultimately forced to admit that there were "murmurings" that student penmanship had gotten worse, not better, and he accordingly conceded that form would have to be reemphasized.[28]

Palmer purists had their own answers, of course—be patient, require consistency—but it was difficult to remain a purist in the face of pedagogical skepticism, parental pressure, and student recalcitrance. When we say that the Palmer method ruled in the early decades of the twentieth century, then, we must be prepared to imagine schools where penmanship supervisors argued to no avail for strict enforcement of Palmerian principles across the curriculum; classrooms in which teachers critiqued the accuracy of letter forms even as they led muscular-movement drills; and students who wrote as they wanted whenever they could get away with it.

Where schools appear to have stood firm until at least well into the 1930s was on the issue of left-handedness. One study published in 1929 estimated that, arguments of educational psychologists notwithstanding, schools "interfered with" the natural preference of about two-thirds of left-handed children. Clarence E. Meleny, a devoted Palmerian and associate superintendent of the New York City public schools, would not hear of left-handed penmanship. "If his right hand is paralyzed," he wrote of a hypothetical southpaw, "that is different, but if he is simply left-handed, I say the right hand is the right hand to work with." Meleny himself was left-handed, as were two of his sons, but he wrote with his right hand and had insisted that his boys do the same. In St. Louis, the penmanship supervisor agreed. Among the reasons he gave for "the propriety of urging upon such children the advantage of learning to write with the right hand" were the "much greater difficulty for such a child to acquire skill in using the pen with his left hand" and "the advantage of conformity to a usual practice." Tom Sawyier, the penmanship supervisor for the state of Ohio, declared that "writing is fundamentally a right-handed act." Brushing aside the "theorists" who countenanced left-handed penmanship, Sawyier suggested that young lefties be sent to the blackboard, instructed to hold an eraser behind their backs with their left hands, and ordered to write on the board with their right hands.[29]

Many left-handed pupils received harsher treatment. One study appearing in the *Journal of Educational Psychology* stated that lefties were routinely subjected to "excruciating ordeals" designed to curb their preference. Another researcher listed just what these ordeals included: "tying gourd over left hand, wrapping cloth over left hand, compelling the wearing of a mitten," "cuffing, slapping, spanking, whipping, boxing ears, cracking the knuckles with a ruler," "ridiculing, scolding, threatening," and "confining in closet." Among these bound and battered, cuffed and closeted children, a full half developed speech disorders.[30]

Academic authorities appear to have had little success in influencing the teaching of handwriting. Any watering down of the muscular-movement method that did occur came about more from its inherent weaknesses than from any expert critique, and officially it remained the technique of choice. Left-handed pupils faced correction and coercion. But this is not to say that the scientific pedagogues were without effect. Academics made their real mark in school practice not by banishing muscular motion from the classroom or making lefties feel welcome in it, but by introducing quantitative scales to measure and rank handwriting skill. The same administrators who advocated the Palmer method in their school systems also measured its success with the kind of achievement testing developed and advocated by Freeman, Thorndike, and Ayres. Ayres himself conducted handwriting surveys in fifty-five cities, and other school systems followed suit. They also established research departments, set numerical standards for each grade, administered tests, and directed teachers to keep records on individual students and classes as a whole. Palmer's rewards for excellence—buttons and certificates—were superseded by the more scientific measure of success, a rising curve on the graph of handwriting test scores. Indeed, by the 1920s the Palmer company recognized that it made little financial sense to buck the trend. The company hired a Ph.D., set up its own research department, and marketed its own handwriting scale.[31] Following World War I, then, the standard urban and suburban public school penmanship program consisted of right-handed muscular-movement instruction supplemented by the standardized testing of results.

SOLDIERS IN THE PENMANSHIP ARMY

What made muscular movement so popular among school officials and why did the academic critique of it fall on deaf ears? Why did school authorities ignore educational psychologists when they pled the cause of lefties? Why, on the other hand, did administrators take so readily to these same academics' program for standardized testing? How can we explain the logic behind this selectivity?

Part of the answer lies with the professional status of school administrators during the progressive era, the early 1900s. School administration was only just defining itself as a profession, calling on all the associations of impartial expertise and scientific efficiency that the term carried. The testing movement in particular epitomized this set of values and goals; in effect, it certified school administration as a proper profession.[32] No doubt many credentialed administrators identified with men like Freeman and Thorndike as fellow educational professionals who subscribed to the same credo of expertise and efficiency. By jumping on the testing bandwagon and by joining the professors in sneering at men like Palmer, administrators demonstrated their affinity concretely.[33]

On the other hand, administrators of an older school or with more traditional qualifications might balk at the university men as elitist and impractical. Joseph S. Taylor, for example, superintendent of New York City schools, may have shared this attitude when he wrote that in the field of penmanship pedagogy, "vast resources of time and money and human energy have been expended to prove what every writing teacher knew long ago from personal experience. It is something to have this experience confirmed by scientific methods and expressed in technical terms; but the teacher is properly resentful when he sees a bit of truth that he always knew strutting about in the fine feathers of Professor Peacock." Such administrators might have felt a good deal more comfortable with plain old Mister Palmer from Iowa, the man who shunned the theory offered by the "newer books on psychology and pedagogy" for the concrete results achieved by his methods.[34]

In place of university scholars who claimed the authority of science, Palmer and his followers cited business leaders as the real experts in the practical world of handwriting. Business colleges had been the first to use muscular-movement penmanship, it was pointed out—Palmer himself, of course, ran a few—and penmanship supervisors argued that businessmen looked for trained Palmerians when they hired employees. At the high school level, penmanship played its most prominent role in the commercial course of training. And many administrators regarded schools as a whole as preparation for a world of work shaped by the demands of business. More generally, they looked to corporate leaders as professional role models whose personal bearing and managerial strategies could be imitated in the running of schools.[35] When the business community placed its imprimatur on the Palmer method, how could the schools look elsewhere?

The attitudes held by school administrators toward academe and the business world only partly explain the popularity of the Palmer method; they do not account for the willingness of these same people to compromise or even delete aspects of that method or their enthusiasm for aspects of the academics' program. To grasp the logic behind these choices, we must look to the larger agenda administrators set for their schools, for it was compatibility with this agenda that determined how handwriting would be taught in the public schools of progressive America. Palmerian drill and the enforcement of right-handedness on the one hand and quantitative measurement on the other, though components of conflicting approaches to handwriting instruction, met that criterion.

As school administrators saw it, the task of the school was not narrowly instructional but more broadly social, economic, and even cultural. For them, the fact of compulsory education meant that classrooms would be filled with children who in other times or societies would never have been there—the half-fed, the half-washed, the half-witted. It was the school's job to reform delinquents, assimilate foreigners, and produce workers of the right kinds and in the right numbers to meet the demands of business. Schools were to neutralize threats to the established order and graduate boys and girls who fit into that order with a maximum of efficiency and a minimum of complaint.[36]

Of course, many of these goals had been shared by antebellum educators. They too had faced the problems of urban poverty, foreign immigration, and a changing set of social relations and workplace realities. Where they differed from educators of the early twentieth century was in the means they employed to achieve their ends. Whereas their instructional regimen took as its highest goal the strengthening of the conscious will, later educators dispensed with the will, indeed with any conscious mental process, in their pedagogical approach. The new method of choice was the training of the body, and nothing less than the authority of science would be cited to explain and justify this approach. Ultimately, the shift in pedagogical methods amounted to a reconceptualization of the educational process—and of its subjects. Victorians perceived students as characters to be formed. Moderns perceived them as bodies to be disciplined.

In the late nineteenth and early twentieth centuries, a wide variety of academics, professionals, and policy makers reconceptualized the human being as a human body, rather than as a human mind. That reconceptualization occurred in fields as diverse as occupational medicine, scientific management, and pedagogy—indeed, wherever it was desirable to imagine control over a human subject as the relatively simple one of physical rather than mental control. In disciplining bodies, experts from many fields could draw on the prestige of the biological, physical, and social sciences. The doctrine of evolution underpinned an understanding of the individual as an organism; the laws of thermodynamics, as a human motor.[37]

The new science of psychology adopted these same paradigms, especially as it developed into an applied field.[38] In the new laboratories that justified the psychologist's self-image as a pure scientist, human consciousness might continue to play some role through the first decade of the twentieth century, but as applied in the clinic, the factory, and especially the school, psychology had no use for consciousness. From the second decade of the twentieth century, behaviorism, which dismissed consciousness as epiphenomenal, dominated psychological thinking, but even before the doctrine of behaviorism was enunciated, psychologists had disposed in their applied work of older notions of the human mind that emphasized such conscious and volitional processes as reason and will; they focused instead on the unconscious functioning of the brain and consequent behavior of the human organism.

Nowhere was this trend more clear than in the field of education, which dominated applied psychology, indeed, American psychology in general, from the 1890s. According to psychologists, learning consisted of neither the progressive strengthening of mental faculties nor the progressive mental control of physical ones but the physiological imprinting of habits into the neuromuscular structure of the human organism (fig. 37). Education was habit formation, plain and simple: the use of repetition to ingrain behavior into the physical organism so that it becomes automatic. Clearly, scientific pedagogues like Frank Freeman and educational psychologists like Charles Judd drew on this understanding of education when they represented writing as a neuromuscular reflex. But so too did Palmer. As we have seen, Palmer, like the professors, stressed movement over form, placed pedagogical emphasis on drill as the method of implanting unconscious muscular habits, and denied the conscious will any role in the mature act of handwriting. Palmer was no psychologist (although in the 1920s he did begin to cite the literature of educational psychology), and academics had spent decades attacking him as an amateur.[39] But he was acting on the same cultural impulse as his academic opponents, the desire to control students by imagining them as little other than bodies that required physical discipline. School officials also acted on this impulse, so that from their point of view, it made little difference whether they allowed themselves to be guided by Palmer on the one hand or Freeman on the other. School penmanship programs may appear to have been eclectic; in fact, they reflect a deeper cultural coherence.

Given the understanding of learning as motor learning, it stood to reason that instruction would focus on the body. In the concrete setting of the school, that interpretation made particular sense in the case of those pupils perceived as intellectually undistinguished and therefore destined for manual labor. In such cases—and given the needs of the modern economy, they would have to constitute the majority of students—training the body would logi-

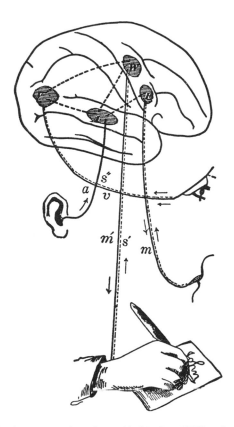

37. Handwriting as physiological habit, from William James,
Principles of Psychology, 1890.

cally occupy the center of the curriculum. Manual and vocational education, in particular, were justified as appropriate ways to educate what one principal called the motor-minded child. But motor learning functioned as a type for the transmission of all socially desirable behaviors. When playground reformers supervised schoolchildren in exercises and games, for example, they looked to provide urban youth with a wholesome recreational alternative to the streets, but they also hoped to develop in their charges a willingness to follow directions, move to an externally imposed rhythm in tandem with others, and subordinate individual energies to the good of the "team." These were lessons educators hoped would carry over into the adult world of work.[40]

When, therefore, in the first three decades of the twentieth century, penmanship was reclassified out of the three R's into the manual arts, handwriting instruction did not take a secondary place in the curriculum. On the contrary, as a skill appropriate to "motor-minded" children and as a form of motor learning, it fit squarely within the school's social and cultural agenda. Not surprisingly, penmanship used many of the methods of physical education to achieve many of the same goals. Often penwork was preceded by a series of preparatory calisthenics, for example, which, like the handwriting drills themselves, were executed precisely and simultaneously by the school-children in time to the military-style commands of their teachers (fig. 38). (Leta Severance Hiles suggested that teachers commence with "At Attention!" while J. Albert Kirby's students were ordered to "Present Arms!")[41] Like both manual education and supervised playground activity, penmanship would reform the dangerous, assimilate the strange, discipline the unruly, and accustom the dissatisfied to their role in life.

Handwriting educators were among the most vocal advocates of penmanship training as the way to reform the behavior of school toughs, implicitly identified as belonging to the social class destined for manual labor. Speaking before the Eastern Palmer Penmanship Teachers' Association in 1910, Joseph S. Taylor outlined the disciplinary value of muscular-movement writing. By training the body, one trained the mind—"cultivation of motor control is mental discipline"—and therefore the entire pupil. Even more remarkable were Taylor's claims for the "ethical value" of the Palmer method. "Children who are inapt at book-study and intellectual pursuits always take to any kind of manual exercise," he explained, whether that exercise be drawing, shop, or handwriting. Take the next step—praise the good penmanship of an otherwise troublesome child—and watch the pupil's self-respect rise. Penmanship training therefore ranks "among the most valuable aids in reforming 'bad' children" and has been "the initial step in the reform of many a delinquent."[42]

Across the country, the supervisor of penmanship for the Long Beach, California, schools agreed. "Many are the pupils who have great difficulty in gaining book lore, but who find the manual arts attractive," wrote Leta Severance Hiles. "To such the consciousness that they can do even one thing well is a powerful inducement toward the mastery of something less attractive." Like Taylor, Hiles hailed the confidence-building effects of penmanship training as a way of turning around problem pupils. "Who cannot recall at least one 'bad boy' who has been completely reformed by some one of the manual arts?" she asked rhetorically. "Muscular movement penmanship has many such to its credit. Teachers and supervisors are called upon quite as much to reform as to form and inform." Hiles was explicit about just what reformation entailed. "Pupils learn before they finish the elementary school that proper conventions must be observed in order to preserve social order and relations," she wrote. "In no subject can a tendency to tear down conventions be discovered more easily than in penmanship and nowhere can we

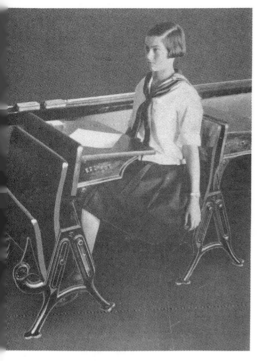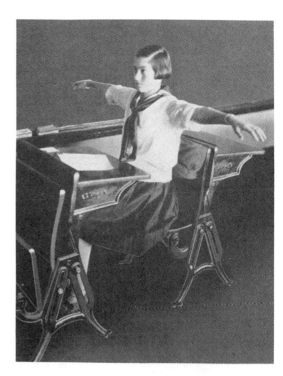

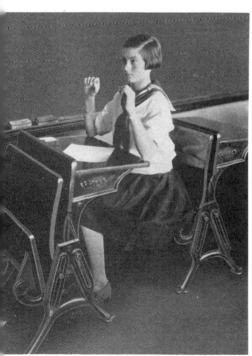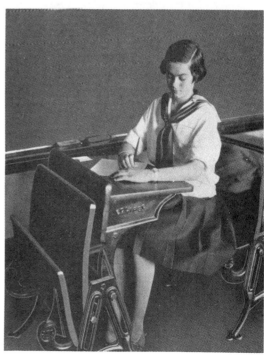

38. Penmanship calisthenics, 1924.

better impress upon pupils the desirability of obeying, to a reasonable degree, the conventional lines which all social beings are bound to recognize."[43]

If conformity to the rules of the Palmer method engendered conformity to the conventions of society, then deviation from penmanship conventions was a form of antisocial behavior. Left-handedness in particular became a proxy for social deviance. It is well known that lefties had long been regarded with mistrust as "sinister" human beings. That mistrust was not dismissed as superstition in the early twentieth century, despite the scientific cast of the era. Indeed, science was used to validate the suspicion of left-handed people, transforming the mistrust into the kind of fear and loathing usually reserved for those who are deemed to pose a social or cultural threat. But this is precisely how lefties were perceived. For Cesare Lombroso, the noted criminologist, left-handedness was primarily associated with the mentally and morally inferior, which was why it was "ordinarily found among women, children, and savages"; why women button their clothes, children trace a line, and Arabs (a "people little civilized") write from right to left; and why felons and lunatics are disproportionately left-handed. Further scientific investigations claimed to verify the correlation of left-handedness with criminal behavior and insanity and to prove its association with mental retardation, epilepsy, and psychopathic tendencies.[44]

These "scientific" studies were immediately popularized. The *Literary Digest* wondered "Are the Left-Handed Inferior?" and *McClure's* ran an exposé of "The Ways of the Left Hand." Edwin Tenney Brewster, the *McClure's* muckraker, noted "a disproportionate number of left-handed adults among criminals, insane persons, imbeciles, epileptics, vagrants, and social failures of various sorts." He argued as well "that sinisterity is slightly more common, in the lower strata of society than in the higher, among negroes than among white persons, and among savages than among civilized races." (But on the greater proportion of sinistrals among females than males: "This fact has probably no significance.") "All these unfortunate beings have something the matter with them"—the "brain is jerry-built," Brewster elaborated elsewhere—"and that something is, in most cases, congenital and beyond all hope of avoidance or reform." Just in case any of his readers had missed what was really represented by left-handedness, Brewster continued:

> The curious thing about the inheritance of left-handedness
> —which, as we have seen, depends on a peculiarity of
> the brain—is that it resembles closely the inheritance of
> two other peculiarities which are also dependent on brain
> structure—namely, mental ability and moral excellence. A
> sound and capable stock, like a right-handed one, breeds

true generation after generation. Then something slips a cog, and there appears a left-handed child, a black sheep, or an imbecile. An imbecile or scapegrace parent married to a normal spouse may have half his children like himself. Two weak-minded, criminal, or degenerate parents always have all their children bad.

Drawing the eugenical noose even tighter, Brewster concluded with the observation that "the one overwhelming and significant difference among men is in the native quality of their brains," while "the one difference in human brains that is most easily made out and most conveniently studied, as it is transmitted from one generation to another, modified by training or affected by breeding" is handedness.[45] If left-handedness could symbolize or even directly point to a whole range of the most dangerous social pathologies, then it is small wonder that it became a target of pedagogical eugenics.

Lefties symbolized social danger, but immigrants were the real thing. Here penmanship training held great promise, much as it had with the "delinquents" of New York City or the "bad boys" of Long Beach, California. Many drew the link between the dangers posed by foreigners and their inability to read and write—indeed, many of the legislative attempts to restrict the influx of Southern and Eastern Europeans had focused on a literacy test—and that logic suggested that immigrants be trained to read and write in carefully managed ways.[46]

One obvious way was to lace instructional materials with a heavy dose of assimilationist and nationalist ideology. Thus among the pages of the Bureau of Naturalization's *Federal Citizen Textbook* were a series of handwriting copy texts that made clear the importance of adopting American ways and adhering to American laws. One series began with fill-in-the-blank sentences: "My name is _____. I live in _____. My address is _____. I attend evening class at _____. My wife's name is _____. My children's names are _____." But the final statements in the series would admit of no individual variation: "They are American children. I wish to be an American citizen. My wife wishes to make an American home." Ideological conformity and patriotic obedience would have to follow on cultural assimilation. "I am not bound to be loyal to the United States to please myself," copied the prospective citizen by way of handwriting practice. "I am bound to be loyal to the United States because I live under its laws and am its citizen; and whether it hurts me or whether it benefits me I am obliged to be loyal."[47]

More often, though, it was the process rather than the content of handwriting instruction that was represented as having positive effects on the foreign-born and their children. In 1911 journalist Philip Robert Dillon

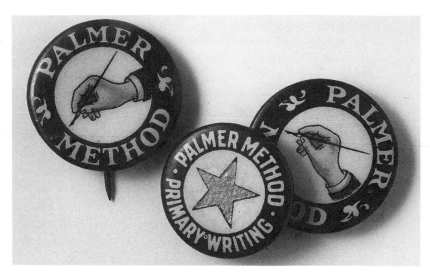

39. Palmer method buttons.

visited an elementary school in New York City's Lower East Side, a neighborhood populated largely by Eastern European Jewish immigrants, and described the "dark-eyed, strangely pale-faced" pupils practicing their handwriting. Dillon reported that the Palmer method had a "powerful hygienic effect" on these immigrant pupils, imparting physical grace where once there was only coarseness. More critical, it transformed a potentially unruly mob into a well-disciplined regiment. Watching the Palmer drill from the back of the schoolroom, remarked Dillon, "the sensation is as pleasing as the feeling one gets when looking at the backs of a fine platoon of soldiers moving away in a level street."[48]

As Dillon presented it, however, students loved practicing their penmanship. "Do you like to write?" he asked Martha Bovitz, a third-grader whose father "keeps the baths." A smiling Martha answered " 'Yes, sir,' " then added that she practiced not only in school but at home as well. "Last night," she reported with pride, "we made capital I's." Some children, like Abraham Krasnow, the ten-year-old son of a suspenders peddler, looked forward to receiving a Palmer pin for their efforts (figs. 39, 40), but according to Dillon, the enthusiasm these children felt for learning how to write sprang from a far more profound source, what he described as a kind of spiritual thrill the children experienced as they participated in the Palmer drills. " 'Heads up high!" the teacher announced as she commenced the drill, " 'Dip! 1-2-3-4-5-6-7-8-9-Ten'—like a watch ticking—'up-down-in-out-swing-out-up-down-in-out-come-out-swing-along-swing-along'—she beats the time two hundred syllable counts a minute." The pupils are carried away, reported Dil-

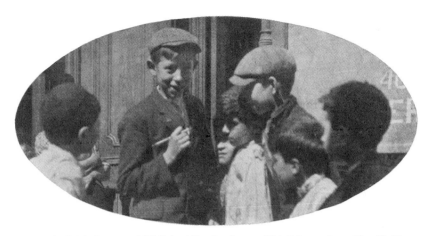

40. "Ain't Mickey grand!" Michael Butsky shows off his Palmer pin on New York's
Lower East Side, 1911.

lon, swinging "in time with the wonderful rhythm. Why, it could get to be
an ecstasy. It could arouse the poet." What was so emotionally satisfying, not
to say exquisite, about the Palmer drill was the degree to which it suggested
the cadence of modern American life. The pupil could feel, elaborated Dillon, that in "this method of handwriting is the same impulse that is moving
all the civilization of the era."[49]

Dillon was not alone in linking the Palmer method to cultural assimilation through the medium of the "rhythm" of modernity. James J. Roberts, an
insurance executive, explained that the Palmer method "embodies a subtle,
dynamic force . . . in perfect harmony with the spirit of the age, the spirit of
fast progress. . . . The day of the copy book and the teaching injunction—
'Now children, slow and careful!'—has passed. In penmanship, as in all other
mediums of the life of today, the dominant thought is 'Swing along fast!'"
If "the great work of New York schools is the making of intelligent and
competent citizens out of the vast body of conglomerate material that comes
from Europe," concluded Roberts, then "it has seemed to me that the new
system of writing is one of the strongest factors in the accomplishment of
this task."[50]

With all the talk of ecstasy and energy, one might be tempted to understand the gospel of Palmerism as a kind of liberation theology. Indeed,
Palmer represented the automatism of the writing movement as something
that relieved the conscious mind of its burdens and released the marvelous
energies of the body. In some respects, then, the Palmer method can be numbered among the harmonial faiths of the day, stretching from Christian Science through New Thought and Mind Cure, all of which represented the

unconscious as a bottomless reservoir of rejuvenating energy. In this context, it is not surprising that writer's cramp was identified as a symptom of neurasthenia, a disease characterized as one of nervous debilitation.[51]

But Palmer's image of the writing arm as a kind of perpetual motion machine fits more squarely into schools of thought that sought to regulate rather than liberate. It is reminiscent of the scientific research that redefined the laboring body as a human motor, identified bodily fatigue as the source of worker discontent, and pointed to the sciences of the human body as the solution to labor problems. Thus one penmanship manual of 1904 defined the human body as "a machine by which writing is done," and in her discussion of muscular movement handwriting, Leta Severance Hiles noted: "We carefully consider how to minimize waste of energy in a machine. Is the human machine of less importance?" Palmer's tireless writing arm also recalls the ideology of scientific management. Small wonder that Frank Freeman used F. W. Taylor's stopwatch and Frank Gilbreth's camera in conducting his research. What Palmerians described as the exhilarating rhythm of modernity might have been nothing other than the deadening regimen of the factory or office. Even the inspirational Dillon compared the beat of the Palmer drill to the "regularity and sureness of machinery."[52]

In this sense, the effect of penmanship training could be expanded beyond the cultural assimilation of immigrants to the assimilation of all Americans into a more broadly defined cultural milieu, namely, the world of modern social and labor relations. Thus, one penmanship authority compared the automatization of the handwriting movement to the Taylorized, hierarchical workings of a modern office. "After the work has been arranged, systematized, and methodized by the head," explained the *Zanerian Theory of Penmanship*, "it can then be handed down to the subordinates or assistants for execution."[53] Emphasizing the role of hand over head in handwriting accustomed penmanship pupils to the fact that they were far more likely to become factory hands than company heads.

Hiles was even more explicit about the use of penmanship training as a dry run for the postschooling realities of life. Penmanship pupils, she wrote, "must follow with military precision the directions of the leader," much as in the future they would have to obey their bosses. Nor did Hiles pretend that the foot soldiers in the penmanship—and by extension, the industrial—army would march with gladdened feet. "Everyone must learn, sooner or later, that much discipline may be gained by keeping steadily at work not interesting in itself," she wrote, adding chillingly: "The muscle should work with a fatalistic steadiness." In New York City, superintendent Joseph Taylor concurred. It is best to interest children in their penmanship drills, he wrote, but not absolutely necessary. "When the law of interest fails to achieve our purpose, we must apply force. Children will have to learn that we live in a world where we can not always do only what we like. Many hard and disagreeable things must be done by people who would rather be doing something else. The dead must be buried, sewers must be cleaned, dishes must be washed three times a day. It is just as well to let children know from the start that some parts of school work are not very interesting, but that they must nevertheless be done."[54]

Penmanship training had long been used as a method to produce character types who would play the economic roles defined by the leaders of that economy as desirable. It had also been used in a larger sense to exert control over the bodies of penmanship pupils in order to discipline the body politic. The two goals overlapped. In the Victorian era, the physical regimen of handwriting instruction was supposed to produce individuals who could control their "lower" impulses through acts of will. These people would make good producers. In the early twentieth century, penmanship pedagogy aimed to make good workers, and it promised to do so by neutralizing the will and transforming the body into a machine. The thousands of ovals executed by penmanship pupils would one day translate into the thousands of bolt-tightenings executed by Henry Ford's workers—or by Charlie Chaplin in *Modern Times*. Automatic writing would produce automatons.

If the classroom was a preview of the world of work, then students had best be evaluated in comparison with their schoolmates and given assigned places in the hierarchy. It was already time to get accustomed to the postgraduate experience of classification. This was the job of standardized tests. Although some school authorities hoped to bring students within a particular grade up to a uniform handwriting standard, the message delivered by school surveys, in which test scores were all over the map, seemed to be that some students were natural-born penmen and others natural-born scribblers. Penmanship supervisors and teachers acknowledged differing levels of competence when they tracked students in handwriting ability groups. Some groups spanned grade level and age boundaries. Others segregated students within a particular class. Hiles, for example, recommended that pupils in each classroom be divided into A and B groups, "it being understood that those who prove themselves unworthy of being in the 'A' group will have a place in the 'B' group." Hiles allowed for some movement back and forth between A and B, but the same cannot be said of the Z students, who seem to have been classified as permanent handwriting dullards.[55] This experience of classification and segregation carried over into life beyond graduation, when the battery of ability and achievement tests proved to be self-fulfilling prophecies of social and economic status.

Whatever it lacked in pedagogical consistency, then, the handwriting program that combined Palmer drills, forced right-handedness, and Thorndike scales featured a broader, internal coherence, based on social and cultural rather than strictly educational concerns. Each component of that program served either to minimize the social threat posed by America's diverse school population or to maximize the economic benefit it offered. Some—like Dillon's exhilarating, assimilating, regulating penmanship drills—promised to do both. Handwriting can therefore take its place alongside other components of the progressive school curriculum that both reflected and served the needs of society.

INDIVIDUALITY, STATISTICALLY CONSIDERED

There was an even deeper significance to handwriting instruction in the early twentieth century, however, one that granted it a unique place in the school curriculum. Looming in the background, largely unacknowledged by pedagogues but deeply coloring the meaning of their work, was the practice of handwriting analysis. Not everyone agreed with graphologists when they claimed that handwriting was an index to character, but given the currency of graphological concepts, it could not be missed that how one chose to "read" handwriting indicated how one chose to define and value individuality. And under those circumstances, the teaching of handwriting could hardly remain a neutral proposition free from cultural statements about individual uniqueness and social conformity.

Penmanship authorities rarely made direct reference to graphology. Probably the most widespread indication that they were aware of its popularity was their acknowledgment that many people took pride in a distinctive hand as a sign of individuality and considered handwriting instruction hostile to that individuality. But there is more direct evidence that handwriting pedagogues knew about handwriting readers. Joseph Taylor included an entire chapter on graphology in his *Supervision and Teaching of Handwriting;* similar works included books on handwriting analysis in their bibliographies. Educational psychologists were almost certain to run across reviews and abstracts of graphological works in scholarly journals and to be familiar with the work of fellow psychologists like June Downey. The popularity of graphology and its postulate of universal, characterological individuality could hardly have escaped members of the penmanship establishment.[56]

Certainly nothing in Palmerian teaching methods—the calisthenics, the commands, the counting, the drills—encouraged students to assert their individuality through stylistic innovation. The academic approach to penmanship pedagogy, on the other hand, rested on the explicit recognition of individual differences. Judd's analysis of the acquisition of handwriting skills assumed that each pupil would develop those neuromuscular pathways appropriate to his or her individualized physiological makeup. Freeman's penmanship pedagogy allowed for variations stemming from physiological idiosyncrasy. Thorndike's handwriting scales measured just those differences in handwriting performance; the graded norms they yielded were simply the midpoints of assumed distributions of individual specimens.

Indeed, differences among individuals stand out as one of the primary intellectual concerns of late nineteenth- and early twentieth-century psychologists. The philosophically oriented psychology of the mid-nineteenth century had ignored individual differences because, as Thorndike explained in a 1911 monograph entitled *Individuality*, "it believed in a typical or pattern mind, after the fashion of which all minds were created, and from which they differed only by rare accidents." By contrast, the new physiologically oriented science of psychology, taking its cue from the evolutionary postulate of biological variation, began with precisely these differences and regarded them not as accidental but as the very stuff of the human mind. Each human being, wrote Thorndike, "has an individuality which marks him off from other men. Each has not only *a* mind, the mind of the human species, but also his own specialized, particular, readily distinguishable mind."[57]

Accordingly, psychologists set about studying and measuring what distinguished one mind from the other. In the 1880s the Englishman Francis Galton measured individual differences in such physiological functions as physical strength, keenness of sensory discrimination, and reaction time. In the following decade James McKeen Cattell, who was trained by Galton and later became Thorndike's mentor at Columbia University, undertook similar investigations into individual physiological differences. Meanwhile, the Harvard psychologist Hugo Münsterberg and Alfred Binet began testing individual differences in such *psychological* functions as memory. Binet, of course, later extended this research into the testing of intellectual differences, as did a whole generation of mental testers.[58]

Statistical analysis proved popular among psychologists precisely because it provided a conceptual framework for a science of individual differences. As it first took form in mid-nineteenth-century Europe, statistics had concerned itself with the quantitative delineation of the "average man," a sort of composite human being. By the mid-nineteenth century, however, statisticians— including the father of Alphonse Bertillon—attacked this statistical concept as a meaningless abstraction. They shifted the focus from the norm or average, which was calculated from the quantitative distribution of individual differences, to the distribution itself.[59] Thus the "surface of distribution," often generalized as the bell curve, replaced the average man as the conceptual tool of choice. This form of statistical thinking set the individual within a hierarchy, ranking him with respect to his fellow points along the curve.

Few chose this analytical approach more enthusiastically or pursued its social implications more relentlessly than American psychologists and educators of the early twentieth century. Leta S. Hollingworth, a psychologist and professor at Columbia's Teachers College, celebrated the fact of human individuality as it lends "sparkle" and "charm" to living but, more fundamental, because "organized society needs and will use capacity of all degrees, from that of a man who can load sand on a carrier, and be satisfied thereby, to that of the man who can with satisfaction work out a new theory of inflammation, or construct a drama to interpret existence anew." Given "the shape of the curve of distribution for mental capacities"—Hollingworth assumed a bell curve of I.Q.s—the full range of individuals would appear in America's classrooms, but given the increasing numbers of foreign and poor students, one could expect rather more sand loaders than had gone to school in times past. Thorndike understood individuality in the same terms, not as a celebration of uniqueness but as the building block of social and economic hierarchy. "There is indeed no one habit of thought about human nature more important for the understanding of individuality," he wrote, "than the habit of thinking of the different amount or degrees of each single quality or trait as distances along a scale and of men and women as distributed along that scale each at his proper point."[60] (One recalls here Thorndike's penmanship "thermometer.")

Unlike the Palmerians, who under pressure grudgingly conceded the possibility of individual variation in handwriting, then, academic handwriting authorities like Freeman and Thorndike assumed variation. Indeed, they could not think about handwriting in any other terms. But that did not make them graphologists. How they characterized and accounted for individual differences in handwriting and what they proposed to do with those differences bore little resemblance to the answers provided by the likes of Louise Rice.

To begin with, academics attributed stylistic variations in handwriting to physiological, rather than characterological, idiosyncrasy. For Charles Judd, "one's individual writing is the expression of his individual habit of movement," and those habits could in turn be traced to highly individualized systems of neuromuscular coordination. Freeman noted differences in the proportions and structure of the hand, in handedness, in natural posture, and in neuromuscular coordination as accountable for individual styles of script. The development of an individual handwriting style was not to be prohibited, but the academics hardly meant to encourage variations as a sign of originality; they merely wished to allow for natural variation in the pupils' physiological makeup. By contrast, American graphologists often presented the irrelevance of physiology as proof that their science was valid. They pointed out, for example, that handwriting executed with the nondominant hand or even with the foot is executed in the characteristic style. Similarly, they seized on the automatic writing of hypnotized subjects, multiple personalities, and psychic mediums as evidence that handwriting emanates from the personality, not the body.[61]

Then too, statistical analysis had taught psychologists that "variations usually cluster around one and only one type," rather than the endless variety of types assumed by graphology. Handwriting therefore varied with respect to a single variable, and that variable—handwriting ability—said nothing about personality. Instead, stylistic variations tended to be reduced to those that were good and those that were bad. Frank Freeman, for example, although tolerant of physiologically induced variations, could not help but conceptualize them as deviations and to wonder how many of them might "seriously impair the legibility of the letter" or have a deleterious effect on handwriting efficiency. Indeed, in explaining why some people were good writers and others poor ones, Freeman again pointed to physiological rather than mental characteristics.[62]

Furthermore, many academics conceptualized the level of handwriting ability as characteristic of genetically defined groups, not individuals. Certainly when it came to analyzing actual test scores, the variables that penmanship authorities pinpointed as relevant to handwriting ability were genetic and collective. Experts disagreed on whether handwriting ability correlated with intelligence, the latter perceived as an inherited trait. The psychologist Arnold Gesell said yes (although he felt constrained to qualify just what sort of intelligence that might be since girls performed better than boys), Thorndike said no, but at any rate the question seemed worth pursuing. Most authorities agreed with Gesell that there were sex differences in handwriting ability, and test scores were accordingly broken down along gender lines. It was usually concluded that girls exceeded boys in legibility because of their greater diligence and aesthetic sense. Gesell speculated that whereas girls delight in "the ornamental, the individual, the concrete" (not unlike "imbeciles" who "beg to be allowed to write for 'busy work,' and are content to copy from their readers by the hour"), boys "have a milder interest in form and a more vigorous one in content." Boys exceeded girls in handwriting *speed*, however, because of their greater energy.[63]

Meanwhile, in Virginia, investigators aggregated test scores by race. Because in many cases blacks performed as well as or even better than whites, the results required "interpretation." Thus the survey authors raised the greater age, grade for grade, of black pupils as a factor that potentially skewed test results in their favor, although they ignored other facts relevant to black schools that worked to the disadvantage of black pupils.[64] When psychologists at the University of Denver undertook similar studies on the handwriting ability of blacks and Indians, they ran into similar "anomalies" and explained them away with the same cockeyed reasoning.[65]

Instead of leading back into the hidden recesses of the mind, then, handwriting was a conceptual cul-de-sac, revealing nothing more significant about the individual writer than how large a hand he had or how good a writer he was. For the character and talent revealed by graphologists, the academics substituted physiological traits or handwriting aptitude; for individual uniqueness, genetic variation. If men like Thorndike and Freeman had any say in the matter, people would stop looking in their handwriting for what made them special. They would find no inspirational message there. Given the widespread currency of graphological concepts, however, the statement that handwriting revealed nothing profound about the writer could not be made outside the contemporary conversation about individual identity. It occupied a kind of cultural negative space, open to interpretation as — or even an explicit assertion of — an alternate concept of the self. Under this definition, human beings were not one-of-a-kind individuals; they were the passive products of genetic membership. In these beliefs, the academic psychologists and educators resembled nothing so much as the American scientists who sought to reduce graphology to the same science of genetic differences. Like those scientists, progressive penmanship experts believed that most people must resign themselves to a subordinate status, and they transmitted that message in a debate about handwriting and in the vocabulary of individuality.

THE MANUSCRIPT WRITING MOVEMENT

There was one group of pedagogues, however, who were able to conceptualize handwriting in a new way, a way that was aligned in spirit with the popular urge to read handwriting as an expression of the individualized self. Most of them had received advanced academic training, most of them were lower down on the academic ladder, and most of them were women. Many of the leaders of this group were associated with graduate departments of education; many of the foot soldiers worked in progressive private, public, and university laboratory schools. They agreed with their fellow academics in rejecting commercial systems of penmanship and with experts like Frank Freeman that children are not adults and that handwriting instruction must be adjusted to juvenile motor needs and limitations. Accordingly, they seconded the proposals that small children work with pencil or chalk and practice oversized letters on wide-ruled paper. But their endorsement of these components of the academic handwriting program stemmed from a different logic altogether, which rejected the definition of penmanship as a motor habit. For these innovators, handwriting was a tool of individual expression, and handwriting instruction must take its cue from the individual's inner desire to communicate ideas and feelings to others. A new handwriting program, the likes of which had never been seen before, sprang from these reconceptualizations. It discarded drill; it scrapped cursive; and it placed a premium on individualized writing.

When Bertha E. Roberts, the superintendent of schools in San Francisco, criticized the "lock-step procedure" of the penmanship "penal system" and lamented that "the State is still demanding its pound of fifteen minutes daily," she was referring to that time-honored pedagogical technique endorsed by Palmer and Freeman alike, the formal, synchronized penmanship drill. According to critics like Roberts, this repressive routine flew in the face of the latest scientific findings. "In the past," wrote Edith Underwood Conard of Teachers College, the teacher "stressed handwriting as a skill" and therefore "spent more time on the technique of building up form through endless drill than on finding out what the children wished to write and using this interest and need as a starting point. Recent psychology advocates handwriting as a skill following handwriting as a means of expression." In place of formal drill, then, the modern teacher should substitute what Roberts termed "natural situations for written expression." These might include writing for the yearbook, ordering seeds to plant in the classroom window box, copying poems, filling in invoices of school supplies, sending valentines, recording lunch orders, labeling maps, and making signs.[66]

Even more controversial was the pedagogical use of what we term printing and what was called print-script or, most commonly, manuscript writing. Today we so take it for granted that children print before they learn cursive that it may come as a surprise that this sequence is only a few generations old. Abiah Holbrook, Henry Dean, James French, P. R. Spencer, A. N. Palmer, Frank Freeman all instructed even the youngest of their charges in script. The first manuscript writing promoters called for something even more radical than the system we have today. They wanted to jettison cursive and replace it completely and permanently by printing. Their pedagogical logic allowed no compromise.

English educator Marjorie Wise popularized the new philosophy and technique in America when she arrived in 1922 to teach manuscript writing at Teachers College, Columbia University. By way of this academic connection, manuscript writing enjoyed a rapid and enthusiastic reception among a small circle of progressive private schools and kindred-spirited public schools. Within a year, twenty-seven schools had adopted manuscript writing into their penmanship curriculum, and the numbers rose throughout the decade, leveling off toward the end of the 1920s at 152. Of these, three-quarters were private institutions—experimental, laboratory, and progressive schools—and the rest were public schools located in such wealthy suburbs as Winnetka, Illinois, and Bronxville, New York.[67]

Manuscript advocates emphasized the pedagogical advantages of the new approach: how easy it was to teach and especially to learn, how well it fit the physiological limitations of small children, how legible it was, how it broke down the barrier between reading and writing instruction by scrapping a two-font system. Some of these same claims had been made for other systems of writing, of course—Palmer on legibility, Freeman on juvenile motor skills—but manuscript advocates did not present them as accomplishments in themselves but only as they contributed to a larger end, the facilitation of expression. Because manuscript consisted of simple and discrete letter forms, even the clumsiest children could acquire a serviceable hand in a matter of a few months, at the same time that they were honing their new reading skills. Grasping the meaning of written language for the first time, unburdened by penmanship drill, children would soar almost immediately (by November of the first school year, claimed one authority) into written self-expression.[68]

Many pedagogues, recognizing juvenile motor limitations, had recommended that written work be kept to a minimum in the early grades. In 1901, for example, the penmanship supervisor of the Lakewood, Ohio, schools recommended that students "do very little or no writing until they reach the fourth grade." In 1917 one of Freeman's academic protégés made the same recommendation. Meanwhile Palmer called for early drill in handwriting but made no promises as to form—again, until the fourth grade. Now all that was changed. "Children do not need to become proficient in movement before writing," stated Edith Underwood Conard. "They can produce satisfactory results without resorting to uninteresting, tedious drill. Children write because they have something to tell."[69]

It was because they conceived of handwriting as a means "to tell" rather than as a motor habit—the student as mind rather than body—that most early advocates of manuscript writing insisted that cursive need never be learned, even at a later age, when physiological limitations no longer presented themselves. Supporters of cursive undertook studies to demonstrate the greater legibility or speed of script, and to counter these arguments, manuscript proponents attempted to prove their hand was the clearer or faster one. But for manuscript advocates, these traditional criteria were not the real measures of a successful hand. What really mattered was how conducive a particular hand was to written expression. Why waste time learning cursive, they argued, when that time could be better spent in actual composition?[70]

The new conception of handwriting as a tool of self-expression brought with it a new attitude toward individuality in handwriting. Penmanship authorities had long either discouraged individuality or finessed its existence, but the opponents of drill and promoters of manuscript actively sought to encourage it. Conard, for example, suggested that because the basics of the manuscript alphabet could be acquired so quickly, students would develop "individual characteristic traits" early in their schooling. Indeed, above the third grade, pupils should be encouraged to experiment with "individual original forms" in order to establish "characteristic strokes" and "to work up an attractive signature."[71]

Ironically, one of the objections to manuscript writing was precisely its alleged lack of individual distinctness. For some critics, the problem was a practical one—a manuscript signature could be forged easily and would therefore carry no legal weight—but others fretted that "manuscript writing would result in a uniform, stereotyped handwriting which would destroy individuality." Manuscript supporters insisted that there would be no such consequences. "The feared loss of individuality, would, perhaps, appear an advantage to those critics who for many years preached the doctrine of uniformity, and to the teachers who have with varying degrees of success laboured to obtain it," wrote one such advocate sarcastically. "But in practice it is found that the same mental and physical peculiarities which cause the cursive writing of different persons to show individuality and character operate with at least equal force in the case of print-script."[72]

The pedagogical program that abolished cursive, and standardized drills with it, conceptualized the penmanship pupil as a writer, not a handwriter—in other words, as an individual expressing ideas. Individuality in handwriting constituted a metalayer of expression, revealing the mind and soul that produced those ideas. In their fundamental reconceptualization of what handwriting is, these handwriting reformers partook of the impulse that transformed graphology into a mass phenomenon in the early twentieth century. Thorndike, Freeman, and Wise all spoke of individuality and handwriting in the same breath, but only the last defined these terms and linked them the way Louise Rice did. Only Wise and Rice perceived handwriting as an expression of the soul rather than the body, and only they interpreted the individuality of handwriting as characterological in origin.

What made graphology so popular in this era, of course, was the general sense of embattled individuality, a sense shared by manuscript advocates. For all their academic credentials and scientific experiments, American manuscript advocates viewed school and society through the lens of progressivism but also of antimodernism. It was the fate of many a phenomenon suffused with the antimodern animus to be absorbed into the very system it opposed and to be transformed from a vehicle of protest into one of accommodation.[73] Manuscript writing was one such phenomenon. During the 1930s and 1940s, it spread rapidly from its small circle of progressive private and elite public schools to the public and parochial schools of America. After World War II it was in standard use. Frank Freeman endorsed it. A. N. Palmer's company saw the printing on the wall and began to publish manuscript writing teaching materials.[74]

But when it moved into the pedagogical mainstream, manuscript writing was altered almost beyond recognition, losing the philosophical framework that gave it its original reason for being. It became accepted in the same spirit as were pencils, wide-ruled paper, and oversized letters, as a concession to the motor-skill limitations of small children. If printing made sense only because five-and six-year-olds were clumsy, then it also made sense for children to learn cursive once they were old enough to control their fingers properly. If in the 1920s, the few American schools that did teach manuscript taught it as a lifelong hand, in the 1930s and 1940s, it entered the public school system as a temporary measure, one to be discarded once students were physiologically ready to learn "real" writing. During the Depression some traditionalists protested against any use of manuscript, while a few progressive school teachers held out for manuscript as a permanent hand but, for the most part, pedagogical debates deteriorated into the relatively trivial discussion of when the manuscript-cursive transition should be made (fig. 41).[75] After that, history closed over, and it was forgotten that only two generations earlier children had labored over cursive from their first day in school.

In the first decades of the twentieth century, academic experts set their scientific penmanship against the business penmanship of A. N. Palmer and his ilk. When it came time for school systems to design their penmanship programs, however, they made no distinct choice between the academics and the Palmerians. Instead they chose selectively from both, modifying certain aspects of each. Yet there was a deeper coherence to this seemingly eclectic approach. Educators looked to their penmanship programs to teach children how to write, of course, but also to train and shape students in a much larger sense. They wanted to reform the dangerous, assimilate the foreigner, and prepare all their charges for the limitations and regimentation of life and work after school. Handwriting instruction could carry such an educational agenda because of the way both academics and Palmerians conceived of penmanship—as a motor habit rather than a conscious act of mental will. If learning to write meant becoming a muscular automaton, then penmanship training could indeed imprint habits of discipline and conformity in a highly effective manner.

By removing Palmer and his critics from the narrow context of progressive education and placing them into the framework of broader cultural concerns, we can see that both contributed to a larger cultural debate sparked by graphology. In the first third of the twentieth century, graphology reached

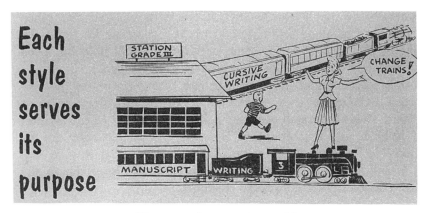

41. The manuscript-to-cursive transition.

Americans in mass proportions for the first time. It was not successful in convincing every American that handwriting is an individualized expression of character, but through its sheer popularity, it did set the terms under which any conception of handwriting would have to operate. When, therefore, both Palmerians and academics characterized individual variations in handwriting styles in ways that minimized or trivialized their significance, theirs was an unspoken but nonetheless palpable challenge to the graphological vision of uniqueness. And when in the 1920s a new group of handwriting pedagogues, the advocates of manuscript writing, reconceived of handwriting as self-expression, their ideological kinship with graphology was equally unmistakable.

What is perhaps most telling about these controversies, what places them so identifiably in the early twentieth century, is the fact that they took place in the same conceptual space, defined by two sets of oppositions: individuality and conformity, body and mind. Graphologists and manuscript writing advocates celebrated the uniqueness of every human being, identified it as characterological in nature, and represented it as the basis of human freedom and potential. Academic educators and psychologists also accepted individuality as a fact of life, but they defined individuality in such a way that its implications were anything but liberating. For them, differences among individuals were ultimately physiological or genetic in origin. They added up to a statistical distribution of ability, and turning that bell curve on its side gave one a picture of the social order. Individuals did not realize unique potentials; they simply accepted the lot granted to them by their location along the curve, their place in the hierarchy. As they had for decades, then, Americans expressed their most dearly held, earnestly conceived visions of human destiny and social organization in visions of the self, and they read and they inscribed those selves in their handwriting.

THE SYMBOLIC FUNCTIONS
OF OBSOLESCENCE

"Is it time to boot out cursive writing?" reads the title of a recent article in an educational periodical. For Jack McGarvey, a middle-school teacher in Connecticut, the answer is obvious. "Word processing technology is speeding ahead at such a rapid rate," he writes, "that right now we may be living in the last days of the pencil-and-paper age." He recommends "the booting out of cursive and the booting up of computers to teach typing" in its stead.[1]

Long before word processors signaled the imminent end of the pencil-and-paper age, other forms of technology—the telegraph, telephone, dictaphone, copy machine, and, above all, the typewriter—posed the same threat to the handwritten word. True, when the typewriter was first introduced in the 1870s, its superiority to handwriting was not immediately obvious. Professional copyists averaged twenty-five to thirty words a minute; early typewriters, employed by untrained operators and prone to mechanical jamming, could not produce the same results. But from the 1880s, with the tremendous expansion in office work and technical improvements in typewriters, the typist, often working in combination with a stenographer, quickly displaced the traditional office copyist. Such rapid change boded ill for the future of the pen.[2]

"In these days," wrote handwriting instructor Daniel Ames in 1894, "when labor-saving devices of stupendously revolutionary import have become so common as to almost cease to excite wonder, no one has a license to say how long . . . it will be before the urgent commercial need which called the typewriter and shorthand writer into being will invoke and materialize some still more potent agency to relieve the busy pen and clicking keys." Ames believed it was "tolerably safe to say, that, so long as one shred of our present commercial and social fabric survives," the pen would remain indispensable, but this was not as reassuring as it might have first appeared. For one, just how much of the social fabric would survive into the twentieth century was not entirely clear in 1894; it was not just labor-saving devices that were stupendously revolutionary in the year of the Pullman strike. But more important, Ames could not really justify the continuing dominance, or even relevance, of the pen. At best he could claim that just as "Father Spencer" had reformed penmanship to make it faster and more efficient because he recognized that "pens that were good enough to keep apace of the easy-going stage-coach of our grandfathers" would no longer do in an age of steam and electricity, so too would a new generation of reformers organize another speed-up of the penmanship assembly line.[3] Austin Norman Palmer promised to do just that when he turned the handwriter himself into a machine—fast, efficient, reliable, untiring. Unchained from the copybook regime of carefully rendered drawing, liberated from fatigue by whole-arm movement, released into the potential of perpetual motion, the trained Palmerian was the equal of any mechanical device because he had, in fact, become one.

Still the typewriter refused to go away. In 1910 no less a figure than E. L. Thorndike argued that employers who want "high qualities of writing" simply "buy machines to produce them." In 1924 Pittsburgh's supervisor of commercial education reported that "since the introduction of the typewriter in our junior high schools, there is a tendency to minimize the importance of the teaching of handwriting." Within a few years, the typewriter threatened to eliminate even elementary school penmanship as school systems experimented with teaching kindergartners and first-graders how to type instead of how to write. By 1956 an article in *Look* magazine maintained that "handwriting nowadays is as out-of-date as the hand-lettered book." Business letters, government forms, even social correspondence, it was argued, are all typed. "Why, then, do we force children to master this archaic system of putting ideas on paper?"[4]

When writing machines threatened to render handwriting obsolete, some people were only too happy to keep up with the times, move into the technological future, and leave penmanship behind as a now archaic skill. But the major consequence of the typewriter and computer for penmanship was not the extinction of handwriting but its symbolic association with the past. Precisely because it seemed to be outmoded, the skill of penmanship came to symbolize a world fast disappearing or already gone. For those who yearned for times past, the resurrection of older pedagogical methods, historic scripts, even traditional writing tools, promised to turn the clock back and stave off the ill effects of modernity. Of course, just what lay in that imagined golden age and just what was wrong with contemporary life were matters of disagreement. For those who advocated the revival of historic calligraphy, the target was the machine itself, for it counted human creativity and individuality among its many casualties. For pedagogues, on the other hand, the target was what they perceived as the laxity and permissiveness of modern society. Individuality had been allowed to run amuck, they believed, with disastrous consequences for society at large. Today, members of the general public remember their early handwriting experiences with nostalgia. Handwritten letters recall the more intimate society of childhood days, while recollections of the Palmer method call forth bittersweet memories of a past when moral certainty still seemed possible.

At the same time that penmanship pedagogues faced down the machine by transforming their students into machines, another group of penmen sought to rescue handwriting from the corrupting influences of machine civilization altogether. Included in this group were those members of the English

Arts and Crafts movement whose particular mission was to revive the art and craft of the medieval scribe. The leader of this calligraphy revival was Edward Johnston, a descendant of such wealthy Quaker families as the Buxtons, Gurneys, and Barclays who had been reared in genteel but diminished circumstances. After graduating from the University of Edinburgh, Johnston devoted his time to studying historic manuscripts at the British Museum, distilling aesthetic and moral wisdom from their pages. Then in 1898 Johnston met W. R. Lethaby, principal of the Central School of Arts and Crafts in London and friend of William Morris, the foremost figure in the English Arts and Crafts movement. By 1899 Johnston was teaching calligraphy at Lethaby's school, and in subsequent years, he offered similar courses of instruction at the Camberwell School of the Arts and the Royal College of Art. In 1906 he published what quickly became the bible of the calligraphy revival in both Britain and America, a combination technical treatise and Arts and Crafts manifesto entitled simply *Writing & Illuminating, & Lettering.*[5]

To anyone familiar with the English Arts and Crafts movement, Johnston's book presents few ideological surprises. At root it was a protest against the soullessness of modernity and the human alienation engendered by the machine. As Lethaby explained in an editor's preface, factory production had transformed the craftsman, who had once derived joy and meaning from the creation of objects both useful and beautiful, into a drudge. The result was both an aesthetic and a human disaster. For separate design from workmanship, thought from labor, and both degrade, the first into empty ornament and silly affectation, the second into "the dreary routine of hack labour." Ugliness and alienation thus went hand in hand.[6]

Calligraphy revivalists from Johnston on represented the history of handwriting as just such a tale of division and degradation. Medieval scribes had produced pure letter forms whose beauty stemmed from the truthful expression of scribal tools and materials. Their labors offered the kind of spiritual satisfaction possible only where the aesthetics of script and the manual labor involved in executing it were understood as inseparable. Into this craftsman's paradise stepped the devil of mechanical reproduction, specifically, the printed copybook filled with copperplate engravings of handwriting models. Engravers had modified handwriting according to the technical idiosyncrasies and requirements of the graver's tool, rounding the letters, increasing the slope, and adding connecting strokes, hairstrokes, loops, and flourishes. The result was the degraded cursive, bereft of the beauty and individuality natural to the hand of the craftsman-scribe but impossible to achieve under the mechanical regimen imposed by the printed copybook.

What was needed was a return to both the conditions of work and the design principles that predated mechanical reproduction. Accordingly, Johnston

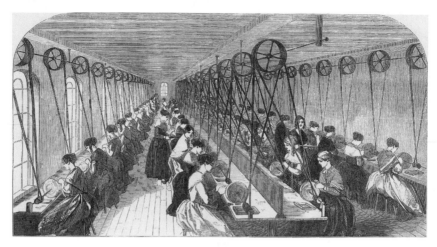

42. The mass production of pens, 1851.

discarded the steel pen in favor of the quill and machine-manufactured paper in favor of parchment (figs. 42, 43). He even recommended that the modern-day scribe work only by daylight. As for the scripts themselves, these must be the pure unconnected hands of the pre-copperplate, pre-printing press era, letter forms based in the properties of scribal tools and materials. Johnston described the uncials and half-uncials of Roman, English, and Irish origin as "true pen-forms," which had "the characteristic, simple strokes and beautiful, rounded shapes which flow from the rightly handled reed or quill." From now on, the calligrapher and his pen must reassert their priority—historic and aesthetic, ultimately moral and social—over the typographer and printer, establishing the art of the manuscript as the foundation for the art of the printed book. "The foundations of typography and book decoration," wrote Johnston, "may be mastered—as they were laid—by the planning, writing, and illuminating of MSS. in book form."[7]

Johnston was no simple reactionary. His idea was not to adhere slavishly to the past but to bring its spirit into the present. Modern scribes should not be mere copyists, reproducing the hands of the past as mechanically as printing presses. To be sure, "developing, or rather *re*-developing, an art involves *the tracing in one's own experience of a process resembling its past development*," he wrote, but "it is by such a course that we, who wish to revive Writing & Illuminating, may *renew* them, evolving new methods and traditions for ourselves, till at length we attain a modern and beautiful technique." The new day at hand would thus entail a revival of personal creativity and individual expression. Indeed, writing could not be considered good unless it had what Johnston called personality, that is, unless it had "the characteris-

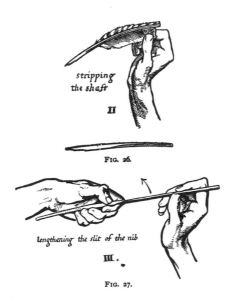

FIG. 26.

lengthening the slit of the nib

III.

FIG. 27.

43. The craft of quill pen-making as revived by
Edward Johnston, 1906.

tics which distinguish one person's hand from another's." Personality would
come gradually, naturally, and invariably as the scribe, allowing his hand first
to be trained by the pen, eventually came "to master and control the pen,
making it conform to his hand and so produce Letters . . . as much his own
as his common handwriting."[8] To affirm the value of human individuality,
then, Johnston reasserted the dominance of the hand over the pen and the
human over the machine. The contrast with the Palmer method, the dominant pedagogy of the time, could not have been greater, for Palmer—and his
academic critics as well, for that matter—visualized the writing hand as passive to unconscious habit and the human being engaged in the act of writing
as little other than a machine.

The revival of interest in historic calligraphy bore many fruits: the establishment of calligraphical societies, the use of traditional hands by fine-book
designers, and scholarly research in the history of handwriting. It achieved
its widest impact, however, in an area where its role has been largely forgotten—namely, in the introduction of manuscript writing into the schools.
Johnston himself gave impetus to this movement when in 1913 he spoke before a conference of London schoolteachers. His Arts and Crafts sensibility
was not lost in the subsequent pedagogical enthusiasm for the new style of

handwriting. Manuscript advocates accepted Johnston's version of the history of handwriting as a narrative of degradation and traced the provenance of their letter forms to the purer hands of a preindustrial era. So convinced were British manuscript advocates of the link between mechanical reproduction and aesthetic and human degradation that Marjorie Wise rejected the term *print-script* to describe the new alphabet. "Printing is a mechanical device for multiplying copies of written material," she wrote sharply. ". . . It is as misleading to suggest that children model their handwriting on anything as uniform and characterless as printing, as it was for earlier penmen to base their writing on the work of the engravers."[9]

As we have seen, the manuscript writing movement lost something in the translation from England to the United States. What began as a form of social criticism and a program for social reform on one side of the Atlantic became an aesthetic critique and style on the other. The same is true of the calligraphy revival. Americans who advocated a revival of historic scripts did so almost wholly on aesthetic grounds; for them it promised the revival of a "leisurely art of writing" characterized by charm and beauty. Thus Johnston's book inspired a generation of American book designers but not a generation of social reformers.[10]

Still, Johnston's spirit was not completely forgotten. Throughout the twentieth century, there remained small but loyal groups of calligraphical devotees. Then, in the late 1960s and early 1970s, historic calligraphy experienced a second renaissance. Broad-edged pens sold briskly; a rash of instruction and pattern books appeared; classes in calligraphy drew healthy audiences. This new revival was not a duplicate of the movement Johnston had inspired—it advocated different kinds of writing materials and styles—but it appropriated much of the philosophy of the original Arts and Crafts movement. "People are reacting against slickness and mass production," commented Lou Strick, president of a calligraphic supply company, in 1975. Explaining why her calligraphical manual contained mistakes, Jacqueline Svaren penned: "REJOICE IN HUMANESS! Machines can't make mistakes." One journalist classified the "massive resurgence of interest in formal calligraphy" with the phenomenon of subway graffiti. "Both," he noted, "have elements of rebellion." Just what might incite rebellion was made clear in the subtitle of his article: "In which it is revealed that *your very own handwriting* has been determined by giant technohistorical forces beyond your control and what many people are doing to combat the situation." Perhaps the clearest indication that this revival, like its Arts and Crafts precursor, combined social criticism with the envisioning of a social alternative was the inclusion of a section on calligraphy in that countercultural wishbook, the *Whole Earth Catalog*.[11]

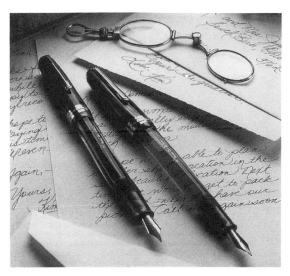

44. The symbolic associations of the fountain pen, from an
advertisement in an upscale catalog, 1993.

In the 1990s the impulse behind the calligraphy revival has taken a con-
sumerist turn. Manufacturers of expensive fountain pens link individuality
not with traditional writing styles but with traditional writing *instruments*
(fig. 44). A pen can be "a tool to help you focus your thoughts into self-
expression and hence, self-fulfillment," reads one upscale catalogue. Unlike
the ballpoint and rollerball pen, the fountain pen "accentuates personal expression." The catalogue specifically recommends a Waterman Le Man fountain pen (price: $279), noting that the company "was 14 years old when it won
its medal at the World Exhibition in Paris in 1900," and that "a Waterman
was used to sign the Treaty of Versailles." While "other pens merely write,"
the advertising copy reads, "a Waterman expresses." Not to be outdone, the
Parker company markets its Sonnet fountain pen (price: $250) with the ques-
tion: "Is your life going to be poetry or prose?"[12]

What is implicit in these advertisements is the notion that individuality is
not only a purchasable commodity but an expensive one; only wealthy people
can afford the luxury of individuality. That notion is reflected and reinforced
by the commercial use of script in general, however generated, to indicate
status and wealth. Invitations to social functions, for example, if they have
any pretense to elegance and class, must be in script. Compare, too, the signature of the Lord and Taylor department stores—visually lavish, unrestrain-
edly sprawling, purposefully illegible—with the block-letter logo of K-Mart
(figs. 45, 46). Clearly, script functions as a sign of both status and individu-

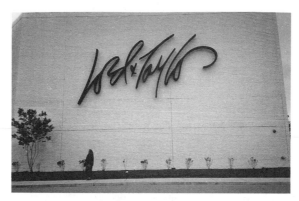

45. The commercial symbolism of illegible script.

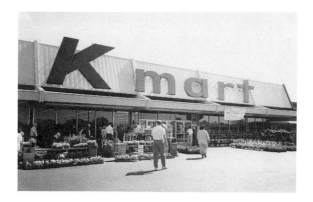

46. The commercial symbolism of block print.

ality. Only the well-off can afford to learn, and then to flaunt, the rules of penmanship.

What horrified most observers of penmanship in postwar America, however, was not its lack of individuality but its illegibility. Invariably, that illegibility was contrasted with the high quality of handwriting that allegedly existed in earlier generations. As early as 1934, one pedagogue compared penmanship samples from 1879, 1912, and 1931 and found the most recent specimens to be significantly inferior. Yet by the time such evaluations took center stage in debates over handwriting, in the postwar era, it was the Depression decade that was cited as the last decade of quality handwriting. In the fifties and sixties, penmanship jeremiads appeared by the dozens in both educational periodicals and such popular magazines as *Time*, *McCall's*, the *Saturday Evening Post*, the

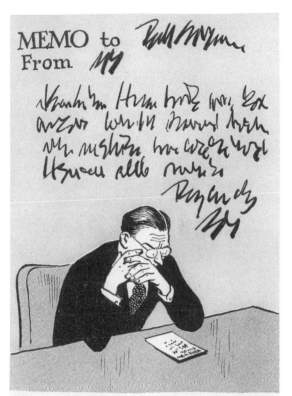

Executives have secret codes of their own.

47. A lighthearted penmanship jeremiad from the 1950s.

Saturday Review, Reader's Digest, and *Science Digest* (fig. 47). These articles carried such dramatic titles as "Nation of Scrawlers," "What Ever Happened to Good Penmanship?" "The Lost Art of Handwriting," "Why Our Kids Can't Write," and "The Moving Finger Writes—But Who Can Read It?"[13]

In explaining the decline in penmanship quality, educators and journalists pointed to changes in instruction. During the Depression, penmanship supervisors had been fired in the interests of economy. When prosperity returned, they were never replaced. Meanwhile, teachers' colleges ceased training future teachers in the techniques of penmanship. When the novice teachers did enter the classroom, they taught their students how to print, and the transition to cursive was never accomplished satisfactorily. Then in the postwar years, many educators accepted the principle first articulated by early advocates of manuscript writing, namely, that since the purpose of writing is to communicate, handwriting must be regarded as a tool, not an end in itself.

Accordingly, they deemphasized formal drill, eliminated the use of handwriting scales, integrated handwriting instruction into the rest of the curriculum, and generally gave penmanship a lower priority than had teachers of the prewar years.[14]

Outside of the school, technology made further inroads in the practice of handwriting. "Nowadays," noted one observer in 1955, "people compose all their letters on a typewriter, or dictate them to a tape recorder, or sign them with a rubber stamp, and, as a result, the muscles of the thumb and forefinger which were formerly employed to grip a pen have fallen largely into disuse, except for picking olives out of Martinis or occasionally pinching stenographers in crowded elevators." For most commentators, the erosion of penmanship skills by technology evoked darker thoughts. "Slogans like, 'Don't Write —Telegraph!' and the increasing reliance on the telephone, typewriter, dictating machines and electronic brains," commented the *Saturday Evening Post*, "would seem to be making handwriting as obsolete as smoke signals" and turning America into "a nation of scrawlers." Even grade-schoolers, noted an article in the *Reader's Digest*, are likely to type their school compositions. "While older folks shake their heads and remember the delight of being complimented on 'writing a good hand,'" this author concluded, "the hum and click of dictating, duplicating, photo-copying, calculating, card-punching and teleprinting goes on, and an automation-bent world asks the advocate of better penmanship, 'Why?'" (fig. 48).[15]

There was at least one quick answer to this question. Bad handwriting cost the nation's businesses money, *big* money, seventy million dollars a year, ran the estimate in 1955. Illegible inventory lists, long-distance telephone records, sales receipts, packing slips, and address labels translated into economic inefficiency that sapped not only company revenues but also our nation's economic strength. "Assassins of the written word lurk in every community," warned the *Saturday Evening Post* with typical Cold War paranoia. Ten years later, the fear that poor penmanship might sabotage America in its battle against communism was made explicit in a headline that appeared in the *Pittsburgh Press:* "Scribblers Pour Millions Down Drain; Omitted Hyphen Doomed Space Rocket."[16]

More was at stake than dollars, though, more even than America's ability to compete efficiently with the Soviet Union. The real problem was moral decay. Schoolchildren had been allowed to avoid the hard work of learning how to write; they had been held to progressively lower penmanship standards; freedom and self-expression had won out over legibility and speed. As a result, handwriting in this country had "hit an all-time low." Critics laid the blame at the feet of progressive educators. "Harsh rigidity has no place in schools and should have been eliminated without mourning," wrote

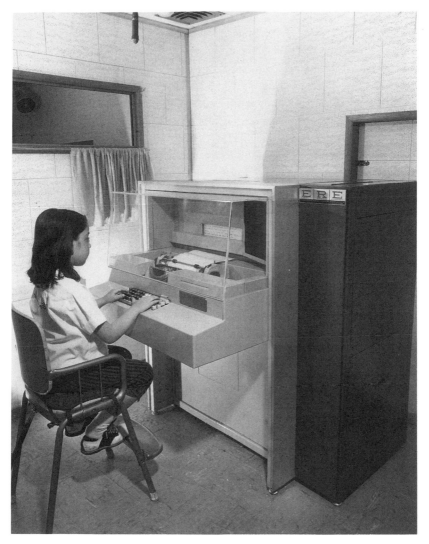

48. The author learning to read and write at a computer keyboard, 1963.

handwriting educator E. A. Enstrom in 1965, but "permissiveness is equally difficult to defend." Enstrom excoriated those teachers who "tore down" conventions without replacing them, who latched onto "new, bizarre, spectacular, and unusual" notions in favor of the "old, reliable essentials," and who thereby assumed a "laissez faire attitude" toward the acquisition of handwriting skills to the point of "criminal neglect."[17]

Ten years later professor of education Patrick Groff also contrasted standards of penmanship quality enforced by teachers before the war with "the indefinite requirements of the new 'legibility.'" Clearly, all that was asked of students today was for their handwriting to approach some minimum "threshold of recognizability." Groff especially bemoaned the jettisoning of handwriting scales. Evidently, some new-style educators had argued that the use of scales coerced students into copying the handwriting on the scale, while others had equated their use with the imposition of a uniform model. Either way, what Groff regarded as a foolish fixation with individuality had eliminated a sound pedagogical practice.[18]

Enstrom, Groff, and their fellow critics were reacting to some real changes in handwriting instruction. Thorndike scales had indeed been left by the wayside, and many a teacher supplemented rote copying of penmanship models with more substantive assignments integrated into the "language arts" curriculum. On the other hand, when we look at actual practice in the postwar classroom, if it was not a continuation of the Palmer method, nor was it so different from what these critics recommended. Model cursive alphabets still ran the length of the blackboard, children still copied individual letters over and over in workbooks, and teachers continued to put a premium on neatness in handwriting, even if they no longer attached a number to their evaluations. Indeed, as the "new math" displaced the old, and "whole language" displaced phonics, penmanship instruction in many ways remained a quaint remnant of the past. That essential conservatism is evident in, for example, the reluctance to adopt up-to-date writing instruments for penmanship instruction. Long after fountain pens became common, even long after they were used for other school subjects, they were largely prohibited from penmanship practice in favor of the antiquated pen staff and steel pen. Ballpoint pens faced similar resistance. Certainly the days of Palmerian push-pulls were gone by the fifties, but then again, even the harshest critics of "permissive" penmanship pedagogy never called for their return. One may not even be able to point to a decline in legibility as the root cause of criticism, since many studies challenged the notion of a precipitous descent into slovenliness.[19]

What really provoked critics of the new penmanship pedagogy was not classroom practice or even classroom results so much as the rhetoric of progressive penmanship pedagogy. That rhetoric was suffused with ideals of self-expression, individuality, and freedom (fig. 49). "Handwriting was one of those early school experiences I have tried to repress," wrote Donald Graves, one such progressive educator. "Recollections of endless circles, precise spacing, and comments about my untidiness take away my energy. I had no idea that handwriting was for writing. . . . Handwriting was punishing, mindless, and mechanical, whereas composing with ideas was lofty and worthwhile." For others, it was the transition to cursive that shaped their subsequent ap-

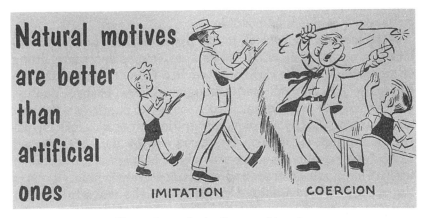

Natural motives
are better
than
artificial
ones   IMITATION   COERCION

49. Progressive methods of penmanship pedagogy.

proach to handwriting. "My papers were always returned covered with directions for more cursive practice," recalled Jack McGarvey. "So, while most of the other kids got to play with white paste, I spent my time with eyes turned upward, meditating upon the charts of perfect cursive above the chalkboards. I tried hard to copy what I saw, but no amount of practice helped. And because my cursive was unattractive, I thought I had nothing important to say. My teacher agreed."[20]

Inasmuch as the new penmanship philosophy championed individuality and self-expression, it represented the permissiveness of American schools and, in an even larger sense, the general societal permissiveness that was thought to have led to the softness of youth in the fifties and their unruliness in the sixties. "I know Donald Graves says not to worry about handwriting; it will come," one teacher was quoted as saying. "But I can't help wonder if it really will, so I teach handwriting." Such teachers were held up as islands of commonsense discipline in an era in which the philosophy of "letting it all hang out" and "taking it easy" had produced a generation of lazy, indulged, and undereducated children. Critics also took to task those educators who objected to traditional methods of penmanship instruction as inhibiting individuality in handwriting. "Handwriting may become so personalized," wrote one such commentator in 1972, "that no standard form or style will be used to guide initial instruction." The result is chaos, not freedom, illegibility, not self-expression. During the next decade, permissiveness seemed to pose more of a threat to American economic competitiveness than social order. "The 1960s notion that handwriting reflects one's personality," maintained an educator in 1986, "is no longer seriously considered in times of increased demands for legible handwriting." Businessmen in particular, the argument

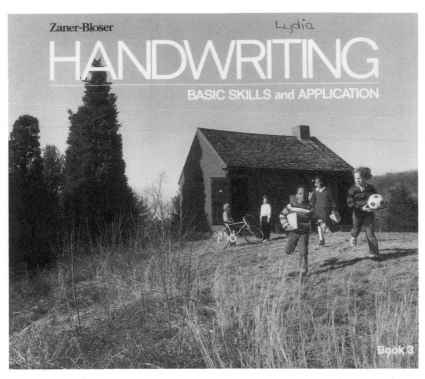

50. Ye Olde Penmanship. Nathan Hale's schoolhouse on the cover of a present-day handwriting workbook.

continued, recognize the hidden costs of illegibility fostered in the name of self-expression.[21]

Under such circumstances, even the Palmer method could be recalled approvingly, not despite the monotony and discipline it entailed but precisely for those qualities. Two Palmer-trained pedagogues, for example, remembered practicing row upon row of ovals and circles and letter elements. "That is the way it is done and someone made us do it," they wrote sharply in 1975. "Children are rarely *made* to do anything in school any more. They have more freedom of choice, which is good,"—or so they felt they must say—"but, given freedom of choice, who among us would elect the dullness and repetition which characterized the penmanship lessons of yore?" These educators admitted that "the old way of learning penmanship isn't right for the child of today" but seemed reluctant to let go of it. Good penmanship seemed less at issue than the discipline and conformity that had been supplanted by freedom and self-expression. What needed to be recovered was not so much "the penmanship lessons of yore" as "yore" itself (fig. 50).[22]

It is not just educators for whom penmanship has taken on symbolic meaning. Americans as a whole respond to handwriting as resonant of the past. For some, this is a past of close-knit social relationships and easy familiarity; they implicitly contrast it with the impersonality and even the self-estrangement of modern life. "It was like a little time capsule," is the way one journalist described a handwritten letter she had received. "The words weren't evenly spaced and the lines weren't straight. This was friendlier than a letter dashed off on a computer. . . . It was a real letter—the kind people don't have time to write anymore." Reporting on her decision to handwrite a letter of condolence, another journalist remarked that "when you write your own hand, those loopy tracks reveal much more about you than the cold impersonality of laser print." She characterized "the erosion of the role of handwriting" as "one more way we let machines separate us from ourselves and from each other."[23]

When in 1994 Ronald Reagan revealed himself to be a victim of Alzheimer's disease in a handwritten farewell letter to the American public, it was as much the medium as the message that lent his words their emotional intensity. "After nine years of studying him with objective coldness," wrote Edmund Morris in the *New Yorker,* "I confess that I, too, cried at that letter, with its crabbed script and enormous margin (so evocative of the blizzard whitening of his mind)." Had it "been keyboarded to the world," the letter would have lost half its poignancy, continued Morris, for "matrix dots and laser sprays and pixels of L.C.D." can never convey "the cursive flow of human thought" embodied in script, "every waver, every loop, ever character trembling with expression." The association of handwriting with the past was so strong for Morris that the term he chose to describe "the human immediacy of script" was an archaic one: "*Quick.* Perhaps that's the word—used in its old, full sense of 'quick with life.'" Meanwhile, in St. Cloud, Minnesota, a company called Written by Hand exploits that same association between script and a lost world of intimate human contact by employing 150 workers to pen thousands of handwritten appeals for charity. The ink is blue, a sign that the letters are not computer generated. Ballpoint pens are used, even though—in fact, precisely because—they are messy. "You can't smudge a laser job," explains the company's marketing agent.[24]

When in 1991 television talk-show host Phil Donahue recalled his childhood, he too crystallized the past in images of handwriting. What he remembered with painful ambivalence, however, was not a world of intimacy but of certainty. He was not so much saddened by the anomie of modern society as terrified by the intellectual freedom it allows and the moral relativism it sustains. In a "letter" sprinkled with facsimiles of handwriting, he confessed to

Sister Mary Andrew, his recently deceased teacher, that he somehow missed "the law and order of Catholic school in the '40s," and felt curiously unfulfilled and insecure, "pushing uneasily forward and occasionally looking back at the absolutes that enabled us to sleep so well in childhood." Once those absolutes had been imprinted upon him too. "From my fifth year to my 13th," he recalled lovingly, "you were the chalk, I was the slate—the *tabula rasa* in which you wrote so profoundly, so beautifully," in "the unmistakable hand of a Catholic nun." For Donahue, that hand stood as a symbol of the discipline and certainty of a bygone era. "Your penmanship, the excellent standard to which we all aspired, was the ultimate expression of a soon-to-be-extinct fine art that had its root in the Palmer Method, which began with the slow rendering of what seemed like a million ovals on thin blue lines across plain white paper of 'official' size. You made your way slowly through rows of perfectly aligned desks, reviewing the work of each oval-maker and adhering strictly, as did each student, to the one-word admonition you had written majestically on the blackboard. Silence." As a boy, Donahue had done well in penmanship, but as he now admitted, and as his signature—reproduced for all the world to see—witnessed, he had long strayed from the Palmerian model. "You would call this 'backsliding,'" he wrote Sister Mary Andrew. "This small sin of the flesh is just one reminder of the many shortfalls between doing what you said and doing what I do. My adult life has been, like my penmanship, sliding backward."[25]

Like enthusiasts of historic calligraphy, then, both conservative penmanship pedagogues and souls troubled by modernity hope to recover a lost past by recovering the way we used to write. Calligraphers turned to historic scripts to place themselves in a time before machines squelched individuality. Educators turned to traditional instructional methods and writing instruments to place themselves in a time before the softness and permissiveness of the postwar world created disorder and degeneration in the name of individuality. Ordinary people, unnerved by modern society, remember the past of penmanship with yearning and nostalgia. As an "obsolete" phenomenon, handwriting in the twentieth century, especially in the postwar world, acquired a new symbolic association with the past. Clearly, there was more to the meaning of handwriting than the literal content of its message.

But then, that had long been the case. Since at least the eighteenth century, when print endowed script with its own set of cultural meanings and functions, handwriting has acted as a medium of the self, capable of defining, regulating, and revealing the self. Penmanship pedagogues used handwriting instruction to create individuals of a particular type. Their students did not always cooperate, and once grown up, they looked in script, perhaps their own, perhaps those of the famous, for alternate visions. Handwriting experts, graphological detectives, and legal theoreticians did not always share those visions, but they also understood that handwriting could be read for both authorial sense and authorial identity. We too must be sensitive to the many meanings earlier generations inscribed in their scripts. Then, as historians, we can learn the art and mystery of graphology and read the character of the past.

NOTES

PROLOGUE

1. Robert Darnton, *The Great Cat Massacre and Other Episodes in French Cultural History* (New York: Basic, 1984), 78.
2. While overlapping in theory and practice, each of these subfields addresses different interests and relies on different methods and assumptions. See Roger Chartier, "Frenchness in the History of the Book: From the History of Publishing to the History of Reading," *PAAS* 97, Part 2 (1987): 299-32, and David D. Hall, "Readers and Reading in America: Historical and Critical Perspectives," *PAAS* 103, Part 2 (1993): 337-57.
3. The literature in this field is vast and rapidly growing; so far it has focused mainly on France, Britain, and America. For an introduction to the field as a whole, see Carl F. Kaestle, "The History of Literacy and the History of Readers," *Review of Research in Education* 12 (1985): 11-53; Roger Chartier, "Texts, Printings, Readings," in Lynn Hunt, ed., *The New Cultural History* (Berkeley: University of California Press, 1989), 154-75; and Robert Darnton, "History of Reading," in Peter Burke, ed., *New Perspectives on Historical Writing* (University Park: Pennsylvania State University Press, 1991), 140-67. As the study of reading applies to American history, see William L. Joyce et al., eds., *Printing and Society in Early America* (Worcester, Mass.: American Antiquarian Society, 1983); David D. Hall and John B. Hench, eds., *Needs and Opportunities in the History of the Book: America, 1639-1876* (Worcester, Mass.: American Antiquarian Society, 1987); Cathy N. Davidson, ed., *Reading in America: Literature and Social History* (Baltimore: Johns Hopkins University Press, 1989); and Carol Armbruster, ed., *Publishing and Readership in Revolutionary France and America* (Westport, Conn.: Greenwood, 1993).

4. For an overview of these methodological controversies, see Kaestle, "History of Literacy," 20–36.

5. Walter J. Ong, *The Presence of the Word* (New Haven: Yale University Press, 1967), 51–69. See also Jack Goody and Ian Watt, "The Consequences of Literacy," in Jack Goody, ed., *Literacy in Traditional Societies* (Cambridge: Cambridge University Press, 1968), 27–84; Elizabeth Eisenstein, *The Printing Press as an Agent of Change: Communications and Cultural Transformations in Early-Modern Europe* (Cambridge: Cambridge University Press, 1980); Walter J. Ong, *Orality and Literacy* (New York: Methuen, 1982), 117–23; and Walter J. Ong, "Writing Is a Technology That Restructures Thought," in Gerd Baumann, ed., *The Written Word: Literacy in Transition* (Oxford: Clarendon, 1986), 99–102.

6. David D. Hall, *Worlds of Wonder, Days of Judgment: Popular Religious Belief in Early New England* (Cambridge: Harvard University Press, 1990); Brian V. Street, *Literacy in Theory and Practice* (Cambridge: Cambridge University Press, 1984), and Michael Warner, *The Letters of the Republic: Publication and the Public Sphere in Eighteenth-Century America* (Cambridge: Harvard University Press, 1990), 20–21; Chartier, "Frenchness in the History of the Book," 309–14.

CHAPTER ONE

The Lost World of Colonial Handwriting

1. John Locke, *An Essay Concerning Human Understanding*, ed. Peter H. Nidditch (1690; Oxford: Clarendon, 1975), 104; Locke, *Some Thoughts Concerning Education*, 5th ed. (London, 1705), in *The Educational Writings of John Locke*, ed. James L. Axtell (Cambridge: Cambridge University Press, 1968), 263–64, 264n.

2. Benjamin Franklin, *The Autobiography of Benjamin Franklin* (New York: Modern Library, 1981), 112.

3. David D. Hall, "Introduction: The Uses of Literacy in New England, 1600–1850," in *Printing and Society in Early America*, ed. William L. Joyce et al. (Worcester, Mass.: American Antiquarian Society, 1983), 1–47; E. Jennifer Monaghan, "Literacy Instruction and Gender in Colonial New England," in *Reading in America: Literature and Social History*, ed. Cathy N. Davidson (Baltimore: Johns Hopkins University Press, 1983), 58–59, 68–70; Mary Beth Norton, *Liberty's Daughters: The Revolutionary Experience of Women, 1750–1800* (Ithaca: Cornell University Press, 1980), 257–59; Kenneth Lockridge, *Literacy in Colonial New England: An Enquiry into the Social Context of Literacy in the Early Modern West* (New York: Norton, 1974), 38–43; Alan Tully, "Literacy Levels and Educational Development in Rural Pennsylvania, 1729–1775," *Pennsylvania History* 39 (July 1972): 301–12; Ross W. Beales, Jr., "Studying Literacy at the Community Level: A Research Note," *Journal of Interdisciplinary History* 9 (Summer 1978): 93–102; Linda Auwers, "Reading the Marks of the Past: Exploring Female Literacy in Colonial Windsor, Connecticut," *Historical Methods* 13 (Fall 1980): 204–14; William J. Gilmore, "Elementary Literacy on the Eve of the Industrial Revolution: Trends in Rural New England, 1760–1830," *PAAS* 92 (April 1982): 87–177; Robert E. Gallman, "Changes in the Level of Literacy in a New Community of Early America," *Journal of Economic History* 48 (September 1988): 567–82; F. W. Grubb, "Growth of Literacy in Colonial America: Longitudinal Patterns, Economic Models, and the Direction of Future Research," *Social Science History* 14 (Winter 1990): 451–82; Joel Perlmann and Dennis Shirley, "When Did New England Women Acquire Literacy?" *William and Mary Quarterly*, 3d ser. 48 (January 1991): 50–67; Gloria L. Main, "An Inquiry into When and Why Women Learned to Write in Colonial New England," *Journal*

of Social History 24 (Spring 1991): 579-89; Mary Beth Norton, "Communications," *William and Mary Quarterly,* 3d ser. 48 (October 1991): 639-45.

4. Monaghan, "Literacy Instruction," 54-58; Hall, "Uses of Literacy."

5. *A Copy Book of the Newest and Most Useful Hands* (London, 1649); Lewes Hughes, *A Copy Book* (London, n.d.); Ambrose Heal, *The English Writing-Masters and Their Copy-Books, 1570-1800,* 2 vols. (Cambridge: Cambridge University Press, 1931), 1:62; *New York Gazette or Weekly Post Boy,* 2, 23, 30 September 1762, in Robert Francis Seybolt, *The Evening School in America,* reprint ed. (New York: Arno Press and the New York Times, 1971), 23; Boston Registry Department, *Records Relating to the Early History of Boston,* vol. 15: *A Report of the Record Commissioners of the City of Boston, Containing the Records of Boston Selectmen, 1736 to 1742* (Boston, 1886), 288; [Benjamin Warner], *Manual of the System of Teaching Reading, Writing, Arithmetic, and Needle-Work in the Elementary Schools of the British and Foreign School Society* (Philadelphia: Benjamin Warner, 1817), 20-22; *The Children's Tutor* (London, [1679]); Ray Nash, "American Writing Masters and Copybooks," *Publications of the Colonial Society of Massachusetts* 42 (1952-56): 347-48. Hall and Monaghan also argue that reading instruction preceded writing instruction. For similar arguments with regard to England during this era, see R. S. Schofield, "The Measurement of Literacy in Pre-Industrial England," in *Literacy in Traditional Societies,* ed. Jack Goody (Cambridge: Cambridge University Press, 1968), 316-17; Margaret Spufford, *Small Books and Pleasant Histories: Popular Fiction and Readership in Seventeenth-Century England* (London: Methuen, 1981), 22, 27, 29, 34-35; Spufford, "First Steps in Literacy: The Reading and Writing Experiences of the Humblest Seventeenth-Century Spiritual Biographers," *Social History* 4 (October 1979): 407-35; and Victor E. Neuberg, *Popular Education in Eighteenth-Century England* (London: Woburn, 1971), 55, 93.

6. In a Louisiana case of 1821, for example, the deponent testified that "he is thirty years of age; cannot well read writing . . . cannot do much more than write his own name," and it was further revealed that "his mother wrote often, as his father kept a tavern, and she kept the accounts when he was absent," but that in her old age, she ceased to write and instead "made her cross, or mark, instead of signing." In the antebellum South, many more slaves could read than could write, presumably because access to the Bible was less subversive than access to a written pass. In the United States Census of 1870, respondents were questioned separately on their ability to read and to write, and enumerators were warned that "it will not do to assume that because a person can read, he can, therefore, write." In 1878 one penman recommended "classes for practice in reading various kinds of writing" (10 Martin's Reports [O.S.] 410, 414; Janet Duitsman Cornelius, *"When I Can Read My Title Clear": Literacy, Slavery, and Religion in the Antebellum South* [Columbia: University of South Carolina Press, 1991], esp. chap. 3; United States Census Office, *Ninth Census of the United States, 1870: Instructions to Assistant Marshals* [Washington, D.C., 1870], 11; H. Russell, "Classes in Reading Writing," *PAJ* 2 [December 1878], 1); Edgar Rice Burroughs, *Tarzan of the Apes* (1914; New York: Penguin, 1990), 53-56, 87-88.

7. Monaghan, "Literacy Instruction."

8. Thomas Watts, *An Essay on the Proper Method for Forming the Man of Business* (London, 1716), in *Education for the Mercantile Counting House: Critical and Constructive Essays by Nine British Writers, 1716-1794,* ed. Terry K. Sheldahl (New York: Garland, 1989), 18-23.

9. Nowhere in the literature on colonial penmanship instruction does the name of a female writing master appear. Perhaps the first woman associated with penmanship instruction in America was Sophia Bingham, whose *Ladies Copies,* published in 1802, was likely used by her brother Caleb at his writing school in Boston. There is no evidence, however, that she

was an active teacher. In England, of the 450 writing masters whose biographies appear in Heal's *Writing-Masters,* four—Hester Inglis, Mary Johns, Elizabeth Lucar, and Elizabeth Penniston—are female. Only the last, the daughter of writing master Thomas Topham, appears to have actively taught penmanship, as is evidenced by a trade card dating from the end of the 1600s that advertises instruction to "Young Ladies and Gentlemen" at "the Maidens Writing School in Ave Mary Lane" (Ray Nash, *American Penmanship, 1800-1850: A History of Writing and a Bibliography of Copybooks from Jenkins to Spencer* [Worcester, Mass.: American Antiquarian Society, 1969], 8, 71-72; Heal, *Writing-Masters,* 1:84).

10. *Boston News-Letter,* 10, 17, 24 September, 1 October 1761, and *Boston News-Letter,* 14-21 March 1708/9, in Robert Francis Seybolt, *The Private Schools of Colonial Boston* (1935; Westport, Conn.: Greenwood, 1970), 45, 11; *Pennsylvania Gazette,* 19 February, 19 March, 4, 18 April, 20 June 1751, in Seybolt, *Source Studies in American Colonial Education: The Private School,* reprint ed. (New York: Arno Press and the New York Times, 1971), 39; *South-Carolina Gazette,* 3, 10, 17 September 1744, in *A Documentary History of Education in the South before 1860,* ed. Edgar W. Knight, 5 vols. (Chapel Hill: University of North Carolina Press, 1949), 1:653.

11. *Boston Weekly News-Letter,* 13 September 1753, in Seybolt, *Private Schools of Colonial Boston,* 36; *Boston Evening Post,* 12, 19, 26 September 1748, in Seybolt, *Evening School,* 60.

12. "The Pen," in Charles Snell, *The Art of Writing* (London, 1712), n.p.; Seybolt, *Source Studies,* 69-82. The Longs' advertisement appeared originally in *Rivington's New York Gazetteer,* 27 January 1774.

13. William Carver Bates, "Boston Writing Masters before the Revolution," *New England Magazine,* n.s. 19 (1898-99): 403-18; Ray Nash, "Abiah Holbrook and His 'Writing Master's Amusement,'" *Harvard Library Bulletin* 7 (Winter 1953): 88-90; and E. Jennifer Monaghan, "Readers Writing: The Curriculum of the Writing Schools of Eighteenth Century Boston," *Visible Language* 21 (Spring 1987): 167-213.

14. William Bentley, *The Diary of William Bentley, D.D.,* 4 vols. (Gloucester, Mass.: Peter Smith, 1962), 3:228; T. Cooper and D. J. McCord, eds., *The Statutes at Large of South Carolina* (Columbia, South Carolina, 1836-41), 2:346, in Seybolt, *Source Studies,* 52n; *Pennsylvania Gazette,* 18 December 1750, in Seybolt, *Source Studies,* 98-99; *Virginia Gazette,* 8 June 1769 and 11 April 1771, in Knight, ed., *Education in the South,* 1:657, 659.

15. E. Jennifer Monaghan discusses the content of copybook maxims in "Readers Writing." For an example of a student copybook containing both penmanship and arithmetical material, see that of Andrew Bigelow (1785) in the Penmanship Collection, 1762-1848, American Antiquarian Society, Worcester, Massachusetts. For examples of virtuoso ciphering books, see those of Mary Clough (1762), Rebeckah Salisbury (1788), and Nathaniel Allen (1805) in the same collection. Typically, these contain arithmetical rules and computations, tables of weights and measures, and mercantile word problems that require complex conversions of weights and measures and calculations of compound interest, brokerage, discount, profit and loss, etc.

16. John Ayres, *Arithmetick and Writing* ([London], [1682]); [John Colson], *An Arithmetical Copy-Book* ([London], [1710?]); Joseph Champion, *The Tutor's Assistant in Teaching Arithmetic* (London, [1747]). Among the writing masters who published arithmetic books we find John Ayres, Humphrey Johnson, H. Legg, Francis Walkingame, Charles Snell, George Shelley, and, most prominent, Edward Cocker. Snell also published a number of accounting texts. Heal, *Writing-Masters;* Sheldahl, ed., *Education for the Mercantile Counting House.*

17. John Ayres, *The Accomplish't Clerk or Accurate Penman* (London, [1683]); William Ban-

son, *The Merchants Penman* (London, [1702]); George Bickham, *The United Pen-Men for Forming the Man of Business* (London, 1743); James Scruton, *Mercantile Penmanship* (n.p., [1779]). Many of these copybooks were dedicated to merchant patrons. Ayres, for example, dedicated his book to Francis Boyer, bookkeeper and accountant of the East India Company. Bickham dedicated his to "the Merchants, and Tradesmen of Great Britain."

18. "George Fisher," *The American Instructor: Or, Young Man's Best Companion* (Philadelphia, 1748).

19. Heal, *Writing-Masters*, 1:6, 7, 11, 13, 18, 19, 27, 29, 68, 76, 102, 118, and pl. 3, 6, 14; Nash, "Abiah Holbrook," 91. Heal quotes from Langton's *A New Copy Book of Round Hand* (n.p., [1723?]) on 1:68.

20. *Hamlet*, 5.2.33-36; Thomas De Quincey, *Confessions of an English Opium-Eater*, rev. ed. (1856; Oxford: Oxford University Press, 1955), 82; William Barrow, *An Essay on Education* (London, 1802), 276-77; John Jenkins, *The Art of Writing* (Cambridge: Flagg and Gould, 1813), xlvii.

21. "Fisher," *American Instructor*, 28. For instructions in quill, ink, and paper preparation, see ibid., 27, 29-30, 43-45. For thorough discussions of writing tools and paraphernalia, see Joyce Irene Whalley, *Writing Implements and Accessories: From the Roman Stylus to the Type-writer* (Detroit: Gale Research, 1975); Joe Nickell, *Pen, Ink, and Evidence: A Study of Writing and Writing Materials for the Penman, Collector, and Document Detective* (Lexington: University Press of Kentucky, 1990); and Michael Finlay, *Western Writing Implements in the Age of the Quill Pen* (Carlisle, Eng.: Plains Books, 1990).

22. Jenkins, *Art of Writing*, xlv-xlvii; Nash, "Writing Masters and Copybooks," 349, 358-59; Nash, "Abiah Holbrook"; Bentley, *Diary of William Bentley*, 2:31-32, 96; Nash, *American Penmanship*, 25-30. For a striking example of a virtuoso specimen, see the one executed in 1783 by Joseph Washburn, in the Joseph Washburn Family Papers, Box 1, Folder 1, Yale University, New Haven, Connecticut.

23. John Bancks, "A Poem, On the Universal Penman," in George Bickham, *The Universal Penman* (London, 1743; New York: Dover, 1954), 5.

24. John Bancks, "The Representative," in Bickham, *Universal Penman*, frontispiece; Isaac Disraeli, "The History of Writing Masters," in *Curiosities of Literature*, 9th ed., 6 vols. (London: Edward Moxon, 1834), 5:291-92.

25. Bickham, *Universal Penman*, 37.

26. M. T. Clanchy, *From Memory to Written Record: England, 1066-1307* (Cambridge: Harvard University Press, 1979); Keith Thomas, "The Meaning of Literacy in Early Modern England," in *The Written Word: Literacy in Transition,* ed. Gerd Baumann (Oxford: Clarendon, 1986), 97-131. See also Hall, "Uses of Literacy"; David Cressy, "Literacy in Context: Meaning and Measurement in Early Modern England," in *Consumption and the World of Goods,* ed. John Brewer and Roy Porter (London: Routledge, 1993), 305-19; and Michael Warner, *The Letters of the Republic: Publication and the Public Sphere in Eighteenth-Century America* (Cambridge: Harvard University Press, 1990), chap. 1.

27. Richard D. Brown, *Knowledge Is Power: The Diffusion of Information in Early America, 1700-1865* (New York: Oxford University Press, 1989), 28.

28. "Fisher," *American Instructor; The Complete Letter-Writer Containing Familiar Letters, on the Most Common Occasions in Life* (New York, 1793); *The Fashionable American Letter Writer; or, The Art of Polite Correspondence* (Hartford, Conn., n.d).

29. Warner, *Letters of the Republic*, 19-20; Hall, "Uses of Literacy," 23-36; David S. Shields, "The Manuscript in the British American World of Print," *PAAS* 102, Part 2 (1992): 408-10.

30. My discussion of English handwriting makes use of these accounts: Stanley Morison, "The Development of Hand-Writing: An Outline," in Heal, *Writing-Masters*, 1:xxiii–xl; Herbert C. Schulz, "The Teaching of Handwriting in Tudor and Stuart Times," *Huntington Library Quarterly* 4 (August 1943): 381–425; Anthony G. Petti, *English Literary Hands from Chaucer to Dryden* (Cambridge: Harvard University Press, 1977); Giles E. Dawson and Laetitia Kennedy-Skipton, *Elizabethan Handwriting, 1500–1650: A Guide to the Reading of Documents and Manuscripts* (1968; Chichester, Eng.: Phillimore, 1981); Joyce Whalley, *English Handwriting, 1540–1853* (London: HMSO, 1969). The range of hands and the groups that made use of them can also be traced in the copybooks themselves, of course. Perusal of the rich biographical and bibliographical material in Heal, *Writing-Masters*, is extremely valuable. Individual sources of particular use include Martin Billingsley, *The Pen's Excellencie* (London, 1618); Edward Cocker, *The Guide to Penmanship* (London, 1664); Snell, *Art of Writing;* and Joseph Champion, *Penmanship Exemplified in All the Variety of Hands Used in Great Britain* (London, [1758?]).

31. On handwriting styles in the American colonies, see Laetitia Yeandle, "The Evolution of Handwriting in the English-Speaking Colonies of America," *American Archivist* 43 (Summer 1980): 294–311; Stanley Morison, "Early Printed Manuals of Calligraphy, Italian and American, in the Newberry Library," *Newberry Library Bulletin*, 2d ser. 1 (July 1948): 23; and Nash, "Writing Masters and Copybooks," 346–48.

32. Martin Billingsley, *A Coppie Booke* (London, 1637), 6; Cocker, *Guide to Penmanship*, 5; John Langton, *Small Italian Hand* (London, [1727]); George Bickham, *Penmanship in Its Utmost Beauty and Extent* (London, 1731), 1.

33. Schulz argues that the legal hands essentially disappeared during the reign of George II, when a statute forbidding their use in the courts of justice was enacted. Writing masters continued to publish copybooks that specialized in these hands, however, which indicates their continuing use. And well into the nineteenth century, copybooks, including those published in the United States, included instruction in one or more of the legal hands. Petti adds that legal hands did not lose their official status until 1836, when chancery was abolished by act of Parliament. Schulz, "Handwriting," 417–18; Petti, *English Literary Hands*, 21; Carington Bowles, *Bowles' Young Lawyers Tutor* (London, 1764); Henry Dean, *Dean's Analytical Guide to the Art of Penmanship* (New York: Hopkins and Bayard, [1808]).

34. Monaghan, "Reader's Writing," 180–94; Ray Nash, "A Colonial Writing Master's Collection of English Copybooks," *Harvard Library Bulletin* 14 (Winter 1960), 12–19; *Pennsylvania Gazette*, 15, 22, 29 August 1745 and 31 March, 8 April 1742, in Seybolt, *Source Studies*, 46; *Boston Weekly News-Letter*, 16–23, 23–30 September 1742, in Seybolt, *Private Schools of Boston*, 29; "Fisher," *American Instructor*, 31; Dean, *Analytical Guide*.

35. William S. Reese, "The First Hundred Years of Printing in British North America: Printers and Collectors," *PAAS* 99, Part 2 (1989): 337–53; Lawrence C. Wroth, *The Colonial Printer* (1931; Charlottesville: University Press of Virginia, Dominion Books, 1964), chaps. 2, 11; Warner, *Letters of the Republic*, 31–32; David D. Hall, *Worlds of Wonder, Days of Judgment: Popular Religious Belief in Early New England* (Cambridge: Harvard University Press, 1990), 43–61.

36. My discussion of scribal publication is based on Harold Love, *Scribal Publication in Seventeenth-Century England* (Oxford: Oxford University Press, 1993).

37. J. W. Saunders, "The Stigma of Print: A Note on the Social Bases of Tudor Poetry," *Essays in Criticism* 1 (April 1951): 139–64. The quotation is from Barnabbe Barnes, *Divine Centurie of Spirituall Sonnetts*, quoted in Saunders, "Stigma of Print," 147.

38. Reese, "First Hundred Years of Printing," 351–60; Elizabeth Carroll Reilly, "The Wages

of Piety: The Boston Book Trade of Jeremy Condy," in Joyce, *Printing and Society*, 83-131; Cynthia Stiverson and Gregory Stiverson, "The Colonial Retail Book Trade: Availability and Affordability of Reading Material in Mid-Eighteenth-Century Virginia," in Joyce, *Printing and Society*, 132-73; Rhys Isaac, "Books and the Social Authority of Learning: The Case of Mid-Eighteenth-Century Virginia," in Joyce, *Printing and Society*, 228-49; Victor Neuberg, "Chapbooks in America: Reconstructing the Popular Reading of Early America," in Davidson, *Reading in America*, 81-113; Wroth, *The Colonial Printer*, chaps. 2, 11.

39. Warner, *Letters of the Republic*, 34-72.

40. The early links between calligraphical and typographical design are a major theme of David Berkeley Updike, *Printing Types: Their History, Forms, and Use; A Study in Survivals*, 2 vols., 3d ed. (Cambridge: Belknap, 1962), and Stanley Morison, *Selected Essays on the History of Letter-Forms in Manuscript and Print*, ed. David McKitterick, 2 vols. (Cambridge: Cambridge University Press, 1981). For specific links noted here, see Updike, *Printing Types*, 2:107-16, 159-67; David Greenhood and Helen Gentry, *Chronology of Books and Printing*, rev. ed. (New York: Macmillan, 1936), 14-15, 17, 50, 52, 75, 90; and John Lewis, *Anatomy of Printing: The Influences of Art and History on Its Design* (New York: Watson-Guptill, 1970), 37, 50.

41. Joseph Moxon, *Mechanick Exercises on the Whole Art of Printing*, ed. Herbert Davis and Harry Carter, reprint ed. (London, 1683-84; New York: Dover, 1962), 21-22; Franklin to Bodoni, 14 October 1787, in Updike, *Printing Types*, 2:167-68.

42. Lewis, *Anatomy of Printing*, 55-56; Moxon, *Mechanick Exercises*, 131-33; Updike, *Printing Types*, 1:15-16.

43. Updike, *Printing Types*, 1:24-32, 2:194-97; Greenhood and Gentry, *Chronology of Books and Printing*, 80, 86, 95, 101-2.

44. Walter J. Ong, *Orality and Literacy* (New York: Methuen, 1982), 122.

45. Warner, *Letters of the Republic*, 7-9.

46. Shields, "Manuscript in the British American World of Print," 403-16; Wroth, *Colonial Printer*, 224-26; Warner, *Letters of the Republic*, 18-19; Lewis, *Anatomy of Printing*, 131; James Ronaldson, *Specimen of Printing Type* (Philadelphia, 1816).

47. Shields, "Manuscript in the British American World of Print," 413-16; David Hall, "The Politics of Writing and Reading in Eighteenth-Century America," in *Publishing and Readership in Revolutionary France and America*, ed. Carol Armbruster (Westport, Conn.: Greenwood, 1993), 153-55; Brown, *Knowledge Is Power*, 114-15.

48. Jean-Christophe Agnew, *Worlds Apart: The Market and the Theater in Anglo-American Thought, 1550-1750* (New York: Cambridge University Press, 1986); Lionel Trilling, *Sincerity and Authenticity* (Cambridge: Harvard University Press, 1970); Jay Fliegelman, *Declaring Independence: Jefferson, Natural Language, and the Culture of Performance* (Stanford: Stanford University Press, 1993).

49. Greenhood and Gentry, *Chronology of Books and Printing*, 17, 19, 22, 23, 30, 52, 66, 71; Lewis, *Anatomy of Printing*, 37, 50, 90; Updike, *Printing Types*, 2:88-89, 128-29, 137-141; *Specimen of Printing Type* (Philadelphia, 1816), 3. Harold Love suggests that it was precisely this opacity and the resulting potential for duplicity that formed the subject matter of Swift's early eighteenth-century satires (*Scribal Publication*, 297-307).

50. Franklin to Webster, excerpted in Rollo G. Silver, *The American Printer, 1787-1825* (Charlottesville: University Press of Virginia, 1967), 146, 147; Jean-Christophe Agnew discusses the eighteenth-century tradition of reading facial expressions as indicators of emotion and motive in *Worlds Apart*, 73-96. This physiognomical practice should be distinguished from

the one dating from the last quarter of the eighteenth century, associated with Johann Kaspar Lavater, in which facial *features* are read as indicators of permanent *character* traits. This latter school of thought will be discussed in chapter 2.

51. Richard Bradford, "The Visual Poem in the Eighteenth Century," *Visible Language* 33 (Winter 1989): 9–27; Shields, "Manuscript in the British American World of Print," 413; Francis Hopkinson, "Plan for the Improvement of the Art of Paper War," *American Museum* 1 (1787); William Thornton, *Cadmus: Or, a Treatise on the Elements of Written Language* (Philadelphia, 1793), 90; Franklin to Webster, in Silver, *American Printer*, 147.

52. Fliegelman, *Declaring Independence*, 28–35. The term *dead letter* is from Thomas Sheridan's *A Course of Lectures on Elocution* (1762; Menston, Eng.: Scolar, 1968), xii, quoted in Fliegelman, *Declaring Independence*, 26. See also James R. Knowlson, "The Idea of Gesture as a Universal Language in the XVIIth and XVIIIth Centuries," *Journal of the History of Ideas* 26 (October–December 1965): 495–508.

53. *Cobbett's Complete Collection of State Trials*, 33 vols. (London: R. Bagshaw, 1811), 9:865; T. B. Howell, comp., *A Complete Collection of State Trials*, 33 vols. (London: T. C. Hansard, 1812), 12:297–98; William Bagot to Walter Bagot, 22 April 1622, reprinted in Dawson and Kennedy-Skipton, *Elizabethan Handwriting*, 102–3.

54. Geoffrey Gilbert, *The Law of Evidence* (London, 1726), quoted in John Henry Wigmore, *A Treatise on the System of Evidence in Trials at Common Law*, 4 vols. (Boston: Little, Brown, 1904), 3:2650n.

55. Richard L. Bushman discusses this notion of self-presentation and its constituent arts in *The Refinement of America: Persons, Houses, Cities* (New York: Knopf, 1992). On handwriting as an aspect of self-presentation, see 92–96. On the class and gendered meanings of gesture, see Keith Thomas, "Introduction," in *A Cultural History of Gesture from Antiquity to the Present Day*, ed. Jan Bremmer and Herman Roodenburg (London: Polity, 1991), 7–10.

56. John Clark, *Writing Improv'd or Penmanship Made Easy in Its Useful and Ornamental Parts* (London, 1714), n.p.

57. Lord Chesterfield to his son, 9 July 1750, in *Letters to His Son by the Earl of Chesterfield on the Fine Art of Becoming a Man of the World*, ed. Oliver H. G. Leigh, 2 vols. (Washington: M. Walter Dunne, 1901), 1:330; George Shelley, *The Second Part of Natural Writing* (London, [1714]), pl. 12.

58. Clark, *Writing Improv'd*, pl. 23; Thomas Ollyffe, *Young Clerk's Tutor Enlarged* (London, 1728), n.p.

59. "Reputation, and the Credit of the Merchant," in Bickham, *Universal Penman*, 137, quoting *Othello*, 3.3.154–60; Ayres, *Accomplish't Clerk*, n.p.; "Credit," in Bickham, *Universal Penman*, 123.

60. Lord Chesterfield to his son, 8 January 1751, in *Letters to His Son by the Earl of Chesterfield*, 1:361; M[artin] Clare, *Youth's Introduction to Trade and Business* (London, 1758), in Sheldahl, *Education for the Mercantile Counting House*, 145.

61. Annotated bibliographical entry for Edward Cocker, *Young Lawyer's Writing Master* (London, [1674]), in Heal, *Writing Masters*, 2:143; George Bickham, *British Youth's Instructor* (London, 1754), preface; William Leekey, *A Discourse on the Use of the Pen* (London, 1794), 19, 27. On scriveners, see Donald Jackson, *The Story of Writing* (New York: Taplinger, 1981), 145–48.

62. J. Radcliffe, *The New British Penman* (London, [ca. 1790]), 13; Edward Cocker, *A Guide to Penmanship* (London, 1664), 5; Martin Billingsley, *The Pen's Excellencie* (London, 1618).

63. Radcliffe, *New British Penman*, 13; Cocker, *Guide to Penmanship* (London, 1664), 5; Billingsley, *Coppie Book*, 6.

64. "The Author's Advice to Young Gentlemen," in Jenkins, *Art of Writing,* 68; Bickham, *Penmanship,* 3. The couplet appears originally in Bickham's *Universal Penman,* 29.

65. Thomas Jefferson, letter of 1814, quoted in Yeandle, "Evolution of Handwriting," 306; Bickham, *Universal Penman,* 9. For examples of aristocratic insouciance, see Lord Chesterfield to his son, 20 July 1747, 17 May and 30 December 1848, in *Letters to His Son by the Earl of Chesterfield,* 1:18, 74, 151.

66. *The Character of an Honest Merchant* (London, 1686), quoted in John Money, "Teaching in the Market-place, or 'Caesar Adsum Jam Forte: Pompey Aderat': The Retailing of Knowledge in Provincial England during the Eighteenth Century," in Brewer and Porter, *Consumption and the World of Goods,* 339; Daniel Defoe, *The Complete English Tradesman,* 2d ed., reprint ed. (London, 1727; New York: Augustus M. Kelley, 1969), 19-20; Watts, "Man of Business," 19, 135-36; Clare, *Youth's Introduction,* 145; Snell, *Art of Writing,* preface.

67. Daniel Defoe, *An Essay upon Projects* (London, 1697; Menston, Eng.: Scholar, 1969), 7-8.

CHAPTER TWO

Men of Character, Scribbling Women

1. James French, *Gentlemens' Writing Book* (Boston: James French, 1845); French, *Ladies' Writing Book* (Boston: James French, 1845).

2. Ray Nash, *American Penmanship, 1800–1850: A History of Writing and a Bibliography of Copybooks from Jenkins to Spencer* (Worcester, Mass.: American Antiquarian Society, 1969), 57–60; Nash, *Some Early American Writing Books and Masters* (n.p., 1943), 22–23.

3. "From Turnbridge, Vermont, to London, England—The Journal of James Guild, Peddler, Tinker, Schoolmaster, Portrait Painter, from 1818 to 1824," *Proceedings of the Vermont Historical Society,* n.s. 5 (September 1937): 277. On itinerants, see Janice Harriet Weiss, "Educating for Clerical Work: A History of Commercial Education in the United States since 1850" (Ed.D. diss., Harvard Graduate School of Education, 1978), 18–19; Nash, *American Penmanship,* 17–21, 52–56; A. N. Hinman, "Traveling Penmen," *PAJ* 1 (March 1878): 1; "How to Conduct and Organize Writing Schools," in G. A. Gaskell, *Gaskell's Compendium of Forms,* 14th ed. (Chicago: William M. Farrar, 1882), 94–102.

4. "Journal of James Guild," 278, 279, 287, 288, 289.

5. Weiss, "Educating for Clerical Work," chap. 2; Cheesman A. Herrick, *The Meaning and Practice of Commercial Education* (New York: Macmillan, 1904), 178–82; Nash, *American Penmanship,* 71–266.

6. My discussion of common-school penmanship education is based on Barbara Joan Finkelstein, "Governing the Young: Teacher Behavior in American Primary Schools, 1820–1880: A Documentary History" (Ed.D. diss., Columbia University, 1970), 55–66, 190–91, 260, 271–72, 275, 285, 317; William A. Alcott, *On Teaching Penmanship* (Boston: Lilly, Wait, Colman, and Holden, 1833); and A. N. Hinman, "Then and Now," *Western Penman* 4 (February 1873): 34–35.

7. *Twenty-First Annual Report of the Common Schools of New-Hampshire* (Concord: George E. Jenks, 1867), 2.

8. Cincinnati's school system had an elaborate penmanship program, for example. Semi-annual examinations in penmanship were administered by the penmanship superintendent, who in his first year of service visited each of his twenty-four district schools from five to thirty-seven times. One indication of the importance accorded the superintendent was his salary, which exceeded that of elementary school principals. Perhaps even more telling, the superintendent's two assistants, one female and the second employed in the city's "colored

schools" (and possibly himself black), were compensated at a rate that surpassed the pay of female elementary and intermediate school teachers and the teachers at the corresponding colored schools (Common Schools of Cincinnati, *Forty-Second Annual Report* [Cincinnati: Wilstatch, Baldwin, 1872], 119; Common Schools of Cincinnati, *Forty-Seventh Annual Report* [Cincinnati: Times Book and Job Printing Establishment, 1877], 367, 435–50).

9. John Clark, *Writing Improv'd* (London, 1714), n.p.; B. G. Howes, *Howes's Model Copy Book* (Worcester, Mass.: B. G. Howes, 1861), n.p.; S. A. Potter, *Penmanship Explained* (Philadelphia: Cowperthwait, 1868), 56–58.

10. See, for example, John Jenkins, *The Art of Writing* (Boston: Isaiah Thomas and Ebenezer T. Andrews, 1791); Henry Dean, *Dean's Analytical Guide to the Art of Penmanship* (New York: Hopkins and Bayard, [1808]); Potter, *Penmanship Explained*; B. H. Rand, *The American Penman* (Philadelphia, 1833); Thomas E. Hill, *Hill's Manual of Social and Business Forms* (Chicago: Moses Warren, 1875); *The Scholar's Plain and Easy Guide to the Art of Penmanship* (New Haven: J.W. and J. Barber, 1878); J. W. Payson, S. Dunton, W. M. Scribner, G. H. Shattuck, A. S. Manson, *The Payson, Dunton, and Scribner Manual of Penmanship* (New York: Potter, Ainsworth, 1873), 69; J. L. Burritt, *How to Teach Penmanship in Public Schools*, 2d ed. (Syracuse: C. W. Bardeen, 1886), 41.

11. *Dictionary of American Biography*, s.v. "Spencer, Platt Rogers"; "History of Spencerian Penmanship for Twenty-Five Years," *PAJ* 1 (May 1877): 1; Stanley Morison, *American Copybooks: An Outline of Their History from Colonial to Modern Times* (Philadelphia: William F. Fell, 1951), 32–42; Nash, *American Penmanship*, 64–67; Joan G. Sugarman, *The Spencerian Heritage: Reawakening the Tradition of Good Penmanship* (Cleveland: Dyke College, 1976); William E. Eaton, "American School Penmanship: From Craft to Process," *American Journal of Education* (February 1985): 259–62.

12. H. C. Spencer, *Spencerian Key to Practical Penmanship* (New York: Ivison, Phinney, Blakeman, 1869), 14–15, 39–40, 166. On the natural aesthetics of Spencerian script, see John Higham, *From Boundlessness to Consolidation: The Transformation of American Culture, 1840–1860* (Ann Arbor, Mich.: William Clements Library, 1969), 1–5.

13. Spencer, *Spencerian Key*, 13, 40; G. A. Gaskell, *Gaskell's Guide to Writing, Pen-Flourishing, Lettering, Business Letter-Writing, Etc., with Photo-Engraved Specimens from the Leading Penmen of America and Europe; Selections for Autograph and Writing Albums, Etc.* (New York: Office of "The Penman's Gazette," 1883), 6; Fielding Schofield, "Penmanship—The Queen of Arts," *Penman's Gazette* 1 (May 1876): 1; Paul Pastnor, "The Pen as a Means of Culture," *PAJ* 2 (June 1878): 1; Uriah McKee, "The Elevating Tendency of the Study of Artistic Penmanship," *PAJ* 4 (October 1880): 82.

14. Jenkins, *Art of Writing*, 10–11; Copybook of Simon Ray Greene, 1801, in Penmanship Collection, 1762–1848, American Antiquarian Society, Worcester, Mass.; Francis McCready, *The Art of Penmanship in Verse* (Baltimore: Lovegrove, Dell, 1818), 11.

15. George W. Winchester, *Theoretical and Practical Penmanship* (Hartford: J. H. Mather, 1844); William Davison, *A Complete, Analytic, and Practically Progressive System of Written Copies . . . ; Being, in Connection with the Muscular Guide, a Perfect Self-Instructor* (n.p., 1841); *Guide to Williams and Packard's System of Penmanship for Teachers and Adepts* (New York: Slote, Woodman, 1869), 4.

16. Spencer, *Spencerian Key*, 114–18, 131–33, 143–45; Potter, *Penmanship Explained*, 45, 75–78, 89–98; *Payson, Dunton, and Scribner Manual*, 18–19, 31–33; *Williams and Packard's System of Penmanship*, 4–5; L[angdon] S[hook] Thompson and [?] Bowlers, *A Hand-Book to Accompany the Eclectic System of Penmanship* (Cincinnati: Van Antwerp, Bragg, 1870), 16–18, 26–28. Michel Foucault links just such overt techniques of physical control to the desire to

increase the body's economic utility while diminishing its political power in his *Discipline and Punish: The Birth of the Prison* (New York: Vintage, 1979), 135–69.

17. Copybooks of Alce Arnold, Reuben Commins, and Lincoln Varney, Penmanship Collection, American Antiquarian Society, Worcester, Mass. Copybook of Melissa Wilson Holmes, Old Sturbridge Village, Sturbridge, Massachusetts. My conclusions are based on a perusal of the dozens of copybooks, ranging from the late eighteenth century to the 1850s, contained in these two collections.

18. Boston School Committee, *Annual Report, 1858* (Boston: George C. Rand and Avery, 1859), 62, quoted in Finkelstein, "Governing the Young," 66.

19. Carl F. Kaestle, *Pillars of the Republic: Common Schools and American Society, 1780–1860* (New York: Hill and Wang, 1983), esp. chaps. 4, 5, 7; David Tyack, *The One Best System: A History of American Urban Education* (Cambridge: Harvard University Press, 1974), esp. 66–77, 104–25; Barbara Finkelstein, "Reading, Writing, and the Acquisition of Identity in the United States: 1790–1860," in *Regulated Children/Liberated Children: Education in Psychohistorical Perspective*, ed. Barbara Finkelstein (New York: Psychohistory Press, 1979), 114–39; Edward Stevens, Jr., "The Anatomy of Mass Literacy in Nineteenth-Century United States," in *National Literacy Campaigns: Historical and Comparative Perspectives*, ed. Robert F. Arnove and Harvey J. Graff (New York: Plenum, 1987), 99–122. Finkelstein, "Governing the Young," details the militaristic classroom methods used throughout the curriculum to achieve these goals.

20. William Alcott, *The Young Man's Guide*, 15th ed. (Boston: T. R. Marvin, 1844), 28; Alcott, *On Teaching Penmanship*.

21. J. S. Montgomery, "Remarks on Penmanship," *PAJ* 1 (July 1877): 2; "Penmanship," *Penman's Gazette* 1 (January 1876): 8. See also "Penmanship," *PAJ* 3 (March 1879): 2; Gideon F. Thayer, "Letters to a Young Teacher," *American Journal of Education* 4 (December 1857): 450; "Judging Character by Handwriting," *PAJ* 5 (April 1881): 28; and *Southern Penman* 1 (February 1886): 3.

22. On Victorian conceptions of the relation between mind and body, especially the key role assigned to the will, see Bruce Haley, *The Healthy Body and Victorian Culture* (Cambridge: Harvard University Press, 1978), and Anita Clair Fellman and Michael Fellman, *Making Sense of Self: Medical Advice Literature in Late Nineteenth-Century America* (Philadelphia: University of Pennsylvania Press, 1981), chap. 7.

23. Spencer, *Spencerian Key*, 15, 27–28, 31. For similar treatments of writing position and movement, see, for example, Potter, *Penmanship Explained*, 24–34; *Payson, Dunton, and Scribner Manual*, 19–31; and Thompson and Bowlers, *Eclectic System of Penmanship*, 19–26.

24. "Spencerian Authors," *Theory of Spencerian Penmanship* (New York: Ivison, Blakeman, Taylor, 1874), 11; Fielding Schofield, "Remarks on Penmanship, before a Class of Teachers," *Western Penman* 1 (October 1871): 1; *Payson, Dunton, and Scribner Manual*, 33–36, 106; Spencer, *Spencerian Key*, 35–36; Potter, *Penmanship Explained*, 89–98.

25. B. F. Foster, *Practical Penmanship, Being a Development of the Carstairian System* (Albany: O. Steele, 1832), xxii; Spencer, *Spencerian Key*, 14–15, 35; [E. T. Martin], *Martin's System of Practical Penmanship* (Worcester, Mass.: n.p., n.d.), unpaginated. On Foster, the American promoter of the talantograph, see Thomas H. Littlefield, "Before Spencerian: A Development of B. F. Foster and the American System," *Print* 3 (1945): 33–40; and Ray Nash, "Benjamin Franklin Foster," in *Calligraphy and Paleography: Essays Presented to Alfred Fairbank on His 70th Birthday*, ed. A. S. Osley (New York: October House, 1966), 155–67.

26. Warren I. Susman, " 'Personality' and the Making of Twentieth-Century Culture," in *New Directions in American Intellectual History*, ed. John Higham and Paul K. Conklin (Balti-

more: Johns Hopkins University Press, 1979), 212–26; Karen Halttunen, *Confidence Men and Painted Women: A Study of Middle-Class Culture in America, 1830–1870* (New Haven: Yale University Press, 1982), 49–50; and Joan Rubin, *The Making of Middlebrow Culture* (Chapel Hill: University of North Carolina Press, 1992), 3–4.

27. On these distinctive forms of individualism, see Jean V. Matthews, *Toward a New Society: American Thought and Culture, 1800–1830* (New York: Twayne, 1990), 75–76, 120–23; Stephen Lukes, *Individualism* (New York: Oxford University Press, 1973); Koenraad W. Swart, "'Individualism' in the Mid-Nineteenth Century (1820–1860)," *Journal of the History of Ideas* 23 (January–March 1962): 77–90; and Georg Simmel, "Individual and Society in Eighteenth- and Nineteenth-Century Views of Life," and "The Metropolis and Mental Life," in *The Sociology of Georg Simmel*, ed. Kurt Wolff (New York: Free Press, 1950), 58–84, 409–24.

28. Benjamin Rush, *Thoughts upon Female Education, Accommodated to the Present State of Society, Manners, and Government of the United States* (Philadelphia, 1787), reprinted in *Essays on Education in the Early Republic*, ed. Frederick Rudolph (Cambridge: Belknap, 1965), 28, 29; Henry Dean, *Observations on the Art of Writing* (New York: Samuel Wood, 1807), 3; Nathaniel Fisher, "An Address Delivered to the Pupils of Henry Dean's Writing Academy . . . Salem, October 26, 1804," in Dean, *Analytical Guide*, 104. On republican notions of womanhood and their impact on female education, see Mary Beth Norton, *Liberty's Daughters: The Revolutionary Experience of Women, 1750–1800* (Ithaca: Cornell University Press, 1980), 263–87, and Linda Kerber, *Women of the Republic: Intellect and Ideology in Revolutionary America* (Chapel Hill: University of North Carolina Press, 1980), chap. 7.

29. Benjamin Rand, for example, noted that the mercantile running hand was the fastest of hands because it was the most angular and required that the pen be raised only between words. By contrast, in the case of ladies' hands, it was "necessary to mend and paint the shaded strokes" (Benjamin H. Rand, *A New and Complete System of Mercantile Penmanship* [Philadelphia: n.p., (1814)], 13, 19).

30. *PAJ* 1 (February 1878): 3; *Annual Reports of the [New Hampshire] Board of Education and Superintendent of Public Instruction* (Manchester: John B. Clarke, 1870), 91, 93; Weiss, "Educating for Clerical Work," chap. 2; advertisement for *Gaskell's Compendium*, in *Penman's Gazette* 1 (November 1876): 8.

31. P. R. Spencer et al., *Spencerian System of Penmanship* (New York: Ivison, Blakeman, 1868–74); Advertisement for Payson, Dunton and Scribner's copybooks, *Payson, Dunton and Scribner's Journal of Penmanship* 1 (January 1868): 2; Thompson and Bowlers, *Eclectic System of Penmanship*.

32. Common Schools of Cincinnati, *Forty-Seventh Annual Report*, 155–56; exercise books of M. Eliza Hovey, Betsey A. Lincoln, Lucy Ann Keyes, Sarah W. Gill, and Mary B. Thomas in the Penmanship Collection, American Antiquarian Society (AAS), Worcester, Mass. Albums of Mary Beach, Marjorie Brooks, Henrietta W. Findey, and Maria H. Segu, Nineteenth-Century Collection, AAS; Clark Louis Barzee, *Oregon in the Making: '60s to Gay 90s* (Salem, Ore.: Statesmen, 1936), excerpted in Finkelstein, "Governing the Young," 317.

33. David D. Hall, "Readers and Reading in America: Historical and Critical Perspectives," *PAAS* 103, Part 2 (1993): 357.

34. On Victorian character formation as a muscular and masculine pursuit, see E. Anthony Rotundo, *American Manhood: Transformations in Masculinity from the Revolution to the Modern Era* (New York: Harper Collins, 1993), 222–27, and Roberta J. Park, "Biological

Thought, Athletics, and the Formation of the 'Man of Character': 1830-1900," in *Manliness and Morality: Middle-Class Masculinity in Britain and America, 1800–1940*, ed. J. A. Mangan and James Walvin (Manchester, Eng.: Manchester University Press, 1987), 7–33.

35. Thompson and Bowlers, *Eclectic System of Penmanship*, 35; "Manliness of Penmanship," *PAJ* 1 (February 1878): 2.

36. There is a good deal of controversy over just when female literacy rates in New England shot up. In 1974 Kenneth Lockridge concluded that only half of the female population was literate after the Revolution, but subsequent studies, making use of new methodological critiques and approaches, suggest that rates of female literacy may have been higher, perhaps even near universal, by the end of the eighteenth century. See Kenneth Lockridge, *Literacy in Colonial New England: An Enquiry into the Social Context of Literacy in the Early Modern West* (New York: Norton, 1974), 38–43; Ross W. Beales, Jr., "Studying Literacy at the Community Level: A Research Note," *Journal of Interdisciplinary History* 9 (Summer 1978): 93–102; Linda Auwers, "Reading the Marks of the Past: Exploring Female Literacy in Colonial Windsor, Connecticut," *Historical Methods* 13 (Fall 1980): 204–14; William J. Gilmore, "Elementary Literacy on the Eve of the Industrial Revolution: Trends in Rural New England, 1760-1830," *PAAS* 92 (April 1982): 87–177; Joel Perlmann and Dennis Shirley, "When Did New England Women Acquire Literacy?" *William and Mary Quarterly*, 3d ser. 48 (January 1991): 50–67; Gloria L. Main, "An Inquiry into When and Why Women Learned to Write in Colonial New England," *Journal of Social History* 24 (Spring 1991): 579–89; and Mary Beth Norton, "Communications," *William and Mary Quarterly*, 3d ser. 48 (October 1991): 639–45. See also Kathryn Kish Sklar, "The Schooling of Girls and Changing Community Values in Massachusetts Towns, 1750-1820," *History of Education Quarterly* 33 (Winter 1993): 511–39.

37. L. Soltow and E. Stevens, *The Rise of Literacy and the Common School in the United States: A Socioeconomic Analysis to 1870* (Chicago: University of Chicago Press, 1981), chaps. 2, 5; Janet Duitsman Cornelius, *"When I Can Read My Title Clear": Literacy, Slavery, and Religion in the Antebellum South* (Columbia: University of South Carolina Press, 1991), esp. chap. 3; Maris A. Vinovskis and Richard M. Bernard, "Beyond Catharine Beecher: Female Education in the Antebellum Period," *Signs* 3 (Summer 1978): 860–64; Perlmann and Shirley, "When Did New England Women Acquire Literacy?" 54, 65n; United States Census Office, *Eighth Census* (1860) (Washington D.C., 1864–66).

38. Michael Warner, *The Letters of the Republic: Publication and the Public Sphere in Eighteenth-Century America* (Cambridge: Harvard University Press, 1990), 14–16. Warner quotes from the *South Carolina Gazette*, 15 January 1732, p. 16.

39. "Thoughts on Letter-writing," in John Pierpont, *The American First Class Book; or Exercises in Reading and Recitation*, 25th ed. (Boston: Charles Bowen, 1836), 341.

40. For an introduction to the substantial literature on female-authored and female-oriented novels, see Cathy N. Davidson, *Revolution and the Word: The Rise of the Novel in America* (New York: Oxford University Press, 1986), and Mary Kelley, *Private Woman, Public Stage: Literary Domesticity in Nineteenth-Century America* (New York: Oxford University Press, 1984). Davidson portrays the novel-reading public as primarily female; more recently, Ronald Zboray argues that the antebellum audience for fiction was evenly divided between men and women. See Ronald J. Zboray, *A Fictive People: Antebellum Economic Development and the American Reading Public* (New York: Oxford University Press, 1993), chap. 11.

41. Catharine Maria Sedgwick to Henry Dwight Sedgwick, 29 March 1822, quoted in Kelley, *Private Woman, Public Stage*, 130; Caroline Howard Gilman to one of her daughters, 2 May

1874, and an autobiographical sketch by Gilman in *The Female Prose Writers of America,* ed. John S. Hart (Philadelphia: E. H. Butler, 1852), 55, quoted in Kelley, *Private Woman, Public Stage,* 180.

42. Davidson, *Revolution and the Word,* 32; Kelley, *Private Woman, Public Stage,* 123, 135.

43. Walter Scott, *Peveril of the Peak* (1822; New York: Waverley Book, 1895), 174-75.

44. Spencer, *Spencerian Key,* 9; Garfield quoted in Ray Nash, *Handwriting in America from Colonial Times to 1850* (Mainz: Gutenberg-Gesellschaft, 1959).

45. Spencer, *Spencerian Key,* 9.

46. "A.H.H.," "Penmanship—Once Practical, Now Beautiful," *PAJ* 1 (September 1877): 1.

47. *Calligraphy and Handwriting in America: Exhibition at the Peabody Institute Library, Baltimore, Maryland* (Baltimore: [Peabody Institute Library, 1961]), n.p.; Carroll Gard, *Writing Past and Present: The Story of Writing and Writing Tools* (New York: A. N. Palmer, 1937), 67-68. On the links between skill in pen art and a penman's commercial success, see Hinman, "Then and Now," 34-35, and "Lessons in Off-Hand Flourishing," *Penman's Gazette* 1 (January 1876): 4.

48. E. F. Richardson, "A Good Handwriting," *Southern Penman* 1 (February 1886): 3; *Southern Penman* 1 (February 1886), 21.

49. D. T. Smith, "E. F. Richardson," *Southern Penman* 1 (June 1886): 2.

50. "Scribo," "Penmanship," *Penman's Gazette* 1 (December 1876): 8; McKee, "Elevating Tendency," 82.

51. See, for example, the chapter "The Ornamental Artist" in *The Young Lady's Book: A Manual of Elegant Recreations, Exercises, and Pursuits,* 2d ed. (Boston: Carter, Hendee and Babcock, [1830]).

52. *PAJ* 2 (September 1878): 8; Robert E. Belding, "The Penman Builds an Empire," *Palimpsest* 61 (1980): 138-45; Carroll P. Gard, "A Romance of the Second 'R,'" *Journal of Education* (5 February 1934): 67-69. Joseph S. Taylor, "A. N. Palmer: An Appreciation," *Educational Review* 76 (June 1928): 15-20; Mary L. Dougherty, "History of the Teaching of Handwriting in America," *ESJ* 18 (December 1917): 284; A. N. Palmer, *Palmer's Guide to Business Writing* (Cedar Rapids, Iowa: Western Penman, 1894); A. N. Palmer, *The Palmer Method of Teaching Practical Writing in Graded Schools* (New York: A. N. Palmer, 1910).

53. See, for example, G. Bixler, *Bixler's Physical Training in Penmanship* (Wooster, Ohio: Bixler's Business College, 1892), and C. P. Zaner, *Arm Movement Method of Rapid Writing* (Columbus, Ohio: Zaner and Bloser, 1904). Like Palmer, Bixler stressed movement over form, writing over drawing, and aimed to establish muscular habits through repetitive drills in ovals. Zaner made a point of giving equal billing to form and movement, but his presentation was essentially no different from Palmer's.

54. A. N. Palmer, "Practical Writing—A Course for Colleges and Public Schools to Answer the Needs of the People," *Journal of the Proceedings of the National Educational Association* 35 (1896): 825-32; Palmer, *Palmer's Guide,* 3; *Cincinnati Public Schools: Eighty-Fifth Annual Report* (Cincinnati: n.p., 1915), 71.

55. Burritt, *How to Teach Penmanship,* 36.

56. Palmer, *Palmer's Guide,* 5-37 passim (quotations on 12, 25, 29, 31); Palmer, *Palmer Method,* 17-24.

57. *Fifty-Eighth Annual Report of the Board of Education of the City of St. Louis, Mo., for the Year Ending June 30, 1912* (n.p., n.d.), 133; Palmer, *Palmer's Guide,* 28.

58. Palmer, *Palmer's Guide,* 4.

59. John Higham, "The Reorientation of American Culture in the 1890s," in *The Origins of Modern Consciousness,* ed. John Weiss (Detroit: Wayne State University Press, 1965), 25-48,

193–97; Carroll Smith-Rosenberg, "The New Woman as Androgyne: Social Disorder and Gender Crisis, 1870–1936," in *Disorderly Conduct: Visions of Gender in Victorian America* (New York: Oxford University Press, 1985), 245–96; Rotundo, *American Manhood,* chaps. 10, 11; Clyde Griffen, "Reconstructing Masculinity from the Evangelical Revival to the Waning of Progressivism: A Speculative Synthesis," in *Meanings for Manhood: Constructions of Masculinity in Victorian America,* ed. Mark C. Carnes and Clyde Griffen (Chicago: University of Chicago Press, 1990), 188–98.

60. Cindy Aron, *Ladies and Gentlemen of the Civil Service: Middle-Class Workers in Mid-Victorian America, 1840–1870* (New York: Knopf, 1970), 36; Olivier Zunz, *Making America Corporate, 1870–1920* (Chicago: University of Chicago Press, 1990), 103–16; Margery W. Davies, *Woman's Place Is at the Typewriter: Office Work and Workers, 1870–1930* (Philadelphia: Temple University Press, 1982), chaps. 2, 3; Rotundo, *American Manhood,* 248–51.

61. Zunz, *Making America Corporate,* 116–21; Davies, *Woman's Place,* chap. 4, app.; Weiss, "Educating for Clerical Work"; Ileen A. DeVault, *Sons and Daughters of Labor: Class and Clerical Work in Turn-of-the-Century Pittsburgh* (Ithaca: Cornell University Press, 1990), chaps. 1, 2; John Allen Rider, "A History of the Male Stenographer in the United States" (Ed.D. diss., University of Nebraska, 1966), chaps. 4–6. The statistics are from Weiss, "Clerical Work," 37–38, and DeVault, *Class and Clerical Work,* 16.

CHAPTER THREE

The Romance and Science of Individuality

1. "Autographs," *National Magazine* 7 (October 1855): 356; Lord Chesterfield to his son, 20 December 1748, in *Letters to His Son by the Earl of Chesterfield on the Fine Art of Becoming a Man of the World,* ed. Oliver H. G. Leigh, 2 vols. (Washington: M. Walter Dunne, 1901), 1:147.

2. "Autographs," 358.

3. [Johann Kaspar] Lavater, *Essays on Physiognomy; Calculated to Extend the Knowledge and the Love of Mankind,* trans. C. Moore, 4 vols. (London, 1797), 4:200. The handwriting section was removed in subsequent English translations. On Lavater's physiognomy, see John Graham, *Lavater's Essays on Physiognomy: A Study in the History of Ideas* (Bern, Switz.: Peter Lang, 1979); Ellis Shookman, ed., *The Faces of Physiognomy: Interdisciplinary Approaches to Johann Caspar Lavater* (Columbia, S.C.: Camden House, 1993); and Martine Dumont, "Le Succès Mondain d'une Fausse Science: La Physiognomie de Johann Kaspar Lavater," *Actes de la récherche en sciences sociales* 54 (1984): 3–30.

4. Edouard Auguste Patrice Hocquart, *L'Art de juger de l'esprit et du caractère des hommes et des femmes, sur leur écriture* (Paris, [1812]) (hereafter *L'Art de juger, 1812*); Hocquart, *L'Art de juger du caractère des hommes sur leur écriture* (Paris, 1816) (hereafter *L'Art de juger, 1816*).

5. [Johann Kaspar] Lavater, *Le Lavater portatif, ou Précis de l'art de connaitre les hommes par les traits du visage* (Paris: Hocquart, 1808); Hocquart, *Physiognomies des hommes politiques du jour* (Paris: A. Royer, 1843). On Hocquart (1787–1870), see the biographical introduction to Hocquart, *L'Art de juger du caractère des hommes sur leur écriture* (Paris: F. Alcan, 1898), by the graphologist J. Crépieux-Jamin, 1–13.

6. Hocquart, *L'Art de juger, 1812,* 14; Hocquart, *L'Art de juger, 1816,* 62–72. Lavater, for example, had interpreted one signature as the "autography of a phlegmatic-melancholic" (Lavater, *Essays on Physiognomy,* 4:203).

7. Thomas Byerley, "On Characteristic Signatures," in *Relics of Literature* (London: T. Boys,

1823), 369, 371-73; Isaac Disraeli, "Autographs," in *Curiosities of Literature,* 9th ed., 6 vols. (London: Edward Moxon, 1834), 5:279, 280, 278n. Italics in original.

8. Benjamin Rush, *Thoughts upon Female Education, Accommodated to the Present State of Society, Manners, and Government of the United States* (Philadelphia, 1787), reprinted in *Essays on Education in the Early Republic,* ed. Frederick Rudolph (Cambridge: Belknap, 1965), 29; diary of Benjamin Henry Latrobe, 8 August 1806, in *Papers of Benjamin Henry Latrobe,* ed. Edward C. Carter II, John C. Van Horne, and Lee W. Formwalt, ser. 1, vol. 3: *The Journals of Benjamin Henry Latrobe, 1799-1820, from Philadelphia to New Orleans* (New Haven: Yale University Press, 1980), 55-56. I am indebted to John C. Van Horne of the Library Company of Philadelphia for this latter reference.

9. R. C. Sands, "Thoughts on Hand-Writing," *Knickerbocker* 12 (October 1838): 319, 320.

10. S. Gilman, "A Week among Autographs," in Caroline Gilman, *The Poetry of Travelling in the United States* (New York: S. Colman, 1838), 378-79.

11. Edgar Allan Poe, "Autography," *Southern Literary Messenger* 2 (February, August 1836): 205-12, 601-4; Poe, "A Chapter on Autography," reprinted in *Edgar Allan Poe,* ed. Edmund Clarence Stedman and George Edward Woodberry (1895; Freeport, N.Y.: Books for Libraries, 1971), 9:224-311. This latter work first appeared in the November and December 1841 and January 1842 issues of *Graham's Magazine.*

12. Poe to Hastings Weld, 14 August 1841, in *The Letters of Edgar Allan Poe,* ed. John Ward Ostrom, 2 vols. (New York: Gordian, 1966), 1:179; Poe to Frederick W. Thomas, 3 February 1842, in ibid., 1:193; Poe, "Chapter on Autography," 227.

13. Reviews in the *Saturday Visitor,* the *Saturday Evening Post,* the *Richmond Compiler,* the *Petersburg Constellation,* and the [Washington] *Index,* in *The Poe Log: A Documentary Life of Edgar Allan Poe, 1809-1846,* ed. Dwight Thomas and David K. Jackson (Boston: G. K. Hall, 1987), 202, 204, 346, 351; Poe to Thomas, 3 February 1842, in *Letters of Edgar Allan Poe,* 1:192-93. On the novelty of the series, see the comments of reviewers for the *Norfolk Sun,* the *Georgetown Metropolitan,* and the *New York Mirror* in *Poe Log,* 204, 356.

14. My understanding of romantic ideals in this and subsequent paragraphs draws from Walter Jackson Bate, *From Classic to Romantic: Premises of Taste in Eighteenth-Century England* (1946; New York: Harper and Brothers, 1961); Russel Blaine Nye, *The Cultural Life of the New Nation, 1776-1830* (New York: Harper and Row, 1960), 6-9; John D. Boyd, *The Function of Mimesis and Its Decline* (Cambridge: Harvard University Press, 1968); Thomas McFarland, *Originality and Imagination* (Baltimore: Johns Hopkins University Press, 1985); Stephen Lukes, *Individualism* (New York: Oxford University Press, 1973); Koenraad W. Swart, " 'Individualism' in the Mid-Nineteenth Century (1820-1860)," *Journal of the History of Ideas* 23 (January-March 1962): 77-90; and Georg Simmel, "Individual and Society in Eighteenth- and Nineteenth-Century Views of Life," and "The Metropolis and Mental Life," in *The Sociology of Georg Simmel,* ed. Kurt Wolff (New York: Free Press, 1950), 58-84, 409-24.

15. Byerley, "On Characteristic Signatures," 370-71, 374. Italics in original.

16. Poe, "Chapter on Autography," 239-40, 270-71, 308, 249, 250. For similar commentary, see ibid., 244, 291, 293, and Francis Jacox, "A Mere Question of Handwriting," *New Monthly Magazine* (London) 133 (January 1865): 47.

17. See Jacox, "A Mere Question of Handwriting," 39, who quotes Scott as commenting in exasperation on his own handwriting: "There goes the old shop again!" Ironically, Scott was also often cited as an early proponent of handwriting analysis, on the basis of his presentation in *Chronicles of the Canongate* (1831) of the "opinion I have heard seriously maintained, that something of a man's character may be conjectured from his hand-writing."

18. Poe, "Chapter on Autography," 229, 231, 232, 234, 252, 261-62, 266, 267, 292.

19. Disraeli, "Autographs," 279. On the romantic reaction to the machine and the mechanical more broadly considered, see McFarland, *Originality and Imagination*, 189-93.

20. Disraeli, "Autographs," 281-82; Poe, "Chapter on Autography," 241, 246, 276.

21. Byerley, "On Characteristic Signatures," 370; Nathaniel Hawthorne, "A Book of Autographs," in *The Dolliver Romance, and Other Pieces* (1864; Boston: Houghton, Mifflin, 1876), 167; Eugene L. Didier, "Peculiarities of Handwriting," *Appleton's Journal* 8 (16 November 1872): 545. On the romantic psychology of sympathy, which blended associationism with a belief in intuition, see Bate, *From Classic to Romantic*, chaps. 4, 5.

22. Jacox, "A Mere Question of Handwriting," 40n, 43, 53; Charlotte Brontë, *The Professor* (1857; Oxford: Basil Blackwell, 1931), 203.

23. [Edward Young], *Conjectures on Original Composition* (London: A. Millar and R. and J. Dodsley, 1759), and Alexander Gerard, *An Essay on Genius* (London: W. Strahan, 1774), quoted in McFarland, *Originality and Imagination*, 5, 89.

24. Jay Fliegelman, *Declaring Independence: Jefferson, Natural Language, and the Culture of Performance* (Stanford: Stanford University Press, 1993), 28-35; James R. Knowlson, "The Idea of Gesture as a Universal Language in the XVIIth and XVIIIth Centuries," *Journal of the History of Ideas* 26 (October-December 1965): 495-508.

25. Hocquart, *L'Art de Juger, 1812*, 2, 14; Hartley Coleridge, *The Life of Andrew Marvell* (Hull, Eng.: A. D. English, 1835), 8n; Byerley, "On Characteristic Signatures," 369, 370. In a single sentence, Lavater had tossed out a related suggestion, that there exists "a wonderful analogy" between the gait of an individual and his handwriting (Lavater, *Essays on Physiognomy*, 4:203).

26. Hocquart, *L'Art de juger, 1812*, 2; Byerley, "On Characteristic Signatures," 370; Gilman, "Autographs," 379. See also Lavater, *Essays on Physiognomy*, 4:201, for the different handwritings of humankind as "so many expressions, so many emanations, of the character of the writer."

27. Lancelot Law Whyte, *The Unconscious before Freud* (Garden City, N.Y.: Doubleday, 1962); Henri Ellenberger, *The Discovery of the Unconscious: The History and Evolution of Dynamic Psychiatry* (New York: Basic, 1970); Robert C. Fuller, *Americans and the Unconscious* (New York: Oxford University Press, 1986).

28. For Disraeli, see note 19, above; Thomas Carlyle, "Characteristics," in *The Works of Thomas Carlyle*, 30 vols. (1839; New York: Peter Fenelon Collier, 1897), 15:244-45.

29. John D. Davies, *Phrenology, Fad and Science: A Nineteenth-Century American Crusade* (New Haven: Yale University Press, 1955); Allan S. Horlick, "Phrenology and the Social Education of Young Men," *History of Education Quarterly* 11 (Spring 1971): 23-38; Arthur Wrobel, "Orthodoxy and Respectability in Nineteenth-Century Phrenology," *Journal of Popular Culture* 9 (Summer 1975): 38-50; Madeleine B. Stern, comp., *A Phrenological Dictionary of Nineteenth-Century Americans* (Westport, Conn.: Greenwood, 1982).

30. A. N. L. Munby, *The Cult of the Autograph Letter in England* (London: Athlone, 1962); David C. Mearns, "Nineteenth Century Comments on Autographs and Collectors," *Manuscripts* 4 (1952): 49-50; "Review of The Autograph Miscellany," *Littell's Living Age* 47 (20 October 1855): 129-33 (quotation on p. 130); "Autographomania," *Overland Monthly* 3 (October 1869): 345-47; A. M. Broadley, *Chats on Autographs* (New York: Frederick A. Stokes, 1910), 319-44 passim; Joseph E. Fields, "The History of Autograph Collecting," in *Autographs and Manuscripts: A Collector's Manual*, ed. Edmund Berkeley, Jr. (New York: Scribner's, 1978), 46; John M. Mulder and Isabelle Stouffer, "William Buell Sprague: Patriarch of American Collectors," *American Presbyterians* 64 (Spring 1986): 1-17.

31. "Gossip on Literature, &c.," *Museum of Foreign Literature, Science and Art* 22 (May 1833): 719-20; "Review of *The Autograph Miscellany*," 130-31; Broadley, *Chats on Autographs*, 338; Fields, "The History of Autograph Collecting," 48-50; J. Thane, *British Autography: A Collection of Fac-similes of the Hand Writing of Royal and Illustrious Personages, with Their Authentic Portraits*, 3 vols. (London: J. Thane, 1789); Gilman, "Autographs," 381, 425-29; *Poe Log*, 197, 201-5, 231, 233, 344-51, 356; "Autographomania," 343. Not all spurned the requests of autograph hunters. Nathaniel Hawthorne remarked: "The autograph of a living author has seldom been so much in request at so respectable a price. Colonel Crittenden told me that he had received as much as fifty pounds on a single day. Heaven prosper the trade between America and Liverpool!" (*Passages from the English Note-Books of Nathaniel Hawthorne*, 2 vols. [Boston: R. Osgood, 1871], 1:13).

32. Frederick G. Netherclift, *The Hand-Book to Autographs* (London: F. G. Netherclift, 1862), 1. See also, "Autographomania," 348.

33. "A Chapter on Autographs," *American Antiquarian* 1 (August 1870): 3; "Autographs," *North American Miscellany* 2 (May 1851): 40; "Autographomania," 343; "Signature-Hunting," *Galaxy* 12 (August 1871): 256-63; "The Miller Correspondence," *Museum of Foreign Literature, Science and Art* 24 (February 1834): 147; "A Forgotten Mania," *Once a Week* 12 (11 March 1865): 318. *Forgotten* in this last refers not to the hobby of autograph collecting, which was alive and well in 1865, but to a related pastime, the collecting of franks (the signature of a member of Parliament, used to send letters postage free) in Britain, which was subsequently made obsolete by legislative changes.

34. On the persistence into the nineteenth century of the desire for magical self-transformation, see Jackson Lears, *Fables of Abundance: A Cultural History of Advertising in America* (New York: Harper Collins, 1994), 40-56.

35. "Autographomania," 342, 343, 349; Jacox, "A Mere Question of Handwriting," 43.

36. "Autographomania," 343-44; "Review of *The Autograph Miscellany*," 132-33; G. P. Thruston, "Autograph Collectors and Historic Manuscripts," *Sewanee Review* 10 (January 1902): 29-30. On public sincerity and the private boudoir, see Karen Halttunen, *Confidence Men and Painted Women: A Study of Middle-class Culture in America, 1820-1870* (New Haven: Yale University Press, 1982), 107-9. On candid photography, see Robert E. Mensel, "'Kodakers Lying in Wait': Amateur Photographers and the Right of Privacy in New York, 1865-1910," *American Quarterly* 43 (March 1991): 24-45.

37. "Autographs," *North American Miscellany*, 39.

38. *Doe v Suckermore*, 5 Ad. & E. 705-6 (Great Britain, 1836). In this chapter, I make use of the standard form for legal citations, supplemented by the date and jurisdiction of the case in parentheses.

39. The judge did in fact follow his uncle and his cousin Hartley in indulging an interest in literature. See *Dictionary of National Biography*, s.v., "Coleridge, John Taylor."

40. For an overview of this shift, see John Henry Wigmore, *A Treatise on the System of Evidence in Trials at Common Law*, 4 vols. (Boston: Little, Brown, 1904), 3:2647-56.

41. For the comparison of the human countenance with handwriting, see, for example, Geoffrey Gilbert, *The Law of Evidence* (London, 1726), and Francis Buller, *Introduction to the Law Relative to Trials at Nisi Prius* (London, 1767), in Wigmore, *Evidence*, 3:2650n, 2651n; *Eagleton v Kingston*, 8 Ves. Jun. 439 (Great Britain, 1803); *Gurney v Langlands*, 5 B. and Ald. 331 (Great Britain, 1822); *Gilliam's Administrator v Perkinson's Administrator*, 4 Randolph 328 (Virginia, 1826); *Rowt's adm'x v Kile's adm'r*, 1 Leigh 225 (Virginia, 1829). Additional relevant judicial opinions are cited and quoted at length in Charles C. Moore,

A Treatise on Facts or the Weight and Value of Evidence, 2 vols. (Northport, N.Y.: Edward Thompson, 1908), 1:606–8.

42. See, for example, *Hawkins v Grimes*, 52 Kentucky (8 Ben. Monroe) 267 (Kentucky, 1852); *Tome v Parkersburg Branch Railroad Co.*, 39 Maryland 91 (Maryland, 1873); *Harriot v Sherwood*, 82 Virginia 8, 13 (Virginia, 1884); Moore, *Treatise on Facts*, 1:610.

43. Wigmore, *Evidence*, 3:791–806, 2654–57; *Brookbard v Woodley*, 27 Peake 30 (Great Britain, 1770); *Page v Homans*, 14 Maine Reports (2 Shepley) 481 (Maine, 1837); *Rowt's adm'x v Kile's adm'r*, 1 Leigh 225. There were some exceptions—if the writer was deceased, if witnesses to the act of writing resided at a great distance, or if the witness had formed his opinion on the basis of a business correspondence that was confirmed by subsequent business transactions as authentic—but in general, the line of questioning commonly commenced with "Have you ever seen this person write?" Indeed, while court rulings may have allowed these exceptions to be made in theory, in practice they were often ignored until the end of the eighteenth century and, in America, even into the nineteenth.

44. *Garrells v Alexander*, 4 Esp. 37–38 (Great Britain, 1801); *Eagleton v Kingston*, 8 Ves. Jun. 446; *Wyche v Wyche*, 10 Martin's [O.S.] 408, 410, 414 (Louisiana, 1821); *Willson v Betts*, 4 Denio 201 (New York, 1847). For a general discussion of the principles underlying these rulings, see Wigmore, *Evidence*, 3:793–95.

45. Wigmore, *Evidence*, 3:2661–74; Burr W. Jones, *Commentaries on the Law of Evidence in Civil Cases*, 5 vols. (San Francisco: Bancroft-Whitney, 1913), 3:613–18.

46. *Eagleton v Kingston*, 8 Ves. Jun. 458, 459; *Doe v Suckermore*, 5 A. & E. 705.

47. Thomas Peake, *A Compendium of the Law of Evidence*, 2d ed. (Philadelphia: P. Byrne, 1806), 104; S. March Phillips, *A Treatise on the Law of Evidence*, 2 vols., 4th ed. (New York: Gould, Banks, 1839), 1:484.

48. On vitalism as a romantic reaction to mechanism, see McFarland, *Originality and Imagination*, 188–95; Alfred North Whitehead, *Science and the Modern World* (New York: Macmillan, 1925), 105–33.

49. Adolphe Desbarrolles, *Les Mystères de l'écriture: Art de juger les hommes sur leurs autographes* (Paris: Garnier frères, 1872); Desbarrolles, *Chiromancie nouvelle* (Paris: E. Dentu, 1859); Desbarrolles, *Mystères de la main* (Paris: Chez l'auteur, 1879). On the popularity of chiromancy and its discrediting as superstition, see "Chiromancy," *Gleason's Drawing-Room Companion* 6 (28 January 1854): 60.

50. "Signs of Character," *American Phrenological Journal* 8 (November 1846): 334–38; "Handwriting," *American Phrenological Journal* 43 (January 1866): 14–16; and the eight-part series "On Indications of Character in Handwriting," by George W. James, beginning with *Phrenological Journal* 81 (July 1885): 21–24.

51. John Henry Ingram, *The Philosophy of Handwriting* (London: Chatto and Windus, 1879), 2, 6, 8, 86, and 9–153 passim.

52. Jean-Hippolyte Michon, *Système de graphologie: L'Art de connaître les hommes d'après leur écriture*, 4th ed. (Paris: Office of *La Graphologie*, 1878); Michon, *Méthode pratique de graphologie*, 3d ed. (Paris, 1885).

53. See, for example, John Rexford, *What Handwriting Indicates: An Analytical Graphology* (New York: Putnam's, 1904), 2; Hugo von Hagen, *Reading Character from Handwriting: A Hand-Book of Graphology for Experts, Students and Laymen* (New York: R. S. Mighill, 1902), 1, 14–15; J. Harington Keene, *The Mystery of Handwriting* (Boston: Lee and Shepard, 1896), 1.

54. Henry Frith, *How to Read Character in Handwriting; or, the Grammar of Graphology De-*

scribed and Illustrated (London: Ward, Lock, 1890), 28, 36; Henry Frith, *Chiromancy; or, The Science of Palmistry*, 4th ed. (London: Routledge, 1884); Clifford Howard, *Graphology* (Philadelphia: Penn Publishing, 1904), 18-19; Keene, *Mystery of Handwriting*, 3.

55. John F. Kasson, *Rudeness and Civility: Manners in Nineteenth-Century Urban America* (New York: Hill and Wang, 1990), 96-98; Halttunen, *Confidence Men and Painted Women*, 40-41; Carsten Zelle, "Soul Semiology: On Lavater's Physiognomic Principles," in Shookman, *Faces of Physiognomy*, 40-63; Horlick, "Phrenology," 27-29.

56. Hocquart, *L'Art de juger, 1812*, 1; Byerley, "On Characteristic Signatures," 369-70.

57. Von Hagen, *Reading Character from Handwriting*, 36; Keene, *Mystery of Handwriting*, 5-6.

58. Mary H. Booth, *Graphology* (Detroit: Book-keeper Publishing, n.d.), 5-6, 8-9; H[elen] S. R[obinson] and M. L. R[obinson], *Talks on Graphology: The Art of Knowing Character through Handwriting* (Boston: Lee and Shepard, 1892), 11-17; Rexford, *What Handwriting Indicates*, 1-2, 4; Frith, *Character in Handwriting*, 8; E. Palmer, *Chirography, or the Art of Telling One's Character by Handwriting* (New York: Knickerbocker, 1888), 17; Seymour Eaton, *How to Read Character from Handwriting* (Boston: Oxford Press, 1891), 4; von Hagen, *Reading Character from Handwriting*, 1-2.

59. "Department of Amplification," *New Yorker* (14 January 1950): 77.

60. Keene, *Mystery of Handwriting*, n.p.

61. Rexford, *What Handwriting Indicates*, 8; R[obinson] and R[obinson], *Talks on Graphology*, 10; Richard Dimsdale Stocker, *The Language of Handwriting: A Text-Book of Graphology* (London: Swan Sonnenschein, 1900), 17; von Hagen, *Reading Character from Handwriting*, 75-76, 103-4, 111, 126.

62. Booth, *Graphology*, 3-4.

63. Stocker, *Language of Handwriting*, 11-14, 18-19; von Hagen, *Reading Character from Handwriting*, 135.

64. Stocker, *Language of Handwriting*, 8-9; von Hagen, *Reading Character from Handwriting*, 2-5.

65. Frith, *Character in Handwriting*, 131. See also Howard, *Graphology*, 40-43.

66. Frith, *Character in Handwriting*, 10-11; Howard, *Graphology*, 7-8; Rexford, *What Handwriting Indicates*, 119-22.

67. William S. Gilbert and Arthur S. Sullivan, *H. M. S. Pinafore; or, The Lass That Loved a Sailor* (1878), in *Martyn Green's Treasury of Gilbert and Sullivan*, ed. Martyn Green (New York: Simon and Schuster, 1961), 86; [E. T. Martin], *Martin's System of Practical Penmanship Taught in 24 Lessons* (Worcester, Mass.: n.p., n.d.), pl. 5. This maxim was a modified version of *Hamlet*, 1.5.106.

68. Halttunen, *Confidence Men and Painted Women*; Kasson, *Rudeness and Civility*, 70-111.

69. "Writing," from the *New York News*, reprinted in *PAJ* 3 (June 1879): 2; "Autographs," *PAJ* 3 (May 1879): 4; "Hints to Letter-writers," from the *Halifax Times*, reprinted in *PAJ* 3 (November 1879): 2. See also "Good Writing," *PAJ* 5 (September 1881): 74, for another comparison of appropriate dress with appropriate penmanship.

70. "Writing," from the *New York News*, 2; Sands, "Thoughts on Hand-Writing," 320, 321; *The Young Lady's Book: A Manual of Elegant Recreations, Exercises, and Pursuits*, 2d ed. (Boston: Carter, Hendee and Babcock, [1830]), 344.

71. Coleridge, *Andrew Marvell*, 8n. See also Disraeli, "Autographs," 279, and *Young Lady's Book*, 343.

72. "Pennstock," "The English Angular Hand," *PAJ* 2 (August 1878): 3; "A Foolish Mania," *PAJ* 8 (June 1884): 86. On the popularity of the angular hand, see *A Complete Course of Ladies' Angular Handwriting in Six Numbers* (New York: George R. Lockwood and Son,

1872) and John P. Gordon, *The Eclectic Angular Hand, a Complete Course of Instruction for Ladies in the Fashionable Style of Penmanship* (Cincinnati: Van Antwerp, Bragg, 1888).

73. Thomas Byrnes, *Professional Criminals of America* (New York: Cassell, 1886), 73, 105; Charles L. Young, *Jim the Penman: A Romance of Modern Society* (London, [1886]); "Contributions to the History of Forgery," *Magazine of Foreign Literature, Science and Art* 36 (May 1839): 111; Julian Hawthorne, *An American Penman: From the Diary of Inspector Byrnes* (New York: Cassell, 1887), 5. See also "History and Anecdotes of Forgery," *Eclectic Magazine* 21 (December 1850): 560–65; "The History of a Forger," *Banker's Magazine* 16 (January 1862): 512–17; and Allan Pinkerton, *Thirty Years a Detective* (New York: G. W. Carleton, 1884), 338–441.

74. In England, the shift came about as a result of an 1854 statute, essentially a change in judicial procedure forced down the throats of the bench. In the United States, the admissibility of expert testimony in handwriting cases varied from state to state. In some jurisdictions, experts were excluded, but they were increasingly allowed to testify either by statute or by judicial ruling. Wigmore, *Evidence*, 3:2671–79; Jones, *Law of Evidence*, 3:632–50; Moore, *Treatise on Facts*, 1:659–85.

75. "Expert Testimony in Detecting Forgeries," *PAJ* 4 (September 1880): 69; William E. Hagan, *A Treatise on Disputed Handwriting* (New York: Banks and Brothers, 1894); Daniel T. Ames, *Ames on Forgery: Its Detection and Illustration* (San Francisco: Bancroft-Whitney, 1899); Persifor Frazer, *Bibliotics; or the Study of Documents*, 3d ed. (Philadelphia: Lippincott, 1901); Jerome B. Lavay, *Disputed Handwriting* (Chicago: Harvard Book, 1909); Douglas Blackburn and Waithman Caddell, *The Detection of Forgery* (London: Charles and Edwin Layton, 1909); Albert S. Osborn, *Questioned Documents* (Rochester: Lawyer's Co-operative, 1910).

76. "The Value of Expert Testimony Regarding Questioned Handwriting," *PAJ* 4 (July 1880): 53–54; "Expertism," *PAJ* 5 (June 1881): 45–46; Hagan, *Treatise on Disputed Handwriting*, 28–36; Moore, *Treatise on Facts*, 1:656–77; "Expertism," *PAJ* 4 (July 1880): 53.

77. D. T. Ames, "Address upon Personality of Handwriting, and Expert Examinations," delivered to the Business Educators' and Penmens' Association, Washington, D. C., 1883, in *PAJ* 8 (January 1884): 3; Ames, "Experts in Handwriting," *PAJ* 1 (December 1876): 7; "Experts on Handwriting," *PAJ* 3 (December 1879): 4.

78. Lavay, *Disputed Handwriting*, 191–202; Blackburn and Caddell, *Detection of Forgery*, 72–77; Rosa Baughan, *The Influence of the Stars; A Book of Old World Lore*, 4th ed. (London: K. Paul, Trench, Trubner, 1904).

79. Frazer, *Bibliotics*, 2; "Personal Identity in Hand-Writing," *PAJ* 2 (May 1878): 4.

80. Osborn, *Questioned Documents*, 213n, 318–21; Ames, *Ames on Forgery*, 276–81.

81. Carlo Ginzburg, "Morelli, Freud and Sherlock Holmes: Clues and Scientific Method," *History Workshop* 9 (Spring 1980): 5–36. See also Alain Corbin, "The Secret of the Individual," in *History of Private Life*, vol. 4, ed. Michelle Perot, trans. Arthur Goldhammer (Cambridge: Harvard University Press, 1990), 457–547.

82. John Anson Ford, "New System Classifies Criminals' Handwriting Accurately," *Illustrated World* 36 (December 1921): 542–43; C. D. Lee and R. A. Abbey, *Classification and Identification of Handwriting* (New York: D. Appleton, 1922); Joyce Anenson, "The FBI's First 75 Years," *FBI Law Enforcement Bulletin* 52 (July 1983): 9; Lee R. Waggoner, "Handwriting Evidence for the Investigator," *FBI Law Enforcement Bulletin* 53 (June 1984): 20–25.

83. [Washington] *Index*, 2 November 1841, in *Poe Log*, 346.

84. "Hand-Writing as a Clew to Character," *Every Saturday* 3 (14 October 1871): 378; Ames, *Ames on Forgery*, 276.

1. Nadya Olyanova, *What Does Your Handwriting Reveal?* (New York: Grosset and Dunlap, 1929), 77.

2. Joseph E. Fields, "The History of Autograph Collecting," in *Autographs and Manuscripts: A Collector's Manual*, ed. Edmund Berkeley, Jr. (New York: Scribner's, 1978), 48–50; Robert Notlep, *The Autograph Collector: A New Guide* (New York: Crown, 1968), 111–13; Lester J. Cappon, "Walter R. Benjamin and the Autograph Trade at the Turn of the Century," *Proceedings of the Massachusetts Historical Society* 76 (1966): 20–37; *TC* 1 (15 December 1887): 2; "Autograph Fiends," *TC* 1 (15 December 1887): 4; "A Plea for the Autograph Collector," *TC* 1 (15 December 1887): 5–6; "Twenty-Five Cent List," portion of an advertisement for W. R. Benjamin, a New York autograph dealer, *TC* 1 (15 December 1887): 14; "A Letter from the Battlefield," *TC* 2 (September 1888): 4; W. S. Alexander, "The Historical Value of Autograph Collections," *TC* 4 (January 1891): 50; "In Retrospect," *TC* 4 (June 1891): 113–14; "The Uses of Signatures," *TC* 5 (June 1892): 150–51; H. T. Scott, "On Autograph Collecting, *TC* 11 (July–August 1898): 112; Edward Bok, *The Americanization of Edward Bok* (1920; New York: Scribner's, 1922), 204, 207; Charles Robinson, "The Confessions of an Autograph Hunter," *Cosmopolitan* (January 1893): 305–13; Adrian H. Joline, "Meditations of an Autograph-Hunter," *Harper's Monthly Magazine* (May 1902): 969.

3. Arthur Howard Noll, "What Constitutes Calligraphic Excellence from an Autograph Collector's Point of View," *TC* 4 (June 1891): 112, 113; Noll, "Some Remarks on Graphology," *TC* 4 (December 1890): 40; *TC* 6 (February 1893): 1. See also "Styles of Writing," *TC* 11 (October 1897): 5.

4. George E. Beauchamp, *Practical Method of Reading Character from Handwriting* (New York: George E. Beauchamp, Harlem Printing Shop, 1911), n.p.

5. Matthew Hale, "History of Employment Testing," in *Ability Testing: Uses, Consequences, and Controversies*, part 2: *Documentation Section*, ed. Alexandra K. Wigdor and Wendell R. Garner (Washington, D.C.: National Academy Press, 1982), 3–38; Donald S. Napoli, *Architects of Adjustment: The History of the Psychological Profession in the United States* (Port Washington, N.Y.: Kennikat, 1981), 30–41, 48; Katherine Blackford, *The Job, the Man, the Boss* (Garden City, N. Y.: Doubleday, Page, 1914). For a psychologist's skepticism of graphology, see Donald A. Laird, "What Is the Letter of Application Worth? Science versus Guesswork on Character Analysis from Handwriting," *Industrial Management* 67 (June 1927): 336–42. For a more open-minded attitude, see Knight Dunlap, "Fact and Fable in Character Analysis," *Annals of the American Academy of Political and Social Science* 110 (November 1923): 74–80. For a survey of students of applied psychology that also suggested the jury was still out on graphology, see Donald G. Patterson, "A Note on Popular Pseudo-Psychological Beliefs," *Journal of Applied Psychology* 7 (March 1923): 101–2.

6. William Leslie French, *The Psychology of Handwriting* (New York: Putnam's, 1922); William Leslie French, "Judging Applicants by Form Value of Their Handwriting," *Industrial Management* 53 (July 1917): 487–94; "Handwriting Analysis," *Industrial Management* 53 (July 1917): 593–94; DeWitt B. Lucas, *Handwriting Analysis in Business* (Philadelphia: n.p., 1924), 9, 10.

7. Carolyn Wells, *The Broken O* (Philadelphia: Lippincott, 1933), 281–85, 315.

8. For an overview of these changes, see Alan Dawley, *Struggles for Justice: Social Responsibility and the Liberal State* (Cambridge: Belknap, 1991), 31–38, 65–85. Particular aspects are taken up by Daniel T. Rodgers, *The Work Ethic in Industrial America, 1850–1920* (Chi-

cago: University of Chicago Press, 1974); Alfred Chandler, *The Visible Hand: The Manage-rial Revolution in American Business* (Cambridge: Harvard University Press, 1977); David Montgomery, *The Fall of the House of Labor: The Workplace, the State, and American Labor Activism, 1865–1925* (New York: Cambridge University Press, 1987); David B. Tyack, *The One Best System: A History of American Urban Education* (Cambridge: Harvard University Press, 1974); and Roland Marchand, *Advertising and the American Dream: Making Way for Modernity, 1920–1940* (Berkeley: University of California Press, 1985).

9. Margery W. Davies, *Woman's Place Is at the Typewriter: Office Work and Workers, 1870–1930* (Philadelphia: Temple University Press, 1982).

10. Marie Tomisetta, comp., *Poetical Selections from Celebrated Authors, Suitable for Inscription in Autograph Albums* (New York: Sharps, 1880); Christopher Lang, comp., *Lang's Collection of Verses for Autograph Albums* (St. Louis: The Compiler, 1882); Abbie Clemens Morrow, ed., *Autograph Album Selections* (New York: N. Tibbals and Sons, 1883); and Carrie L. Wehrman, comp., *Wehrman's Selection of Autograph-Album Verses* (New York: H. J. Wehrman, 1891); W. K. McNeil, "The Autograph Album Custom: A Tradition and Its Schol-arly Treatment," *Keystone Folklore Quarterly* 13 (Spring 1968): 29–40; Robert P. Stevenson, "The Autograph Album: A Victorian Girl's Best Friend," *Pennsylvania Folklife* 34 (1984): 34–43; Katharine Morrison McClinton, *Antiques of American Childhood* (New York: Clark-son N. Potter, 1970), 124–34.

11. My discussion is based on an examination of seventy-seven such albums, almost all dating from the 1820s to the 1850s, in the collections of the American Antiquarian Society, Wor-cester, Massachusetts. For an informative bibliography of these albums, see the AAS guide by Todd S. Bernes, "Check List of Albums and Commonplace Books at A. A. S." (unpub-lished).

12. W. Anderson Smith, *"According to Cocker": The Progress of Penmanship from the Earliest Times* (London: Alexander Gardner, 1887), 24, 25–26 (italics in original); Edward Maunde Thompson, *An Introduction to Greek and Latin Paleography* (Oxford, 1912; New York: Burt Franklin, 1973). Graphologist Louise Rice used the Thompson quotation as an epigraph in her *Character Reading from Handwriting* (New York: Frederick A. Stokes, 1927), vii.

13. "A Foolish Mania," *PAJ* 8 (June 1884): 86.

14. "Good and Bad Handwriting," *Western Penman* 1 (March 1874): 1; "Handwriting of Emi-nent Men," *Penman's Gazette* 1 (July 1876): 4; "Bad Writing as a Mark of Genius," *PAJ* 5 (November 1881): 96; J. H. Bachtenkircher, "Essentials of Practical Penmanship," National Education Association, *Journal of Proceedings and Addresses of the Fiftieth Annual Meet-ing* (Ann Arbor, Mich.: National Education Association, 1912), 1075–76; Milton Wittler, "Factors Affecting Ability in Handwriting," *School and Society* 29 (29 June 1929): 849.

15. "Handwriting," *New York Mail*, reprinted in *Western Penman* 1 (March 1874): 1.

16. H. C. Spencer, *Spencerian Key to Practical Penmanship* (New York: Ivison, Blakeman, Tay-lor, 1872), 92; A. N. Palmer, "Practical Writing—A Course for Colleges and Public Schools to Answer the Needs of the People," *Proceedings of the National Educational Association* 35 (1896): 825. See also George E. Gay, "Penmanship," *Journal of Education* 68 (12 November 1908): 510.

17. Charles N. Crandle, "Business Penmanship," *PAJ* 29 (February 1905): xlvi; Philip Robert Dillon, *The Penmanship of New York* (New York: A. N. Palmer, 1911), 15, 18, 20. For a simi-lar report, see S. I. Kreemer, "Writing," *Education* 25 (May 1905): 547.

18. Dillon, *Penmanship of New York*, 18–21.

19. Lyman D. Smith, *How to Teach Writing* (New York: American Book, 1892), 10–11; *Writing in the Schools* (New York: American Book, 1905), 16–17; A. N. Palmer, *The Palmer Method*

of Business Writing (New York: A. N. Palmer, 1913), 2; Commonwealth of Massachusetts, Bulletin of the Department of Education, *Penmanship in Normal Schools: A Manual for Teachers* (Boston: Wright and Pitter, 1921), 16; Elmer G. Miller, "The Vocational Need for Business Writing in the Junior High School and How to Meet It," National Education Association, *Addresses and Proceedings of the Sixty-Second Annual Meeting . . . 1924* (Washington, D.C.: National Education Association, 1924), 434. See also Leta Severance Hiles, *Penmanship: Teaching and Supervision* (Los Angeles: Jesse Ray Miller, 1924), 108.

20. On Rice, see "Vocational Guiding," *Cosmopolitan* (October 1935): 14; Shirley Spencer, "Graphology—Early American," *BAGS* (May 1947): 8, 9; Meet . . . Louise Rice," *BAGS* (May 1952): 3-4; Shirley Spencer, "Some Recollections," *BAGS* (May 1952): 9-10; "Comeback Proves to be Successful," *BAGS* (May 1953): 9. On the gender of graphologists, see *BAGS* (January 1949): 10.

21. Laura Doremus, *Character in Handwriting* (New York: Charles Renard, 1925); "Grapho," *Character Reading from Handwriting* (Philadelphia: McKay, 1943); Mary B. Mullett, "What Your Handwriting Tells about You," *American* (May 1929): 24; Bill Cavanagh, *The Key to Graphology* (Detroit: Cavanagh and Cavanagh, 1935), 7; "A.G.S. Graph-ites: Shirley Spencer," *BAGS* (October 1944): 3; Helen King, "Commercializing Graphology," *BAGS* (January 1949): 4; "Meet: Helen King," *BAGS* (May 1952): 5.

22. William Leslie French, "Cupid, Graphologist," *Good Housekeeping* (December 1912): 765-71; French, "What Your Handwriting Tells," *Woman's Home Companion* (August 1912): 12; French, "How Your Handwriting Shows Your Character," *McClure's* (September 1913): 130-35; Louise Rice, "How to Read Character in Handwriting," *Saturday Evening Post* (3 October 1925): 44; Dorothy Sara, "Is Your Heart in Your Handwriting?" *Real Romances* (November 1944): 46. Numerous references to publications in pulp magazines can be found in most issues of the *Bulletin of the American Graphological Society*, for example, the September 1947 issue on pp. 4 and 6.

23. "Meet . . . Louise Rice," 3-4; "A.G.S. Graph-ites: Muriel Stafford," *BAGS* (October 1944): 4; King, "Commercializing Graphology," 2; "Profiles: T-Bars and I-Dots," *New Yorker* (24 December 1949): 29-30; Spencer, "Some Recollections," 9-10.

24. *DSM* (24 December 1921): 132; *DSM* (11 March 1922): 129; Shirley Spencer, "Classification of Types," *BAGS* (September 1947): 11; King, "Commercializing Graphology," 2; *BAGS* (July 1951): 12; "Meet . . . Louise Rice," 4; "Meet: Helen King," 5; "Meet: Dorothy Sara," *BAGS* (May 1952): 7; "Meet: Shirley Spencer," *BAGS* (May 1952): 7; Spencer, "Some Recollections," 9-10. Sara, King, and Anne T. Bennett were also assistants of Rice's who became graphologists.

25. "Profiles: T-Bars and I-Dots," 29-30; Advertisement for Chipso detergent, New York *Daily News*, 1 February 1935, 41; "A.G.S. Graph-ites: Dorothy Sara," *BAGS* (October 1944): 1; King, "Commercializing Graphology," 4.

26. For insight into these private practices, see Beauchamp, *Reading Character from Handwriting*, and the intermittent coverage in *BAGS*.

27. Jane Lambe, "Contact Grapho-Analysts," *BAGS* (October 1946): 11; George T. Foldes, "A Graphological Interlude," *BAGS* (October 1946): 10; Ann Dix, "Personal Appearance by Appointment," *BAGS* (January 1947): 1; Alice Cary Gilchrist, "You Are What You Write," *BAGS* (January 1947): 2; King, "Commercializing Graphology, 3, 4; "Meet: Helen Yun," *BAGS* (January 1955): 13; M. N. Bunker, *You Too Can Read Handwriting for Pleasure and Profit* (Springfield, Mo.: International Grapho Analysis Society, 1955); Irma J. Craw, *Your 't' Party* (Springfield, Mo.: International Grapho Analysis Society, n.d.); *BAGS* (May

1948): 9; *BAGS* (May 1949): 11; "Meet: The Lookers, Glen and Lucille," *BAGS* (January 1954): 16.

28. Rice, *Character Reading from Handwriting,* 6; "Meet . . . Louise Rice," 3.

29. "Comeback Proves to be Successful," 9; Spencer, "Some Recollections," 9. On women in psychology, see Elizabeth Scarborough and Laurel Furumoto, *Untold Lives: The First Generation of American Women Psychologists* (New York: Columbia University Press, 1987).

30. Beauchamp, *Reading Character from Handwriting;* Eugene R. Dukette, *Character Portrayed by Handwriting* (n.p., 1926), foreword; Paul E. Jackman, John T. Wentz, and Booth B. Goodman, *Success through Handwriting* (Oakland, Calif.: Institute of Personal Development, 1936), foreword.

31. "Department of Amplification," *New Yorker* (January 1950): 77; "To Our Correspondents: Character in Handwriting," *American Phrenological Journal* 97 (June 1894): 317; Beauchamp, *Reading Character from Handwriting.*

32. A. Henry Silver, *What Handwriting Reveals: How It Determines Character, Ability, Disposition and Health and How To Use This Information for Profit* (New York: Putnam's , 1929), 13–14; L[ouis] G[illespie] Erskine, *Your Signature: What It Reveals* (Larchmont, N.Y.: n.p., 1931), 3; "Andrienne" [Ann Saper], *What Does Your Handwriting Reveal?* (Portland, Or.: West Coast Printing and Binding, 1935), 3, 4; Fritzi Remont, *The Revelation of Character in Handwriting* (Los Angeles: n.p., 1918), 5, 6, 7.

33. Warren I. Susman, " 'Personality' and the Making of Twentieth Century Culture," in *Culture as History: The Transformation of American Society in the Twentieth Century* (New York: Pantheon, 1984), 271–85; Marchand, *Advertising and the American Dream,* esp. 13–24, 53–63; Welham Clarke, *Power and Force through the Application of Memory, the Reading of Character and Personality in Business and Social Life,* section XIII: "Character Reading: The Hand and Fingers, Their Prints, and Handwriting" (Chicago: John C. Winston, 1920).

34. Clifford Howard, *Graphology* (Philadelphia: Penn Publishing, 1904), 11; Hugo von Hagen, *Reading Character from Handwriting: A Hand-Book of Graphology for Experts, Students and Laymen* (New York: R. S. Mighill, 1902), 5–6, 8; H[elen] S. R[obinson] and M. L. R[obinson], *Talks on Graphology: The Art of Knowing Character through Handwriting* (Boston: Lee and Shepard, 1892), 15, 19.

35. *DSM* (21 May 1921): 135; (11 March 1922): 132.

36. My collective profile is based on an analysis of all the columns that appeared weekly in *Detective Story Magazine* in the years 1920–22. On average, each column analyzed the handwriting of about fifteen people.

37. Conviction of distinctiveness: *DSM* (8 April 1922): 132; (19 March 1921): 40–41; (19 February 1921): 136; (23 March 1921): 134; (9 April 1921): 133; (30 April 1921): 136; (7 May 1921): 132; (24 September 1921): 139; (8 October 1921): 136; (23 April 1922): 132. Escape from mediocrity: *DSM* (25 March 1922): 133; (4 February 1922): 130; (17 December 1921): 129; (28 May 1921): 132; (7 January 1922): 131; (7 January 1922): 132; (2 July 1921): 132. Rice, "How to Read Character in Handwriting," 44.

38. Louise Rice, "Yourself—As in a Mirror," *Pictorial Review* (April 1927): 2; Olyanova, *What Does Your Handwriting Reveal?* 27; advertisement for Chipso detergent; "Vocational Guiding," 14. Some 998 other interesting individuals would receive decreasing amounts of money, awarded "in order of merit."

39. Encouragement: *DSM* (28 May 1921): 132; (2 July 1921): 132; (2 April 1921): 135. Immigrants: *DSM* (29 January 1921): 136 ("Fulton Market"); *DSM* (25 December 1920): 138–39; (1 January 1921): 136; (15 January 1921): 134; (19 March 1921): 140; (17 September 1921): 132–

33. Heredity: *DSM* (25 December 1920): 138; (29 January 1921): 134; (19 March 1921): 140; (18 June 1921): 130–31; (2 July 1921): 132; (15 October 1921): 134. Women: *DSM* (1 January 1921): 135; (16 April 1921): 132; (30 April 1921): 135; (14 May 1921): 134; (13 August 1921): 133; (10 December 1921): 133; (8 April 1922): 134.

40. Daniel T. Ames, *Ames on Forgery: Its Detection and Illustration* (San Francisco: Bancroft-Whitney, 1899), 276–77; "Grapho," *Character Reading from Handwriting; BAGS* (October 1944): 1; Gilchrist, "You Are What You Write," 2; Isabelle Clark Swezy, "Graphology as It Should be Practiced," *BAGS* (January 1947): 7.

41. *DSM* (15 January 1921): 135; (23 April 1921): 134; (24 September 1921): 139; (30 April 1921): 136; (8 October 1921): 136; (19 February 1921): 136.

42. *DSM* (25 December 1920): 139; (12 November 1921): 131; (23 July 1921): 133; (4 June 1921): 134.

43. French, "How Your Handwriting Shows Your Character," 135. On adjustment as the paradigm for the profession of psychology, see Napoli, *Architects of Adjustment.*

44. Rice, *Practical Graphology*, 164.

45. *DSM* (25 December 1920): 136. For a similar situation in Shirley Spencer's graphological column, see the (New York) *Daily News*, 15 April 1936.

46. Olyanova, *What Does Your Handwriting Reveal?* 2; Rice, "Yourself—As in a Mirror," 2.

47. T. J. Jackson Lears, *No Place of Grace: Antimodernism and the Transformation of American Culture, 1880–1920* (New York: Pantheon, 1981).

48. Susman, "'Personality' and the Making of Twentieth Century Culture," 271–85; T. J. Jackson Lears, "From Salvation to Self-Realization: Advertising and the Therapeutic Roots of the Consumer Culture, 1880–1930," in *The Culture of Consumption: Critical Essays in American History, 1880–1930,* ed. Richard Wrightman Fox and T. J. Jackson Lears (New York: Pantheon, 1983), 1–38.

49. William Dean Howells, *A Boy's Town* (New York: Harper, 1890), 171.

50. Rice, "How to Read Character in Handwriting," 44; Anton Da Borcka, *Personality in Handwriting* (New York: Reader Mail, 1936). Archer Wall Douglas switched the positions of signature and text with respect to character and personality, but his point was otherwise the same ("The Art and Nature of Graphology," *Atlantic Monthly* [March 1924]: 344).

51. Arthur Howard Noll, "Some Remarks on Graphology," *TC* 4 (December 1890): 40; von Hagen, *Reading Character from Handwriting*, 14; *Dictionnaire de biographie française* (Paris: Librairie Letouzey et Ané, 1965), s.v., "Crépieux-Jamin, Jules." Graphology continues to be taken seriously in Europe, particularly in France, where handwritten letters of application for employment are de rigueur, and graphologists are hired to assess prospective employees much as French and Lucas offered their personnel services (Roger Cohen, "In France, It's How You Cross the T's," *New York Times*, 19 October 1993, D1–D2).

52. Alfred Binet, *Les Révélations de l'écriture d'après un controle scientifique* (Paris: Felix Alcan, 1906), 250–51.

53. Binet, *Révélations de l'écriture*, 21–22, 38–44, 168–71, 250–57. June Downey reviewed Binet's treatise in *Psychological Bulletin* 5 (15 October 1908): 327–30.

54. William T. Preyer, *Zur Psychologie des Schreibens* (Hamburg: L. Voss, 1895); Georg Schneidemühl, *Handschrift und Charakter* (Leipzig: T. Grieben, 1911); Ludwig Klages, *Handschrift und Charakter* (Leipzig: J. A. Barth, 1917); Max Pulver, *Symbolik der Handschrift* (Zurich: Orel Fussli, 1931).

55. Thea Stein-Lewinson, "An Introduction to the Graphology of Ludwig Klages," *Character and Personality* 6 (1937–38): 163–76; Pulver, *Symbolik der Handschrift.*

56. Pulver's tripartite schema in particular became popular in America after World War II

and remains the basis for present-day graphology. See, for example, "Profiles: T-Bars and I-Dots," 26–30; Ann Mahony, *Handwriting and Personality: How Graphology Reveals What Makes People Tick* (New York: Ballantine, 1989); P. Scott Hollander, *Reading between the Lines: The Basics of Handwriting Analysis* (St. Paul, Minn.: Llewellyn Publications, 1991); Andrea McNichol, *Handwriting Analysis: Putting It to Work for You* (Chicago: Contemporary, 1991).

57. Clark L. Hull and Robert B. Montgomery, "An Experimental Investigation of Certain Alleged Relations between Character and Handwriting," *Psychological Review* 26 (January 1919): 63.

58. Ibid., 65.

59. Ibid., 66–74. For a similar dismissal of Binet's results in a learned, nonscientific periodical, see "Impossibility of Inferring Character from Handwriting," *Current Literature* 41 (December 1906): 687–88.

60. "Family Likeness in Handwriting," *Scientific American* (2 December 1911): 496; Leonard Keene Hirshberg, "Curious Things about Handwriting," *Scientific American* (22 August 1914): 130; E. L. Thorndike, "Resemblance of Young Twins in Handwriting," *American Naturalist* (June 1915): 377–79; Webster A. Melcher, "Handwriting from a Psychopathic Viewpoint," *Journal of Criminal Law* 7 (July 1916): 284–87; Clarence Quinan, "Handwriting in Criminals: An Experimental Study," *Archives of Neurology and Psychiatry* (Chicago) 32 (1934): 350–58. Explorations of this sort were far more common in German-speaking Europe, especially and most ominously during the Nazi era. References to German studies of hereditary factors in handwriting, and of correlations of handwriting style with deviant behavior, can be found in the bibliography issued by the Handwriting Foundation (Washington, D.C.) entitled *Handwriting and Related Factors, 1890–1960* (Madison, Wis., n.d.), 65–67, 81–93.

61. Binet, *Révélations de l'écriture*, 21–22; June E. Downey, "Judgments on the Sex of Handwriting," *Psychological Review* 17 (May 1910): 205–16. See also S. M. Newhall, "Sex Differences in Handwriting," *Journal of Applied Psychology* 10 (1926): 151–61; J. S. Kinder, "A New Investigation of Judgments on the Sex of Handwriting," *Journal of Educational Psychology* 17 (May 1926): 341–44; and M. E. Broom, B. Thompson, and M. T. Bouton, "Sex Differences in Handwriting," *Journal of Applied Psychology* 13 (1929): 159–66.

62. Henry Frith, *How to Read Character in Handwriting; or, the Grammar of Graphology Described and Illustrated* (London: Ward, Lock, 1890), 15–16; Louise Rice, *Practical Graphology; or, the Science of Reading Character through Handwriting* (Chicago: Library Shelf, 1910), 149. See also J. Harington Keene, *The Mystery of Handwriting* (Boston: Lee and Shepard, 1896), 19–20; Rosa Baughan, *Character Indicated by Handwriting*, 3d ed., rev. (London: William Rider and Son, 1919), 6–7; and Olyanova, *What Does Your Handwriting Reveal?* 27.

63. Isaac Disraeli, "Autographs," in *Curiosities of Literature*, 9th ed., 6 vols. (London: Edward Moxon, 1834), 5:279; *The Young Lady's Book: A Manual of Elegant Recreations, Exercises, and Pursuits*, 2d ed. (Boston: Carter, Hendee and Babcock, [1830]), 343; "Handling the Pen," *PAJ* 1 (February 1878): 2; Frith, *Character in Handwriting*, 15–16; French, "Cupid, Graphologist," 766; Douglas, "The Art and Nature of Graphology," 346.

64. Keene, *Mystery of Handwriting*, 19; French, "Her Handwriting," *Harper's Weekly* (1 August 1914): 105; Rice, "Yourself—As in a Mirror," 2. See also Louise Rice, "What Handwriting Tells about Men and Women," *The Woman's Journal* (March 1931): 20–21.

65. June E. Downey, *Graphology and the Psychology of Handwriting* (Baltimore: Warwick and York, 1919), 1–3.

66. Ibid.

67. *Notable American Women,* s.v. "Downey, June Etta"; *American National Biography,* s.v. "Downey, June Etta," draft. I am grateful to Professor Laurel Furumoto for providing me with the latter source, of which she is the author.

68. Downey, "Judgments on the Sex of Handwriting," 209.

69. Ibid., 210. Downey published a popular version of her research and conclusions in *The Independent* (30 January 1913): 262–64.

CHAPTER FIVE
Automatic Writing?

1. William James, "Notes on Automatic Writing," *Proceedings of the American Society for Psychical Research* (1889): 551–54, 556–57.

2. Ibid., 555.

3. F. W. H. Myers, "On a Telepathic Explanation of Some So-Called Spiritualistic Phenomena. Part I," *Proceedings for the Society for Psychical Research* 2 (28 November 1884): 222. See also Myers, "Automatic Writing—II," *Proceedings for the Society for Psychical Research* 3 (30 January 1885): 1–63. On Myers, see Gardner Murphy, "The Life Work of Frederic W. H. Myers," *Tomorrow* (Winter 1954): 33–39.

4. Frank N. Freeman and Mary L. Dougherty, *How to Teach Handwriting: A Teacher's Manual* (Boston: Houghton Mifflin, 1923), 19.

5. A. N. Palmer quoted James in "Child Habit Formation in the Elementary Schools," *American Penman* (June 1927): 1.

6. Frank N. Freeman, *The Teaching of Handwriting* (Boston: Houghton Mifflin, 1914), vii, viii.

7. On vertical writing, see John Jackson, *The Theory and Practice of Handwriting* (London: Sampson Low, Marston, 1893); A. F. Newlands and R. K. Row, *Teacher's Manual to Accompany the Natural System of Vertical Writing* (Boston: Heath, 1896); and H. W. Shaylor, *How to Teach Vertical Writing* (Boston: Ginn, 1898). For later perspectives on the vertical vogue, see Frank N. Freeman, "Some Issues in the Teaching of Handwriting," *ESJ* 12 (September, October 1911): 1–5, and Mary L. Dougherty, "History of the Teaching of Handwriting in America," *ESJ* 18 (December 1917): 283.

8. Cloyd N. McAllister, "Researches on Movements Used in Writing," *Studies from the Yale Psychological Laboratory* 8 (1900): 21–63; Charles Hubbard Judd, *Genetic Psychology for Teachers* (New York: D. Appleton, 1903), chaps. 6, 7; Freeman, *Teaching of Handwriting,* 8–29, 64–69. Much of this research is summarized in Mary E. Thompson, *Psychology and Pedagogy of Writing* (Baltimore: Warwick and York, 1911).

9. McAllister, "Researches on Movements Used in Writing," 55–59; Judd, *Genetic Psychology for Teachers,* 170–82.

10. Freeman, "Some Issues in the Teaching of Handwriting," 5–7, 53–59; Freeman, *The Handwriting Movement: A Study of the Motor Factors of Excellence in Penmanship* (Chicago: University of Chicago Press, 1918); Freeman, "Principles of Method in Teaching Writing as Derived from Scientific Investigation," in *The Eighteenth Yearbook of the National Society for the Study of Education,* part 2: *Fourth Report of the Committee on Economy of Time in Education,* ed. Guy Montrose Whipple (Bloomington, Ill.: Public School Publishing, 1919), 11–15; Freeman, "The Scientific Evidence on the Handwriting Movement," *JEP* 12 (May 1921): 253–70; Freeman, "Present-Day Issues in the Teaching of Handwriting," *ESJ* 24 (September 1923): 38–39. Related investigations, many carried out by Freeman's graduate

students, include H. W. Nutt, "Rhythm in Handwriting," *ESJ* 17 (February 1917): 432–45, and 19 (March 1919): 532–40; and Paul V. West, "The Relation of Rhythm to the Handwriting Movement," *JEP* 13 (October 1922): 438–44.

11. Judd, *Genetic Psychology for Teachers*, 219–26; Freeman, *Teaching of Handwriting*, 29–31; Freeman, "Some Issues in the Teaching of Handwriting," 6–7; Harry Houston, "Pedagogical Principles in Teaching Penmanship," *Journal of Education* 83 (2 March 1916): 241–42.

12. Judd, *Genetic Psychology for Teachers*, 226, 232–35; Thompson, *Psychology and Pedagogy of Writing*, 86–90; Freeman, *Teaching of Handwriting*, 77–87, 104–9; Freeman, "Principles of Method in Teaching Writing as Derived from Scientific Investigation," 15–17; Freeman, "Present-Day Issues in the Teaching of Handwriting," 38–39; Freeman and Dougherty, *How to Teach Handwriting*, 21–23.

13. Judd, *Genetic Psychology for Teachers*, 227–31; Freeman, "Present-Day Issues in the Teaching of Handwriting," 39–40; Freeman and Dougherty, *How to Teach Handwriting*, 24–25.

14. The first reference to left-handedness I can find in the dozens of penmanship manuals I have examined came in 1892, in G. Bixler, *Physical Training in Penmanship* (Wooster, Ohio: Bixler's Business College, 1892), 43. The very rare references in penmanship journals came mainly in response to specific requests for guidance on the part of left-handers: "I. B. C., Scale's Mound, Illinois," *Penman's Gazette* 1 (March 1876): 4; "Answers to Correspondence," *PAJ* 3 (May 1879): 6–7; and "Answers to Correspondence," *PAJ* 8 (March 1884): 33. One penmanship journal did note that President Garfield, "left handed by nature," had "conquered the peculiarity," and wrote a beautiful hand, in fact, had once been a penmanship teacher (*PAJ* 4 [July 1880]: 51). For an example of classroom prohibition of left-handedness, see the description of an Uxbridge, Massachusetts, school in the late 1840s in William A. Mowry, *Recollections of a New England Educator, 1838–1908* (New York: Silver, Burdett, 1908), 53–54.

15. Among the earliest scientific references are Thomas Dwight, "Right and Left-Handedness," *Journal of Psychological Medicine* 4 (1870): 541; W. Ogle, "On Dextral Preeminence," *Lancet* (1871): 49; G. Stanley Hall and E. M. Hartwell, "Bilateral Asymmetry of Function," *Mind* 9 (January 1884): 92–109; and J. M. Baldwin, "Origin of Right or Left-Handedness," *Science* 31 (October 1890): 247–48. For a review of the scientific controversies surrounding the nature of handedness, see Laura G. Smith, "A Brief Survey of Right- and Left-Handedness," *Pedagogical Seminary and Journal of Genetic Psychology* 24 (March 1917): 19–35. For an example of a lay "historical" explanation of the evolution of right dominance at its hokiest, see George M. Gould, *Righthandedness and Lefthandedness* (Philadelphia: Lippincott, 1908), which invokes shield holding among our primeval ancestors. For two sides of the heredity versus environment debate, see Francis Ramaley, "Inheritance of Left-Handedness," *American Naturalist* 47 (December 1913): 730–38, and John B. Watson, "What the Nursery Has to Say about Instincts," *Pedagogical Seminary and Journal of Genetic Psychology* 32 (June 1925): 319–22.

16. Freeman, "Present-Day Issues in the Teaching of Handwriting," 38–39, 40–41; Freeman and Dougherty, *How to Teach Handwriting*, 12; Lewis M. Terman, *The Hygiene of the School Child* (Boston: Houghton Mifflin, 1914), 345–46; P. B. Ballard, "Sinistrality and Speech," *Journal of Experimental Pedagogy* 1 (1911–12): 298–310; Thompson, *Psychology and Pedagogy of Writing*, 116–17; W. Franklin Jones, "The Problem of Handedness in Education," National Education Association, *Journal of Proceedings and Addresses of the Fifty-Third Annual Meeting . . . 1915* (Ann Arbor, Mich.: National Education Association, 1915), 962–63.

17. E. L. Thorndike, "Handwriting," *Teachers College Record* 11 (March 1910): 83–175; Leonard P. Ayres, *A Scale for Measuring the Quality of Handwriting of School Children* (New York:

Russell Sage Foundation, 1912); Freeman, *Teaching of Handwriting,* 118-50; Freeman, "An Analytical Scale for Judging Handwriting," *ESJ* 15 (April 1915): 432-41.

18. The secondary literature on the history of intelligence testing is substantial. For a brief introduction, see David B. Tyack, *The One Best System: A History of American Urban Education* (Cambridge: Harvard University Press, 1974), 198-216. The underlying eugenicist outlook is explored in Clarence J. Karier, "Testing for Order and Control in the Corporate Liberal State," in *Roots of Crisis: American Education in the Twentieth Century,* ed. Clarence J. Karier, Paul C. Violas, and Joel Spring (Chicago: Rand McNally, 1973), 108-37. In the same volume, Joel Spring treats intelligence testing as a form of social control in "Education as a Form of Social Control" (30-39). Other assessments include Michael M. Sokal, "James McKeen Cattell and American Psychology in the 1920s," in *Explorations in the History of Psychology in the United States,* ed. Josef Brozek (Lewisburg, Penn.: Bucknell University Press, 1984), 273-323; Henry L. Minton, *Lewis M. Terman: Pioneer in Psychological Testing* (New York: New York University Press, 1988); and Paul Davis Chapman, *Schools as Sorters: Lewis M. Terman, Applied Psychology, and the Intelligence Testing Movement, 1890-1930* (New York: New York University Press, 1988). For the views of early advocates and users of intelligence testing, see the essays in Guy Montrose Whipple, ed., *The Twenty-First Yearbook of the National Society for the Study of Education. Intelligence Tests and Their Use* (Bloomington, Ill.: Public School Publishing, 1923).

19. Walter S. Monroe, "Existing Tests and Standards," in *The Seventeenth Yearbook of the National Society for the Study of Education,* part 2: *The Measurement of Educational Products,* ed. Guy Montrose Whipple (Bloomington, Ill.: Public School Publishing, 1918), 71-104; E. L. Thorndike, "Measurement in Education," *Teachers College Record* 22 (November 1921): 374; Harlan C. Hines, *A Guide to Educational Measurements* (Boston: Houghton, Mifflin, 1923); Ellwood P. Cubberley, *Public School Administration: A Statement of the Fundamental Principles Underlying the Organization and Administration of Public Education,* 3d ed. (Boston: Houghton Mifflin, 1929), 502n. On educational measurements, see also in the *Seventeenth Yearbook,* Leonard P. Ayres, "History and Present Status of Educational Measurements" (9-15); Edward L. Thorndike, "The Nature, Purposes, and General Methods of Measurements of Educational Products" (16-24); and the exhaustive "Selected Bibliography of Certain Phases of Educational Measurement," by Edna Bryner, Ayres' colleague at the Russell Sage Foundation (161-90). Cubberley devotes an entire chapter to "Educational Research and Efficiency" in his *Public School Administration.* Ralph Tyler offers a historical and critical summary of the movement in "The Specific Techniques of Investigation: Examination and Testing Acquired Knowledge, Skill, and Ability," *The Thirty-Seventh Yearbook of the National Society for the Study of Education,* part 2: *The Scientific Movement in Education,* ed. Guy Montrose Whipple (Bloomington, Ill.: Public School Publishing, 1938), 341-55.

20. Ayres, "History and Present Status of Educational Measurements," 9, 12; E. L. Thorndike, *Introduction to the Theory of Mental and Social Measurements,* 2d ed. (New York: Teachers College, Columbia University, 1913); Thorndike, "Nature, Purposes, and General Methods of Measurements of Educational Products"; Geraldine Jonich, *The Sane Positivist* (Middletown, Conn.: Wesleyan University Press, 1968); Leonard P. Ayres, *The Binet-Simon Measuring Scale for Intelligence: Some Criticisms and Suggestions* (New York: Russell Sage Foundation, n.d.); Ayres, *The Measurement of Educational Process and Products* (New York: Russell Sage Foundation, 1912); Ayres, *Laggards in Our Schools* (New York: Russell Sage Foundation, 1909); Frank N. Freeman, *Mental Tests: Their History, Principles and Applications* (Boston: Houghton Mifflin, 1926).

21. Thorndike, "Handwriting," 128–29; Thompson, *Psychology and Pedagogy of Writing*, 114–15; Freeman and Dougherty, *How to Teach Handwriting*, 4–5, 6–7, 9–10, 29.

22. On Palmer's teacher-training requirement and activities, see Joseph S. Taylor, "A. N. Palmer: An Appreciation," *Educational Review* 76 (June 1928): 17–18, and A. N. Palmer, *The Palmer Method of Teaching Practical Writing in Graded Schools* (New York: A. N. Palmer, 1910), 5–11, 36–38.

23. Virginia Education Commission, *Virginia Public Schools: A Survey of a Southern State Public School System*, 2 vols. (Yonkers-on-Hudson, N.Y.: World Book, 1920), 1:106–7.

24. Freeman, "Principles of Method of Teaching Writing as Derived from Scientific Investigation," 11–25; "Penmanship and Arm-Movement," *ESJ* 24 (December 1923): 247; Freeman, "Scientific Evidence on the Handwriting Movement," 253. On the estrangement of the university handwriting experts from school system penmanship supervisors, see, for example, Luella Chapman, "The Problem of the Supervisor of Handwriting—Abstract," *National Education Association, Proceedings of the Sixty-Seventh Annual Meeting* 67 (Washington, D.C.: National Education Association, 1929), 811.

25. Leta Severance Hiles, *Penmanship: Teaching and Supervision* (Los Angeles: Jesse Ray Miller, 1924), 96; *Fifty-Eighth Annual Report of the Board of Education of the City of St. Louis, Mo., for the Year Ending June 30 1912* (n.p., n.d.), 133; Commonwealth of Massachusetts, Bulletin of the Department of Education, *Penmanship in Normal Schools: A Manual for Teachers* (Boston: Wright and Pitter, 1921), 10–12; A. N. Palmer, "Penmanship," National Education Association, *Journal of Proceedings and Addresses of the Fifty-Third Annual Meeting . . . 1915* (Ann Arbor, Mich.: National Education Association, 1915), 888–93; Taylor, "A. N. Palmer," 19. Taylor also reported that three-quarters of the membership of the National Association of Penmanship Teachers and Supervisors had been trained by Palmer, that Palmer's company employed forty-five traveling consultants to participating school systems, that more than 150 summer schools existed to instruct teachers in the Palmer method, and that the Palmer company itself was at that moment training fifty thousand teachers in its own normal department (18–19). Furthermore, Taylor's figure did not include schools that adopted look-alike muscular movement systems.

26. *Colorado Springs Public Schools: Course of Study, Handwriting* (Colorado Springs: Administrative Department, Colorado Springs Public Schools, 1921), 5, 6. See also Commonwealth of Massachusetts, *Penmanship in Normal Schools*, 23.

27. "Penmanship and Arm-Movement," 247; Jackson W. Granholm, "Curse You, Palmer!" *American Mercury* (April 1954): 91, 92, 93; *Fifty-Seventh Annual Report of the Board of Education of the City of St. Louis, Mo., for the Year Ending June 30 1911* (n.p., n.d.), 123; "Handwriting in the Schools," *ESJ* 21 (September 1920): 6–7; Hiles, *Penmanship*, 57, 91.

28. *Annual Report of the Superintendent of Education of the City of Buffalo, 1905–1906* (Buffalo: Hausauer-Jones, 1907), 23; "Penmanship and Arm-Movement," 247; *Annual Report of the Board of Education of the City of St. Louis . . . 1911*, 122–23; *Annual Report of the Board of Education of the City of St. Louis . . . 1912*, 133; *Sixty-First Report of the Board of Education of the City of St. Louis, Mo., for the Year Ending June 30 1915* (n.p., n.d.), 196–98.

29. Ralph Haefner, *The Educational Significance of Left-Handedness*, Teachers College, Columbia University, Contributions to Education, No. 360 (New York: Bureau of Publications, Teachers College, Columbia University, 1929), 79; Charles E. Meleny, *Observations on the Teaching of Penmanship in Elementary Schools* (New York: A. N. Palmer, 1911), 21–22; *Annual Report of the Board of Education of the City of St. Louis . . . 1912*, 132; State of Ohio, Department of Public Instruction, *Manual of Fundamentals in the Teaching of Handwriting in the Public Schools* (Columbus: F. J. Heer, 1918), 36. On the conflict between educational

psychologists and penmanship supervisors on this issue, see Freeman, "Present-Day Issues in the Teaching of Handwriting," 40, and Joseph S. Taylor, *Supervision and Teaching of Handwriting* (Richmond, Va.: Johnson Publishing, 1926), 81–82.

30. Norma V. Scheidemann and Hazel Colyer, "A Study in Reversing the Handedness of Some Left-Handed Writers," *JEP* 22 (March 1931): 191; C. E. Lauterbach, "Shall the Left-Handed Child Be Transferred?" *Journal of Genetic Psychology* 43 (September–December 1933): 458.

31. Ayres, *Scale for Measuring the Quality of Handwriting;* Ayres, *The Public Schools of Springfield, Illinois* (New York: Russell Sage Foundation, n.d), 74–77; *School Survey: Grand Rapids, Michigan, 1916* (n.p., n.d), 129–36; *The Public School System of San Francisco, Cal.* (San Francisco: Education Committee of the San Francisco Teachers' Association, 1917), 18–19; Board of Education, City of New York, Bureau of Reference, Research and Statistics, Publication no. 18, *Grade Standards for the New York Penmanship Scale* (New York: Board of Education, 1920); Hiles, *Penmanship,* 80–81, 84; *Sixty-Ninth Annual Report of the Board of Education of the City of St. Louis, Mo., for the Year Ending June 30 1923* (n.p., n.d.), 41–46; Carrol P. Gard, "A Romance of the Second 'R,'" *Journal of Education* (5 February 1934): 69.

32. Cubberley, *Public School Administration,* 488–89, 499n; Tyack, *One Best System,* 135–36.

33. See, for example, the comments of E. S. Russell, the supervising agent of Connecticut's State Department of Public Instruction, regarding whole-arm movement in handwriting as "a violation of nature" and "clever commercial propaganda" ("Penmanship and Arm-Movement," 247, 248).

34. Taylor, *Supervision and Teaching of Handwriting,* 6; Palmer, *Palmer Method,* 8.

35. A. N. Palmer, "Practical Writing: A Course for Colleges and Public Schools to Answer the Needs of the People," *Proceedings of the National Education Association* 35 (1896): 827; Bixler, *Physical Training in Penmanship,* 44; Tyack, *One Best System,* 139–47.

36. Tyack, *One Best System,* 188–91; David John Hogan, *Class and Reform: School and Society in Chicago, 1880–1930* (Philadelphia: University of Pennsylvania Press, 1985), esp. chap. 4.

37. Anson Rabinbach, *The Human Motor: Energy, Fatigue, and the Origins of Modernity* (New York: Basic, 1990); John M. O'Donnell, *The Origins of Behaviorism: American Psychology, 1870–1920* (New York: New York University Press, 1985); John C. Burnham, "The Mind-Body Problem in the Early Twentieth Century," in *Paths into American Culture: Psychology, Medicine, and Morals* (Philadelphia: Temple University Press, 1988), 26–37, 239–41.

38. My discussion of the history of psychology draws from O'Donnell, *Origins of Behaviorism,* and Burnham, "Mind-Body Problem."

39. Palmer, "Child Habit Formation in the Elementary Schools," 1, 3.

40. William H. Dooley, *The Education of the Ne'er-Do-Well* (Cambridge: Houghton Mifflin, 1916), 26; Hogan, *Class and Reform,* chap. 3; Daniel T. Rodgers, *The Work Ethic in Industrial America, 1850–1920* (Chicago: University of Chicago Press, 1978), 84–87; Marvin Lazerson and W. Norton Grubb, eds., *American Education and Vocationalism: A Documentary History* (New York: Teachers College Press, 1974); Dominick Cavallo, *Muscles and Morals: Organized Playgrounds and Urban Reform, 1880–1920* (Philadelphia: University of Pennsylvania Press, 1981).

41. Hiles, *Penmanship,* 16; J. Albert Kirby, *Penmanship: The Kirby Rhythmic Method* (New York: Newson, 1916), 27. Kirby, head of the penmanship department at New York City's High School of Commerce, modeled his muscular movement system closely on the Palmer method.

42. Joseph S. Taylor, *The Educational Value of Muscular Movement Writing* (New York: A. N. Palmer, 1910), 5–14. The quotations appear on 13, 14.

43. Hiles, *Penmanship*, 13, 14.

44. Cesare Lombroso, "Left-Handedness and Left-Sidedness," *North American Review* 177 (September 1903): 440, 442–44. For other "scientific" treatments of the issue, see E. A. Doll, *Anthropometry as an Aid to Mental Diagnosis*, Research Publication No. 8, Training School, Vineland, N. J. (Baltimore: Williams and Wilkins, 1916), 91; Hugh Gordon, "Left-Handedness and Mirror Writing, Especially among Defective Children," *Brain: A Journal of Neurology* 43 (1920): 312–68; C. Quinan, "A Study of Sinistrality and Muscle Coordination in Musicians, Iron-Workers and Others," *Archives of Neurology and Psychiatry* 7 (March 1922): 352–60; and Ballard, "Sinistrality and Speech," 298–310.

45. "Are the Left-Handed Inferior?" *Literary Digest* (9 July 1921): 45; Edwin Tenney Brewster, "The Ways of the Left Hand," *McClure's* (June 1913): 179, 180, 183.

46. John Higham, *Strangers in the Land: Patterns of American Nativism, 1860–1925* (New York: Atheneum, 1985), 70, 101–5, 106–12, 128–29, 162–64, 189–93, 202–3.

47. United States Department of Labor, Bureau of Naturalization, Division of Citizenship Training, *Federal Citizenship Textbook: Penmanship Sheets* (Washington, D.C.: Government Printing Office, 1919), 11, 13. The copy texts also assumed, of course, that the prospective citizen was male, confining the power of the vote and the power of literacy to men.

48. Philip Robert Dillon, *The Penmanship of New York* (New York: A. N. Palmer, 1911), 15.

49. Ibid., 5, 7, 10–11.

50. Ibid., 22–24.

51. Robert C. Fuller, *Americans and the Unconscious* (New York: Oxford University Press, 1986); James B. Gilbert, *Work without Salvation: America's Intellectuals and Industrial Alienation, 1880–1910* (Baltimore: Johns Hopkins University Press, 1977), 35–36.

52. Rabinbach, *Human Motor*; C. P. Zaner, *The Arm Movement Method of Rapid Writing* (Columbus, Ohio: Zaner and Bloser, 1904), 10; Hiles, *Penmanship*, 49–50; Dillon, *Penmanship of New York*.

53. *The Zanerian Theory of Penmanship*, 2d ed. (Columbus, Ohio: Zanerian Art College, 1894), 42.

54. Hiles, *Penmanship*, 15, 33, 34; Taylor, *Supervision and Teaching of Handwriting*, 53.

55. Daniel Starch, "The Measurement of Efficiency in Writing," *JEP* 6 (February 1915): 114; Charles Hubbard Judd, *Measuring the Work of the Public Schools: Cleveland Education Survey* (Cleveland: Survey Committee of the Cleveland Foundation, 1916), 61–81; *Sixty-Third Annual Report of the Board of Education of the City of St. Louis, Mo., for the Year Ending June 30 1917* (n.p, n.d), 221; Hiles, *Penmanship*, 26–28, 78–79, 88–90.

56. Taylor, *Supervision and Teaching of Handwriting*, 53–59; Thompson, *Psychology and Pedagogy of Writing*, 123. For reviews of graphological studies, including those of and by June Downey, see, for example, *Psychological Bulletin* 2 (1905): 29–30, 5 (1908): 327–30, and 16 (1919): 28–31.

57. Edward L. Thorndike, *Individuality* (Boston: Houghton Mifflin, 1911), 2, 7.

58. O'Donnell, *Origins of Behaviorism*, 32–34, 152–53, 166–67. O'Donnell argues that there is a direct continuity between phrenology and the new psychology, evident in the common interest in the particularized mind and individual differences.

59. Theodore M. Porter, *The Rise of Statistical Thinking, 1820–1900* (Princeton: Princeton University Press, 1986); Lorraine J. Daston, "Rational Individuals versus Laws of Society: From Probability to Statistics," and Bernard-Pierre Lécuyer, "Probability in Vital and

Social Statistics: Quetelet, Farr, and the Bertillons," in *The Probabilistic Revolution,* vol. 1: *Ideas in History,* ed. Lorenz Krüger, Lorraine J. Daston, and Michael Heidelberger, 2 vols. (Cambridge: MIT Press, 1987), 295-304, 317-35. The younger Bertillon, as I noted in chap. 3, was an expert in the identification of criminals by means of individualized physiological characteristics, including handwriting.

60.. Leta S. Hollingworth, *Special Talents and Defects: Their Significance for Education* (New York: Macmillan, 1925), 196-211; Thorndike, *Individuality,* 8-12.

61. Judd, *Genetic Psychology for Teachers,* 169; Freeman, "Present-Day Issues in the Teaching of Handwriting," 40; Freeman and Dougherty, *How to Teach Handwriting,* 24-25, 27; Hugo von Hagen, *Reading Character from Handwriting* (New York: R. S. Mighill, 1902), 5-7.

62. Thorndike, *Individuality,* 13; Arthur I. Gates and Jessie LaSalle, "A Study of Writing Ability and Its Relation to Other Abilities Based on Repeated Tests during a Period of 20 Months," *JEP* 15 (April 1924): 205-16; Frank Freeman, "Contributions of Research to Special Methods: Handwriting," *Thirty-Seventh Yearbook of the National Society for the Study of Education,* part 2, 96-97; Freeman and Dougherty, *How to Teach Handwriting,* 25-30.

63. Arnold L. Gesell, "Accuracy in Handwriting as Related to School Intelligence and Sex," *American Journal of Psychology* 17 (July 1906): 394-405 (quotations, pp. 399, 400); Thorndike, "Handwriting," 161-62; Milton Wittler, "Factors Affecting Ability in Handwriting," *School and Society* 29 (29 June 1929): 847-50; Lena S. Shaw, "Supervisory Activities Involved in Integrating Handwriting Instruction—Abstract," National Education Association, *Proceedings of the Sixty-Ninth Annual Meeting . . . 1931* (Washington, D.C.: National Education Association, 1931), 814-15; and Gates and LaSalle, "Writing Ability and Its Relation to Other Abilities"; Daniel Starch, "The Measurements of Handwriting," *JEP* 4 (October 1913): 458-59.

64. Remarking on the fact that blacks and whites in one-room schoolhouses performed about equally, the survey authors conjectured that "perhaps measurements of a larger number of pupils of each race in one-room schools would have yielded different results," adding for good measure that "in making a comparison the greater age and longer school stay of colored pupils should always be allowed for." That the rural school year was shorter for blacks than for whites (122 versus 144 days), that black students missed more of those days (64 percent versus 58 percent attendance), that class sizes were larger in the black schools (45 versus 31 students), and that, more often than not, black schools lacked adequate materials (blackboards "wholly useless or entirely lacking" in 52 percent of rural black schools compared to 4.7 percent of rural white schools) were not seen as circumstances relevant to test performance. Even more troubling to the survey authors were the results of handwriting tests administered in city schools, where black pupils actually outperformed their white counterparts by a full year's progress. Here again investigators marshaled the fact that black students tended to be older, grade for grade, than white students to explain this "surprising result." About the only set of statistics that did not require the invocation of other variables were those for rural four-room schools, which revealed "decidedly different writing ability for the pupils of the two races" (Virginia Education Commission, *Virginia Public Schools,* 1:105-8, 375-79, 397-99; 2:76, 78-79).

65. Thomas R. Garth, "The Handwriting of Indians," *JEP* 22 (December 1931): 705-9; Elizabeth Weisser, "A Diagnostic Study of Indian Handwriting," *JEP* 23 (December 1932): 703-7; Thomas R. Garth, "The Handwriting of Negroes," *JEP* 30 (January 1939): 69-73. Weisser, for example, concluded that "this study does not indicate any differences that might be attributed to race since in some cases Indians seemed to exceed white children in their ability to write" (707).

66. Bertha E. Roberts, "Formality vs. Informality in Handwriting," *Sierra Educational News* 27 (June 1931): 49; Edith U. Conard, *Trends in Manuscript Writing* (New York: Teachers College, Columbia University, Bureau of Publications, 1936), 11–12; Thelma G. Voorhis, *The Relative Merits of Cursive and Manuscript Writing* (New York: Teachers College, Columbia University, Bureau of Publications, 1931), 49; Paul V. West, "The Motivation of Handwriting Instruction," *Journal of Educational Method* 6 (May 1927): 395–96.

67. S. Lucia Keim, "The Present Status and Significance of Manuscript Writing," *Journal of Educational Research* 24 (September 1931): 117–20; Gertrude Hildreth, "Manuscript Writing after Sixty Years," *Elementary English* 37 (January 1960): 3–4; Conard, *Trends in Manuscript Writing*, 3.

68. Margarette E. Howard, "The Case for Manuscript Writing," *Elementary English Review* 14 (May 1937): 177–78; Marjorie Wise, "Manuscript Writing," *Teachers College Record* 25 (January 1924): 27, 32–33; Keim, "Present Status and Significance of Manuscript Writing," 115–17; Conard, *Trends in Manuscript Writing*, 3, 23–24; Hildreth, "Manuscript Writing," 4.

69. J. F. Barnhart, "Writing in the Grades below the High School When the Commercial Branches Are Taught in the High School," *Journal of the Proceedings and Addresses of the Fortieth Annual Meeting* (Washington, D.C.: National Education Association, 1901), 753; Nutt, "Rhythm in Handwriting," 444; A. N. Palmer, "Penmanship," *Journal of the Proceedings and Addresses of the Fifty-Third Annual Meeting* (Washington, D.C.: National Education Association, 1915), 891–92; Conard, *Trends in Manuscript Writing*, 24.

70. A vast literature quickly developed on this subject. See, for example, W. H. Winch, "Print-Script and Cursive-Script in Schools: An Investigation in Neuro-Muscular Readjustments," *Forum of Education* (London) 4 (June, November 1926): 128–38, 206–22; Arthur I. Gates and Helen Brown, "Experimental Comparisons of Print-Script and Cursive Writing," *Journal of Educational Research* 20 (June 1929): 1–14; W. Henry Gray, "An Experimental Comparison of the Movements in Manuscript Writing and Cursive Writing," *JEP* 21 (April 1930): 259–72; Edith U. Conard and Elizabeth J. Offerman, "A Test of Speed and Quality in Manuscript Writing as Learned by Adults," *Teachers College Record* 31 (February 1930): 449–67; Olive G. Turner, "The Comparative Legibility and Speed of Manuscript and Cursive Handwriting," *ESJ* 30 (June 1930): 780–86; Voorhis, *Cursive and Manuscript Writing;* Howard, "Case for Manuscript Writing," 177–78; Hildreth, "Manuscript Writing," 11.

71. Conard, *Trends in Manuscript Writing*, 8, 17, 24.

72. Carleton Washburne and Mable Vogel Morphett, "Manuscript Writing—Some Recent Investigations," *ESJ* 37 (March 1937): 527–28; S. A. Golds, *A Guide to the Teaching of Manuscript Writing* (London: Blackie and Son, [1919]), 13; and Hildreth, "Manuscript Writing," 9–10. The quotations are from Conard and Offerman, "Speed and Quality in Manuscript Writing," 451; [Great Britain] Board of Education, *Print-Script*, Educational Pamphlets, No. 40, Elementary School Series, No. 4 (London: HMSO, 1923), 12–13.

73. T. J. Jackson Lears, *No Place of Grace: Antimodernism and the Transformation of American Culture, 1880–1920* (New York: Pantheon, 1981).

74. Frank N. Freeman, "An Evaluation of Manuscript Writing," *ESJ* 36 (February 1936): 446–55; Freeman, "Survey of Manuscript Writing in the Public Schools," *ESJ* 46 (March 1946): 375–80; Ada R. Polkinghorne, "Current Practices in Teaching Handwriting," *ESJ* 47 (December 1946): 218–24; Howard, "Case for Manuscript Writing," 177–78; Hildreth, "Manuscript Writing," 4.

75. For an example of a cursive-only traditionalist, see "Shall Beginners Start Writing with

Print?" *Kansas Teacher* 46 (December 1937): 23. For an example of a manuscript-only hold-out, see Washburne and Morphett, "Manuscript Writing," 525. On the manuscript-cursive transition, see, for example, Esther Whitacre Arnold, "The Transition from Manuscript to Cursive Writing," *ESJ* 33 (April 1933): 616–20; Mary Burke, "Cursive Writing: Transition from Manuscript Writing," *Grade Teacher* 64 (April 1947): 38–39, 84–85; and Frank N. Freeman, "The Transition from Manuscript to Cursive Writing," *Elementary English* 25 (October 1958): 366–72.

EPILOGUE

The Symbolic Functions of Obsolescence

1. Jack McGarvey, "Is It Time to Boot Out Cursive Writing?" *Classroom Computer Learning* 6 (March 1986): 36, 37.
2. Margery W. Davies, *Woman's Place Is at the Typewriter: Office Work and Office Workers, 1870–1930* (Philadelphia: Temple University Press, 1982), 28–38; Sue Walker, "How Typewriters Changed Correspondence: An Analysis of Prescription and Practice," *Visible Language* 18 (Spring 1984): 102–3.
3. D. T. Ames, "Hand-Writing of the Future," *Journal of the Proceedings of the National Educational Association* 33 (1894): 976–80. For a similar narrative of the progress of penmanship, see G. Bixler, *Bixler's Physical Training in Penmanship* (Wooster, Ohio: Bixler's Business College, 1892), 27–28, 42.
4. E. L. Thorndike, "Handwriting," *Teachers College Record* 11 (March 1910): 15–18; Elmer G. Miller, "The Vocational Need for Business Writing in the Junior High School and How to Meet It," National Education Association, *Addresses and Proceedings of the Sixty-Second Annual Meeting . . . 1924* (Washington, D.C.: National Education Association, 1924), 433; "Typewriting Instead of Script," *ESJ* 30 (January 1930): 333–34; Matthew Epstein, "Is Handwriting Obsolete?" *Look* (11 December 1956): 153.
5. Priscilla Johnston, *Edward Johnston*, 2d ed. (1959; London: Barrie and Jenkins, 1976); Edward Johnston, *Writing & Illuminating, & Lettering*, 14th ed. (1906; London: Sir Isaac Pitman and Sons, 1925). Johnston's treatise was part of a series edited by W. R. Lethaby entitled The Artistic Crafts Series of Technical Handbooks that included works on stained glass, woodcarving, heraldry, and historic dress design. My discussion of the Arts and Crafts calligraphy revival is based on Johnston's treatise, Grailey Hewitt, *Handwriting* (London: Chiswick Press, 1915), and Marjorie Wise, "Manuscript Writing," *Teachers College Record* 25 (January 1924): 28–32.
6. W. R. Lethaby, in Johnston, *Writing & Illuminating*, vii–ix. On the English Arts and Crafts movement, see Isabelle Anscombe and Charlotte Gere, *Arts and Crafts in Britain and America* (London: Academy Editions, 1978); Peter Stansky, *Redesigning the World: William Morris, the 1880s, and the Arts and Crafts* (Princeton: Princeton University Press, 1985); and Eileen Boris, *Art and Labor: Ruskin, Morris, and the Craftsman Ideal in America* (Philadelphia: Temple University Press, 1986), chaps. 1, 2.
7. Johnston, *Writing & Illuminating*, xiii, 38, 40, 48–70. See also T. J. Cobden-Sanderson, *Ecce Mundus: Industrial Ideals and the Book Beautiful* (Hammersmith, Eng.: Hammersmith Publishing, 1902), quoted in Paul Standard, *Calligraphy's Flowering, Decay, and Restauration* (Chicago, 1947; New York: Pentalic Corporation, 1978), 5–6.
8. Johnston, *Writing & Illuminating*, xvi, 239, 278, 280, 323–24.
9. M. M. Bridges, *A New Handwriting for Teachers*, 4th ed. (1899; Oxford: Oxford University Press, 1907), vi–ix; S. A. Golds, *A Guide to the Teaching of Manuscript Writing* (London:

Blackie and Son, [1919]), 4; (Great Britain) Board of Education, *Print-Script*, Educational Pamphlets, No. 40, Elementary School Series, No. 4 (London: HMSO, 1923); S. A. Golds, "The Introduction of a New Method of Handwriting," *Child-Study* (London) 9 (1916): 66–67; C. W. Kimmins, "Handwriting: Methods and Tests," *Child-Study* (London) 9 (1916): 61–63; Wise, "Manuscript Writing," 29.

10. "Beautiful Writing," *The Nation* (18 November 1909): 485; Standard, *Calligraphy's Flowering*, 13–36. On the Arts and Crafts movement in America see Boris, *Art and Labor;* James B. Gilbert, *Work without Salvation: America's Intellectuals and Industrial Alienation, 1880–1910* (Baltimore: Johns Hopkins University Press, 1977), 83–96; and T. J. Jackson Lears, *No Place of Grace: Antimodernism and the Transformation of American Culture, 1880–1920* (New York: Pantheon, 1981), chap. 2.

11. David McLelland, "The Curse of Commercial Cursive and Other Calligraphic Curiosities," *Harper's* (June 1975): 80, 81; Jacqueline Svaren, *Written Letters: 22 Alphabets for Calligraphers* (Freeport, Maine: Bond Wheelwright, 1975); Stewart Brand, ed., *The New Whole Earth Catalog: Access to Tools* (Sausalito, Calif.: Point, 1980), 506. See also the entire issue of *Visible Language* 17 (Winter 1983), an extended commentary on the association of calligraphy with individuality and its opposition to the technological purism of the machine age.

12. Levenger Company catalogue (1993), 52, 53, 55; Advertisement for the Parker Sonnet, *National Geographic* (November 1994): n.p.

13. Harry Tenwolde, "A Comparison of the Handwriting of Pupils in Certain Elementary Schools 'Now and Yesterday,'" *Journal of Applied Psychology* 18 (June 1934): 437–42; "Nation of Scrawlers," *Time* (10 February 1947): 92; Theodore Irwin, "Why Our Kids Can't Write," *Saturday Evening Post* (10 September 1955): 24–25, 122–24; Robert O'Brian, "The Moving Finger Writes—But Who Can Read It?" *Saturday Review* (1 July 1959): 8–10; Josef Berger, "What Ever Happened to Good Penmanship?" *Reader's Digest* (July 1962): 156–58; Fred R. Zepp, "Please Don't Excuse the Penmanship!" *McCall's* (December 1963): 9–10; Wesley E. Scott, "The Lost Art of Handwriting," *Science Digest* (December 1963): 57–59.

14. Irwin, "Why Our Kids Can't Write," 125; Berger, "What Ever Happened to Good Penmanship?" 157; O'Brian, "Moving Finger Writes," 9; Zepp, "Please Don't Excuse the Penmanship," 9–10; E. A. Enstrom, "The Decline of Handwriting," *ESJ* 66 (October 1965): 22–27; Patrick Groff, "The Future of Legibility," *Elementary English* 52 (February 1975): 205–12, 220.

15. Corey Ford, "Excuse This Hasty Scrawl," *Saturday Evening Post* (6 August 1955): 75; Irwin, "Why Our Kids Can't Write," 25; Berger, "What Ever Happened to Good Penmanship?" 158.

16. "Poor Penmanship Costs Money," *Nation's Business* 43 (April 1955): 101; Irwin, "Why Our Kids Can't Write," 23, 122–23; Scott, "Lost Art of Handwriting," 57–59; Jerry Klein, "Scribblers Pour Millions Down Drain; Omitted Hyphen Doomed Space Rocket," *Pittsburgh Press,* 17 March 1965, 25 ("An unidentified scientist was careless about a hyphen in a set of instructions for the electronic computer guarding the spacecraft. As a result, the rocket flew off course and had to be destroyed.")

17. Enstrom, "The Decline of Handwriting," 22–27.

18. Groff, "The Future of Legibility," 205–9.

19. Henry J. Otto, "The Use of Ink and Fountain Pens in Elementary Schools," *ESJ* 48 (March 1948): 379–84; Virgil E. Herrick, "Writing Tools for Children," *National Education Association Journal* 50 (February 1961): 49–50; Adrienne Erlebacher and Virgil E. Herrick, "Quality of Handwriting Today and Yesterday," *ESJ* 62 (1961): 89–92; Virgil E. Herrick

and Nora Okada, "The Present Scene: Practices in the Teaching of Handwriting in the United States," in *New Horizons for Research in Handwriting,* ed. Virgil Herrick (Madison: University of Wisconsin Press, 1963), 17–32; Polly Addy and Richard E. Wylie, "The 'Right' Way to Write," *Childhood Education* 49 (February 1973): 253–54; Connie A. Bridge and Elfrieda H. Hiebert, "A Comparison of Classroom Writing Practices, Teachers' Perceptions of Their Writing Instruction, and Textbook Recommendations on Writing Practices," *ESJ* 86 (November 1985): 155–72.

20. Donald H. Graves, "Research Update: Handwriting Is for Writing," *Language Arts* 55 (March 1978): 393; Jack McGarvey, "Is It Time to Boot Out Cursive Writing?" 36. See also Don M. Wolfe, "Self-Expression: The Heart of Language Arts," *Elementary English* 34 (November 1957): 450–55.

21. Pamela J. Farris, "Views and Other Views: Handwriting Instruction Should Not Become Extinct," *Language Arts* 68 (April 1991): 313; Kay Huitt, "Handwriting: The State of the Craft," *Childhood Education* 48 (January 1972): 219; M. Lee Manning, "Responding to Renewed Emphasis on Handwriting," *The Clearing House* 59 (January 1986): 211.

22. Joan Kuipers and Mary Lou Riccio, "From Graphomania to Graphophobia and Halfway Back," *Elementary English* 52 (February 1975): 219–20. See also S. Johnson, "The Writing Problem: Whatever Became of Palmer?" *New York Times,* 4 January 1984, 47–48.

23. Renate Robey, "It Says a Lot: Handwritten Letter Is Special," *Denver Post,* 13 March 1994, magazine, 10; Adair Lara, "The Hand Is Connected to the Heart," *San Francisco Chronicle,* 14 July 1994, D-8.

24. Edmund Morris, "Life and Letters: This Living Hand," *New Yorker* (16 January 1995): 66, 67; James P. Sterba, "Old-Fashioned Letter Is Fund Raising's Cutting Edge," *Wall Street Journal,* 18 August 1992, B-2.

25. Phil Donahue, "Dear Sister," *Buffalo News,* 24 June 1991, D-1, D-2.

ACKNOWLEDGMENTS

When I first caught a glimpse of this project, several years ago, I described it very briefly in a letter to David Brion Davis. I think I may have done no more than mention the words *culture* and *penmanship* in the same sentence. He responded characteristically, with enthusiasm and insight into the direction and significance of this new topic of research that I had not yet seen myself. I thank him for his encouragement and his steadfast friendship, and I am honored by both. Since then, many others have helped me at various stages of research and writing. Richard Bushman, Mary Kupiec Cayton, Ann Fabian, David Hall, Richard John, Jackson Lears, Mary Beth Norton, Randolph Roth, James B. Stewart, John R. Stilgoe, and Bill Warner have all commented on earlier stages of this project or on chapters of the manuscript. So too have many of my colleagues at the State University of New York at Buffalo, including Susan Cahn, Jonathan Dewald, Richard Ellis, William Freehling, Michael Frisch, David Gerber, and Gail Radford. Joan Rubin read the entire manuscript, and her thoughtful comments have been a great help to me. I owe a special debt of gratitude to my good friend and best critic Bill Graebner, who read the manuscript with his usual uncommon intelligence and thoroughness. I would also like to thank Ken Williams of the School of Art at the University of Georgia for the beautiful work he has done in penning the book title on the jacket as well as the chapter titles. Ken's work proves that, contrary to all contemporary reports, the genius of calligraphy persists in the modern world.

The National Endowment for the Humanities provided me with a fellowship year during which most of this book was written. Funds from the Lockwood Chair at the State University of New York, Buffalo, enabled me to undertake several research trips, as did a Scholarly Incentive Award and the Amy Everett Memorial Award from the State University of New York, College at Fredonia. I am grateful to the parents of Amy Everett for their generosity in establishing the award and hope that they find their daughter remembered with this book. Finally, a grant from the Julian Park Fund at the State University of New York, Buffalo, helped defray the costs of illustrations.

I feel most fortunate to come from a family that values learning, enjoys thinking, excels at talking, and shares my delight in my own pursuit of scholarship. To my parents, H. Gregory Plakins and Edith Sarah Fischgrund Plakins, and to my sisters, Naomi and Ava, I owe more than I can ever express. I take great strength from them and feel great pride to be one of them. My husband, Jonathan, has been unfailingly supportive of my work, but I think he has helped me most by providing a model of joyful craftsmanship in his own work. Of my daughters, Lydia and Dora, I can only say that they are joy itself.

ILLUSTRATION CREDITS

1. *A Coppie-Booke of the Newest and Most Usefull Hands* (London, [1674]), cover. (Reproduced by permission of the Huntington Library, San Marino, California)
2. Thomas Rowlandson, "A Merchant's Office," 1789. (Courtesy of the Yale Center for British Art, Paul Mellon Collection)
3. Nathaniel Dove, "Bills of Parcels," in George Bickham, *The Universal Penman* (London, 1743), pl. 28. (Courtesy of Dartmouth College Library)
4. "Division," in Rebeckah Salisbury, Ciphering Book, Boston, 1788, Penmanship Collection, American Antiquarian Society, Worcester, Massachusetts. (Courtesy of the American Antiquarian Society)
5. "John Clark, Writing Master and Accomptant, London," 1714, in Ambrose Heal, *The English Writing-Masters and Their Copy-Books, 1570–1800*, 2 vols. (Cambridge: Cambridge University Press, 1931), vol. 1, pl. 6. (Courtesy of Yale University Library)
6. Abiah Holbrook, "The Writing-Master's Amusement," 1767. (Courtesy of the Department of Printing and Graphic Arts, Houghton Library, Harvard University)
7. George Bickham, "The Alphabets in All Hands," in George Bickham, *The Universal Penman* (London, 1743), pl. 52. (Courtesy of Dartmouth College Library)
8. "A New Alphabet," in J. Johnson, *A Copy-Book* (London, 1669). (Reproduced by permission of the Syndics of Cambridge University Library)
9. Geoffrey Tory, *Champ Fleury* (Paris, 1529).
10. "Double Pica Script," in John Ronaldson, *Specimen of Printing Type* (Philadelphia, 1816). (Courtesy of Cary Graphic Arts Collection, Rochester Institute of Technology)
11. "The Art and Mystery of Printing," *Grub-Street Journal Extraordinary* 148 (October 30, 1732). (Courtesy of Kenneth Spencer Research Library, University of Kansas, Lawrence, Kansas)
12. Francis Hopkinson, "Plan for the Improvement of the Art of Paper War," *American Museum* 1 (1787): 440. (Courtesy of Beinecke Rare Book and Manuscript Library, Yale University)
13. "D. H. Leonard, Teacher of plain, practical Penmanship," handbill for a writing school. (Courtesy of Special Collections, Dartmouth College Library)
14. "How to Organize and Conduct Writing Schools," in G. A. Gaskell, *Gaskell's Compendium of Forms* (Chicago: William M. Farrar, 1880), 94. (Courtesy of Dartmouth College Library)
15. Platt Rogers Spencer, from H. C. Spencer, *Spencerian Key to Practical Penmanship* (New York: Ivison, Phinney, Blakeman, 1869), frontispiece. (Courtesy of Yale University Library)

16. "Position of the Hand and Pen" in B. F. Foster, *Practical Penmanship, Being a Development of the Carstairian System* (Albany: O. Steele, 1832), pl. 3. (Courtesy of Dartmouth College Library)

17. Robert Brathwaite Martineau, "Kit's Writing Lesson," 1852, Tate Gallery, London. (Courtesy of Tate Gallery, London/Art Resources, New York)

18. George W. Winchester, *Theoretical and Practical Penmanship* (Hartford, Conn.: J. H. Mather, 1844), cover. (Courtesy of Dartmouth College Library)

19. John Jenkins, *The Art of Writing* (Cambridge: Flagg and Gould, 1813), 40. (Courtesy of Dartmouth College Library)

20. G. A. Gaskell, a business form in Spencerian script, in G. A. Gaskell, *Gaskell's Compendium of Forms* (Chicago: William M. Farrar, 1880), pl. 4. (Courtesy of Dartmouth College Library)

21. Joseph Callender, *Round Text Copies* (Worcester: Isaiah Thomas, 1787), cover. (Courtesy of the American Antiquarian Society, Worcester, Massachusetts)

22. A. H. Hinman, ornamental penwork, in Daniel T. Ames, *Ames' Compendium of Practical and Ornamental Penmanship* (New York: A. J. Bicknell, 1877). (Courtesy of Yale University Library)

23. "Spencerian Authors," *Theory of Spencerian Penmanship* (New York: Ivison, Blakeman, Taylor, 1874), frontispiece. (Courtesy of Yale University Library)

24. A. N. Palmer, *The Palmer Method of Business Writing* (New York: A. N. Palmer, 1915), 29. (Courtesy of Dartmouth College Library)

25. J. Harington Keene, *The Mystery of Handwriting* (Boston: Lee and Shepard, 1896), cover. (Courtesy of Yale University Library)

26. "Explanation of the Signs of the 42 Faculties," in Richard Dimsdale Stocker, *The Language of Handwriting: A Text-Book of Graphology* (London: Swan Sonnenschein, 1900), pl. facing p. 87. (Courtesy of Yale University Library)

27. Thomas Byrnes, *Professional Criminals of America* (New York: Cassell, 1886), photographs 37–42.

28. Persifor Frazer, *Bibliotics; or the Study of Documents,* 3d ed. (Philadelphia: J. B. Lippincott, 1901), 27.

29. John Anson Ford, "New System Classifies Criminals' Handwriting Accurately," *Illustrated World* 36 (December 1921): 542.

30. William Leslie French, "Cupid, Graphologist," *Good Housekeeping* 55 (December 1912): 769. (Courtesy of Cornell University Library)

31. *Hutch-in-Son Calendar,* yearbook of Hutchinson Technical High School, Buffalo, New York, 1919.

32. Advertisement for Chipso detergent, (New York) *Daily News,* 1 February 1935, 41. (Courtesy of the Library of Congress)

33. "The Human Form a Walking Advertisement," F. T. McIntyre, *A Correspondence Course in Radial Character Reading* (New York: Metropolitan Institute of Sciences, 1904), cover. (Courtesy of the Library of Congress)

34. Anton Da Borcka, *Personality in Handwriting* (New York: Reader's Mail, 1936). (Courtesy of the Library of Congress)

35. Charles Hubbard Judd, *Genetic Psychology for Teachers* (New York: D. Appleton, 1903), 171.

36. "Correct Position for Writing on the Blackboard," in State of New Jersey, Department of Public Instruction, *The Teaching of Penmanship* (n.p., 1912), plate between pp. 10 and 11. (Courtesy of Yale University Library)

37. Diagram of "Sensori-Motor Coordination," in William James, *Principles of Psychology*, 2 vols. (New York: Henry Holt, 1890), 1:57. (Courtesy of Cornell University Library)

38. Leta Severance Hiles, *Penmanship: Teaching and Supervision* (Los Angeles: Jesse Ray Miller, 1924), plates between pp. 16 and 17 and opposite 20.

39. Palmer method buttons, early twentieth century, author's collection.

40. "Ain't Mickey grand!" in Philip Robert Dillon, *The Penmanship of New York* (New York: A. N. Palmer, 1911), 5. (Courtesy of the General Research Division, the New York Public Library, Astor, Lennox, and Tilden Foundations)

41. Teacher materials for handwriting instruction, Reed Library, State University of New York, College at Fredonia.

42. "The Pen Grinding Room," in "The Manufacture of Steel Pens in Birmingham," *Illustrated London News* 18, suppl. (22 February 1851): 148.

43. "Stripping the Shaft," and "Lengthening the Slit of the Nib," in Edward Johnston, *Writing & Illuminating, & Lettering,* 14th ed. (1906; London: Sir Isaac Pitman and Sons, 1925), 55.

44. "The Impeccable Pelikan," advertisement in Levenger Company catalogue, 1993.

45. Photograph of Lord and Taylor, Cheektowaga, New York, author's collection.

46. Photograph of K-Mart, Buffalo, New York, author's collection.

47. "Executives Have Secret Codes of Their Own," in Corey Ford, "Excuse This Hasty Scrawl," *Saturday Evening Post* (6 August 1955): 25. (The Curtis Publishing Company; Courtesy of Cornell University Library)

48. Photograph of the author, 1963, author's collection.

49. Teacher materials for handwriting instruction, Reed Library, State University of New York, College at Fredonia.

50. *Handwriting: Basic Skills and Application,* Book 3 (Columbus, Ohio: Zaner-Bloser, 1994), cover.

INDEX

Page numbers in italics refer to illustrations.

Graphology (*continued*)
relationship between handwriting experts and graphologists, 103–5; and adjustment to one's ordinariness, 109, 127–29, 132, 140; and genetic categories of people, 109, 136; and scientific establishment, 109, 132–41; and universal uniqueness of handwriting, 109, 112–18, 124–25, 132, 140–41, 175; for marital counseling, 111; for employment decisions, 111–12, 128, 220n51; in fiction, 112; women as graphologists, 118, 120, 122; advice columns using, 119–20, 124, 125–29, 131; in periodicals, 119–20; marketing of, 120–22, *121, 123;* for analysis of one's personal acquaintances and business associates, 122, *123;* for self-analysis, 122, 124–32, 140; and search for one's extraordinary talents, 125–27; as mirror revealing self, 129–32, *130;* in Germany, 134–35, 138; versus automatism, 144; and penmanship instruction, 166, 174–75; and automatic writing, 168–69. *See also* Handwriting analysis
Graves, Donald, 188, 189
Green, Richard, 8
Groff, Patrick, 187–88
Guild, James, 44–45

Hale, Sarah Josepha, 87
Hall, David, 24
Handedness, 148, 152–53, 160–61
Handwriting: author's early experiences with and attitudes toward, ix–x, *187;* importance of study of, x–xiv; Franklin on practicing, 3; reading of script, 6, 197n6; ancient origins and historical significance of, 15–16; as fine art, 16; as copying, 18, 52; development of, in England, 18–19; anthropomorphism of, 27, *28,* 33; compared with print, 28–30; mental component of, 47, 49–50, 69; as physiological habit, 143–47, 156, *157;* slope of, 146; and race, 169, 228nn64–65. *See also* Colonial handwriting; Gender and handwriting; Graphology; Handwriting analysis; Individuality; Obsolescence of hand-

writing; Penmanship instruction; Self and handwriting; Victorian handwriting; *and specific handwriting styles and methods*
Handwriting ability groups, 165
Handwriting analysis: and individuality of handwriting, 35, 73–74; theory of, 73–74, 79; beginnings of, 74–78, 94; romantic handwriting analysis, 78–86, 94–95, 106, 107; and meaninglessness of most people's scripts, 79; and romantic notions of gestures, 83–84, 94–95; and the unconscious, 84–85, 87, 95; compared with phrenological analysis, 85–86; and autograph collecting, 86–88, 106, 110; of marital incompatibility, 111, *111. See also* Graphology
Handwriting experts, 90, 101–5, *105,* 106–7, 215n74
Handwriting scales, 148–49, 153, 167, 188
Harris, Owen, 7–8
Hawthorne, Nathaniel, 212n31
Hereditary factors in handwriting, 109, 136, 169, 175, 221n60
Higham, John, 69
Hiles, Leta Severance, 150, 158, 164, 165
Hocquart, Edouard Auguste Patrice, 74–75, 81, 83–84, 94
Holbrook, Abiah, 12, 44, 171
Hollingworth, Leta S., 168
Holmes, Oliver Wendell, 110
Holmes, Sherlock, 104
Hopkinson, Francis, 33
Howard, Clifford, 125
Howells, William Dean, 131
Hull, Clark L., 135–36, 138

Illegibility: as mark of gentility, 13–14, 39; as lack of respectability in Victorian handwriting, 53, 100; as mark of genius in early twentieth century, 115; commercial symbolism of, 183–84, *184;* of postwar penmanship, 184–88, 231n16; business costs of, 186, 189–90, 231n16
Immigrants, 161–64, 227n47
Indians, 169, 228n65
Individuality: and legal evidence of handwriting, 34–35, 41, 88–92; of

handwriting, 35, 73–74, 78–86; and beginnings of handwriting analysis, 73–86, 94; romantic version of modern self and handwriting analysis, 78–86, 94–95, 106, 107; and autograph collecting, 86–88, 106; and the sciences of detection, 95–105; and handwriting analysis, 95–105, 107; and handwriting experts compared with graphologists, 103–4, 107; in Victorian era, 106–7; characterological model of, 107; physiological model of, 107; graphology and universal uniqueness of handwriting, 109, 112–18, 124–25, 132, 140–41, 175; threats to, in twentieth century, 113–14, 115, 129, 131, 140; and illegibility of handwriting, 115, 183–84, *184;* and penmanship instruction, 116–18, 186–90; Palmer on, 117; in women's handwriting, 137–40; and handedness, 148; statistical analysis of, 167–70; and manuscript writing movement, 170–74, *175;* and calligraphy revival, 183–84; script as sign of, in twentieth century, 183–84; and permissiveness of penmanship instruction in postwar years, 186–90. *See also* Self and handwriting

Inglis, Hester, 198n9
Ingram, John Henry, 92
Ink. *See* Writing tools
Instruction. *See* Penmanship instruction; Schools
Intelligence testing, 133, 149, 167
Irving, Washington, 86
Italian hands, 18–19, *20,* 37, 38, 55
Italic chancery, 19
Itinerant writing masters, 44–45, *45*

James, William, 143, 144, *157*
Jefferson, Thomas, 39
Jenkins, John, 50, 53
Johns, Mary, 198n9
Johnston, Edward, 179–82, 230n5
Judd, Charles H., 146, 156, 166, 168
Jung, Carl, 134

Keene, J. Harington, 93, *93,* 95–96, 99, 122, 137

Kirby, J. Albert, 158, 226n41
Klages, Ludwig, 134, 138

Ladies' hands: in colonial era, 19, 23, 37–39; in mid-nineteenth century, 43, 44, 57–58; in late eighteenth century, 55; in Gilded Age, 100–101, 115; individuality in, 137–40; in early nineteenth century, 206n29. *See also* Women
Lamb, Andrew, 8
Langton, John, 12, 19
Latrobe, Benjamin, 75–76
Lavater, Johann Kaspar, 74, 78, 82, 84, 86, 134, 202n50, 209nn3,6, 211nn25–26
Lears, T. J. Jackson, 131
Left-handedness, 148, 152–53, 160–61
Legal evidence of handwriting, 34–35, 41, 88–92, 101, 104–5, 212–13nn41–46, 215n74
Legal forms, 30
Legal hands, 22, 37–38, 200n33
Lethaby, W. R., 179, 230n5
Literacy, x–xii, 16–23, 59, 66, 207n36
Locke, John, 3, 4
Lockridge, Kenneth, 207n36
Lombroso, Cesare, 160
Long, Sarah, 8
Long, William, 8
Love, Harold, 201n49
Lucar, Elizabeth, 198n9
Lucas, Dewitt B., 112

McAllister, Cloyd N., 146
McCready, Francis, 50, 53
McGarvey, Jack, 177, 189
Machines: printing press, 4, 24–27, 115; typewriter, 114, 177–78, 186; bodies as, 162–64, 177–78; computers, 177, 178, *187;* and calligraphy revival, 178–84; erosion of handwriting by, 186, 191
McKee, Uriah, 51
Male hands. *See* Gender and handwriting; Legal hands; Men; Merchants
Manuscript-cursive transition, 174, *175,* 188–89
Manuscript writing movement, 170–74, *175,* 182
Materot, Lucas, 19

Mather, Cotton, 19
Meleny, Clarence E., 152
Men: and different Italian hands, 19, 23, 38; gentlemen's handwriting, 19, 22–23, 25, 35–36, 39; Victorian ideal of, 55, 99–101, 105–6; physical appetites of, 58; act of handwriting as inherently male during Victorian era, 58–59; penmanship instruction for, in Victorian era, 58–59; inner reality versus outward appearances in Victorian era, 99–101. *See also* Gender and handwriting; Legal hands; Merchants; *and specific men*
Mental component of handwriting, 47, 49–50, 69
Merchants: and writing in colonial America, x, 6–12, *7*, 37, 39–40, 199n17; Italian hands used by, 18–19, 22; forms used by, 30, *30*, 31; running hand of, 39–40, 43, 44, 206n29. *See also* Business
Michon, Abbé Jean-Hippolyte, 92–93, 96, 98, 102, 103, 132–33, 134
Mirror of self, graphology as, 129–32, *130*
Montgomery, J. S., 53
Montgomery, Robert B., 135–36, 138
Moreau, Pierre, 26
Morelli, Giovanni, 104
Morgan, J. P., 110
Morris, Edmund, 191
Morris, William, 179
Motor learning, 156–60, *159*
Movements. *See* Bodily movements
Moxon, Joseph, 27
Multiple scripts, 18–23, *20–21*, 37, 41
Münsterberg, Hugo, 167
Muscularity, 50, 58–59, 68–69. *See also* Bodily movements
Myers, F. W. H., 143

Nethercliff, Frederick, 87
New Woman, 69, 70, 109, *111*, 137–38
Novels, 60–63, 207n40

Obsolescence of handwriting: and typewriter, 177–78; and handwriting as symbol of past, 177–78, 191–93; and calligraphy revival, 178–84, 192; and

illegibility in postwar years, 184–88, *184*, *185*; and postwar penmanship instruction, 185–90
Occult, 92–93, 103, 106–7, 120, 134
Occupations. *See* Business; Legal hands; Merchants
O'Donnell, John M., 227n58
Olyanova, Nadya, 109, 129
Ong, Walter, xii, 28
Oratory, 33
Ornamental penwork, 63–66, *64*

Palmer, A. N.: development of handwriting method of instruction, 66–71, 145, 147; and handwriting as muscular movement, 103, 156, 177–78, 208n53; on individuality in handwriting, 117; on automatism of handwriting, 144; criticisms of, 154; and handwriting drill, 171; company of, and manuscript writing teaching materials, 174
Palmer method: masculinity of, 66–70, *68*; business use of, 67–68, 154; form of letters in, 67–68, *68*; movement over form and drill in, 68–69, 103, 156, 162–64, 171, *172*; and destruction of individuality in handwriting, 116–17; academics' critique of, 144–49, 153, 156, 174–75; classroom instruction in, during progressive era, 149–53, *151*; teacher and student complaints on, 151–52; and handedness, 152–53, 160–61; reasons for use of, 153–66; calisthenics as preparation for, 158, *159*; disciplinary value of, 158, 160; for immigrants, 161–64; buttons and pins, 162, *162*, *163*; student enjoyment of, 162–63; and preparation for employment, 164–65; and legibility, *172*; nostalgia for, 190, 192; training of teachers in, 225n25
Palmistry, 93. *See also* Chiromancy
Pastnor, Paul, 49
Pelham, Peter, 8
Pen art, 63–66, *64*
Penmanship. *See* Handwriting
Penmanship drill, 50–51, 68–69
Penmanship instruction: by Locke, 3, 4;

in colonial America, 5–12, 15, 22, 40–41; by women, 7, 197–98n9; gender differences in, 8, 55–59, *56, 57;* for women and girls, 8, 55–59, *56, 57;* and multiple scripts of colonial era, 22; and character formation, 43, 46–55, 58–59; in Victorian America, 44–59, *44, 45, 56, 57;* and contemplation of natural forms, 49–50; drill in, 50–51, 68–69; militaristic methods of, in nineteenth century, 50–51; student reactions to regimen of, 51; and bodily discipline in the Victorian era, 53–55, *54,* 71; and bodily movement in the Victorian era, 53–55, 68–69, 83–84, 146; and talantograph, 54–55, *54;* for men and boys in Victorian era, 58–59; Palmer method, 66–70, *68,* 116–17, 145–66; and individuality in handwriting, 116–18; automatism in progressive era, 143–66; academic experts and critique of Palmer method, 145–49, 153, 156; and handedness, 148, 152–53, 160–61; measurement of success of, 148–49, 153; classroom instruction in progressive era, 149–53; reasons for use of Palmer method in progressive era, 153–66; and motor learning, 157–60, *159;* calisthenics as preparation for, 158, *159;* disciplinary value of, 158, 160; for immigrants, 161–64; and transformation of students into machines, 162–64, 177–78; and preparation for work in progressive era, 164–65; ability groups in, 165; and graphology, 166, 174–75; manuscript writing movement, 170–74, *175;* and typewriter, 178; and illegibility of postwar penmanship, 184–88; teacher training in, 185, 225n25; in postwar years, 185–90; and permissiveness during postwar years, 186–90; nostalgia for Palmer method, 190

Penmanship manuals, 45–47, 50. *See also* Copybooks

Penniston, Elizabeth, 198n9

Pens. *See* Writing tools

Perlmann, Joel, 59

Petti, Anthony G., 200n33

Phrenology, 85–86, 92–96, *97,* 98, 111, 227n58

Physiognomy, 85, 94, 95, 111, 133, 135

Poe, Edgar Allan, 77–81, 92

Poetry, printing of, 33

Potter, S. A., 50–51

Pratt, John, 8

Preyer, William, 134, 135, 138

Print: versus script, 24–35, 115; impersonality of, 26, 27–30, 41, 115; blankness of, 31–33; duplicity of, 31–33, *32, 34,* 41, 201n49; versus oratory, 33

Printing press, 4, 24–27, 115

Print-script (printing). *See* Manuscript writing movement

Progressive era: penmanship instruction during, 143–66; conception of learning process in, 144, 156–57, *157;* reasons for use of Palmer method during, 153–66; status of school administrators during, 154; human being conceptualized as human body in, 155–56

Psychoanalysis, 104

Psychology: and graphology, 111–12, 134–36, 138–40, 166; critique of Palmer method, 143, 144–49, 174–75; and conception of learning in progressive era, 144, 156–57, *157;* left-handedness, 148, 152–53; handwriting scales, 148–49, 153, 167; applied psychology in late nineteenth and early twentieth centuries, 156; behaviorism, 156; statistical analysis of individuality, 166–70

Pulver, Max, 134, 220–21n56

Quill pens. *See* Writing tools

Quintilian, 13–14

Race, and handwriting ability, 169, 228nn64–65

Radcliffe, James, 38

Rand, Benjamin, 206n29

Reading: study of, x–xi; in colonial America, 4–6, 17, 18, 40–41, 59; of printed versus handwritten word, 6, 197n6; of fiction, 60–61, 207n40; by slaves, 197n6

Word processing. *See* Computers

Writer's cramp, 164

Writing. *See* Handwriting

Writing masters: in colonial America, 7-8, 23, 35-36, 44; lowly origins of, 12; in England, 12-13, *13, 14,* 26; as craftsmen, 12-16, 35-36; and view of penmanship as fine art, 15-16; in France, 19, 26; and multiple scripts, 23; as typeface designers, 26; itinerants, 44-45, *45;* in Victorian America, 44-46, *44, 45,* 58-59; displacement of, by classroom teachers, 46; as publishers of arithmetic and accounting books, 198n16;

and legal hand, 200n33. *See also specific people*

Writing tools: steel pens, 14, 46, 180, *180,* 188; in colonial America, 14-15; quill pens, 14-15, 180, *181;* in Victorian America, 46; and calligraphy revival, 180, *180, 181,* 182-83, *183;* fountain pens, 183, *183,* 188; in postwar classrooms, 188; ballpoint pens, 191

Young, Edward, 82

Zaner, C. P., 208n53

Zboray, Ronald, 207n40